OFF THE BEATEN PATH®
MICHIGAN →

Help Us Keep This Guide Up to Date

We would love to hear from you concerning your experiences with this guide and how you feel it could be improved and kept up to date. Please send your comments and suggestions to:

editorial@GlobePequot.com

Thanks for your input, and happy travels!

ELEVENTH EDITION

OFF THE BEATEN PATH®
MICHIGAN →

A GUIDE TO UNIQUE PLACES

JIM DuFRESNE

Revised and Updated by
JACKIE SHECKLER FINCH

gpp®
travel

Guilford, Connecticut

All the information in this guidebook is subject to change. We recommend that you call ahead to obtain current information before traveling.

Editor: Kevin Sirois
Project Editor: Lauren Szalkiewicz
Layout: Joanna Beyer
Text Design: Linda R. Loiewski
Maps by Equator Graphics © Morris Book Publishing, LLC

ISSN 1542-4804
ISBN 978-0-7627-8648-0

Printed in the United States of America
10 9 8 7 6 5

Many thanks to the wonderful tourism folks of Michigan for answering my endless questions. My appreciation to the excellent public relations officials and to the Michigan residents and business owners who took the time to share what makes Michigan special.

Gratitude to my Globe Pequot Press editor Kevin Sirois and to my project editor Lauren Szalkiewicz for inviting me to take this treasure-filled trip through Michigan. It has been a delight and a pure pleasure.

This book is dedicated to my family—Kelly Rose; Mike Peters; Sean, Devin, Dylan, and Emma Rose; Stefanie, Will, Trey, and Arianna Rose; and Logan, Olivia, and Grayson Peters.

A special remembrance to my husband, Bill Finch, whose spirit goes with me every step of the way through life's journey.

Jackie Sheckler Finch

Contents

About the Author

Jim DuFresne is a Clarkston-based travel and outdoor writer whose articles appear in newspapers and magazines across the state. Formerly a sports and outdoors editor for the *Juneau Empire* in Alaska, DuFresne wrote his first travel book, *Tramping in New Zealand,* in 1982 for Lonely Planet. His other books include *Isle Royale National Park: Foot Trails and Water Routes; Michigan State Parks; Michigan's Best Hikes with Children; The Complete Guide to Michigan Sand Dunes; Backpacking In Michigan;* and *Twelve Classic Trout Streams in Michigan.*

About the Reviser

Jackie Sheckler Finch has written about a wide array of topics—from birth to death, with all the joy and sorrow in between. An award-winning journalist and photographer, Jackie has done about a dozen travel guidebooks for Globe Pequot, and is a member of the Society of American Travel Writers and the Midwest Travel Writers Association. She has been named the Mark Twain Travel Writer of the Year a record five times, in 1998, 2001, 2003, 2007, and 2012. Jackie shares her home with resident guard and entertainer, a black dog named Pepper. One of her greatest joys is taking to the road to find the fascinating people and places that wait over the hill and around the next bend.

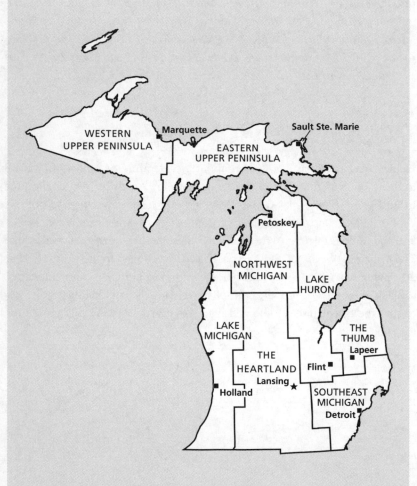

WESTERN
UPPER PENINSULA

Marquette

Sault Ste. Marie

EASTERN
UPPER PENINSULA

Petoskey

NORTHWEST
MICHIGAN

LAKE
HURON

LAKE
MICHIGAN

THE
THUMB

Lapeer

THE
HEARTLAND

Flint

Lansing

Holland

SOUTHEAST
MICHIGAN

Detroit

Introduction

If you look at a map of the United States or spin a globe, you'll discover that the most prominent state is Michigan. It always stands out, regardless of the size of the map or how obscured the detail.

Michigan is set off from much of the country by water. Four of the five Great Lakes surround it and have turned its borders into 3,200 miles of lakeshore where you can sit in the sand and look out on the watery horizon of the world's largest freshwater seas.

Michigan is inundated with water. It's not only outlined by blue, but its history was shaped by the Great Lakes. Today travelers search the state over for a bit of their own sand and surf, and there is no short supply. Stand anywhere in the state and you are no more than 85 miles from the Great Lakes and only 6 miles from one of the 11,000 sparkling inland lakes or 36,000 miles of streams and rivers. Come winter, Michigan's water turns fluffy and white and gently lands all around, much to the delight of skiers.

Michigan is water, yet beaches and boating, swimming and sunbathing are only part of the state's attractions. To the adventurous traveler, to those who love to swing off the interstate highways onto the country roads that wander between the woods and the lakes, there are quaint villages to discover and shipwrecks to explore, art fairs and mushroom festivals to enjoy, wine-tasting tours to savor, a stretch of quiet trail to soothe the urban soul.

All you need is time, a good map of Michigan, and this book. The map can be obtained by calling Pure Michigan Travel toll-free at (888) 784-7328; or by checking the website michigan.org. The map will lead you away from the six-lane highways to the scenic country roads and then back again when you are ready to return home.

Michigan Off the Beaten Path points out those half-hidden gems that travelers rejoice in discovering, from a lighthouse that has become a country inn to party-fishing boats that let novice anglers stalk and catch the Great Lakes' tastiest offering, the yellow perch. Because addresses, phone numbers, and hours of operation can change from summer to summer, the regional chapters contain a list of tourist associations that can provide the most up-to-date information.

The same holds true for prices. Inflation, with its annual increases in everything from room rates and restaurant prices to entry fees at parks and museums, will quickly outdate anything listed. Therefore, only the prices for substantial items (rooms, meals, and major attractions) have been provided in this book to help readers judge whether a restaurant or hotel is affordable.

Most of all, more than this book and a map, you need time. Don't short-change Michigan. Don't try to cover half the state in a weekend holiday. You will only be disappointed at the end of your trip. You could spend a summer exploring Michigan and never leave the shoreline. I have spent a lifetime here, yet my never-ending list of places to go and adventures to undertake only grows longer with each journey in the Great Lakes State.

Michigan Facts

Nickname: Great Lakes State

Capital: Lansing

Population: 9,833.640, eighth in the country

Area: 56,804 square miles, 23rd in the country

Admitted to Union: Michigan became the 26th state when it was admitted on January 26, 1837.

Major Cities: Detroit, population 713,777; Grand Rapids, 188,040; Warren, 134,056; Sterling Heights, 129,699; Flint, 102,434; Lansing, 114,297; Ann Arbor, 113,934; Livonia, 96,942

Famous Residents: Henry Ford, Thomas Edison, Gen. George Custer, President Gerald Ford, Charles Lindbergh, Diana Ross, Stevie Wonder, and Eminem

National Park Units: Isle Royale National Park, Pictured Rocks National Lakeshore, Sleeping Bear Dunes National Lakeshore

Travel Information: Pure Michigan, 300 N. Washington Sq., Lansing 48913; (888) 784-7328; michigan.org, will send you a free travel guide to Michigan along with a road map. The West Michigan Tourist Association, 741 Kenmoor Ave., Suite E, Grand Rapids 49546; (800) 442-2084 or (616) 245-2217; wmta.org, covers accommodations, attractions, and visitor facilities in the western half of the Lower Peninsula. The Upper Peninsula Travel and Recreation Association, P.O. Box 400, Iron

Mountain 49801; (800) 562-7134 or (906) 774-5480; uptravel.com, covers the Upper Peninsula.

State Parks: For a guide to the Michigan State Parks system, contact the Michigan Department of Natural Resources, Parks & Recreation Division, Box 30257, Lansing 48909; (517) 373-9900; michigan.gov/dnr.

Major Newspapers: *Detroit Free Press, Detroit News, Grand Rapids Press, Flint Journal, Lansing State Journal*

Public Transportation: Michigan's major regional air center is Detroit Metro Airport, located in the suburb of Romulus 15 miles southwest of Detroit. The main carrier is Delta Airlines/Northwest Airlines (800-221-1212; delta.com), which uses Detroit as a major hub. Both Greyhound Bus Service (800-231-2222; greyhound.com) and Amtrak (800-872-7245; amtrak.com) maintain service throughout the state.

Climate: Michigan is split in the middle by the 45th Parallel; this northern position means that it has a very temperate, four-season climate. Summers reach the high 90s but rarely break triple digits. Winters can dip to minus 10 or 20 degrees at times in the northern half of the state but usually hover between 10 and 20 degrees in southern Michigan. Thanks to the Great Lakes, Michigan receives an abundance of snow, with some towns like Munising and Calumet totaling more than 250 inches by the end of March. Autumn colors are spectacular in the state, with trees beginning to change in late September in the Upper Peninsula and late October in Southern Michigan.

SOUTHEAST MICHIGAN

Southeast Michigan, a region of seven counties, revolves around metropolitan **Detroit,** which sprawls into three of them. And Detroit revolves around automobiles. It's as simple as that.

Known best throughout the country as Motor City, Detroit carries several other titles, including Motown, after the recording company that produced such famous singers as Diana Ross and Stevie Wonder before it fled to Los Angeles from its studio on Woodward Avenue. The city was also home to the nation's oldest state fair (the Michigan State Fair dated to 1849) until it was closed after funding cuts in 2009. On May 30, 2012, it was announced that the Michigan State Fair would be replaced by the Great Lakes State Fair, which was held August 31 through September 3, 2012 at the Suburban Collection Showplace in the Detroit suburb of Novi.

Detroit and its neighboring suburbs wear many faces; some are good, some others are unjustly earned, but the least recognized one is that of a destination for travelers. Detroit is the eighteenth largest city in the country, yet despite its size many tourists consider it very much "off the beaten path." Depart from the city and the rest of Southeast

SOUTHEAST MICHIGAN

Michigan changes quickly, from the urban sprawl to the rolling hills and lakes of northern Oakland County, the blue water of St. Clair and Port Huron, and the culture and carefree college ways of Ann Arbor, the home of the University of Michigan.

Wayne County

Until the 1870s, Detroit was a commercial center for farmers, but at the end of that century the first automobiles appeared, as Ransom E. Olds and Henry Ford began tinkering with "horseless carriages." By 1903, Ford had organized the Ford Motor Company, and when he pioneered the assembly-line method of building cars and introduced the Model T, the vehicle for the common man, Detroit's place as the automobile capital of the world was established.

Cars are a way of life in Detroit. Michigan boasts of having the first mile of concrete rural highway (1909), the first traffic light (1915), and the first urban freeway free of those annoying stoplights (1942). The best-known place to view this history of cars and their immense effect on the American way of life is The Henry Ford, home of Greenfield Village and *Henry Ford Museum* (313-982-6001 or 800-835-5237; thehenryford.org), a 260-acre complex with one hundred historic buildings in *Dearborn* that has become the nation's largest indoor and outdoor museum.

A $200 million upgrade of Greenfield Village in 2004 resulted in "America's Greatest Historical Attraction" being extensively redesigned and for the first time open from mid-April through New Year's Eve. Now the streets of the turn-of-the-20th-century village are lined with 331 lampposts, while such famous buildings as Thomas Edison's laboratory from Menlo Park, New Jersey; the Wright Brothers' Ohio cycle workshop; and the Logan County Courthouse where Abraham Lincoln first practiced law are heated for visitors who arrive other than in the summer. The adjacent Henry Ford Museum also features new exhibits, including the bus where in 1955 Rosa Parks refused to give up her seat, thus igniting America's civil rights movement.

So much history, so little time to absorb it all. Keep in mind that the village and the museum are each a separate attraction with a separate admission price, and each requires a good part of a day to view. Car buffs are fascinated by Henry Ford Museum, especially its main attraction, the

AUTHOR'S TOP TEN PICKS

Ann Arbor Hands-On Museum
Ann Arbor
(734) 995-5437
aahom.org

Detroit Zoo
Royal Oak
(248) 541-5717
detroitzoo.org

Eastern Market
Detroit
(313) 833-9300
detroiteasternmarket.com

Ford Drive-in
Dearborn
(313) 846-6910
forddrivein.com

The Henry Ford
Dearborn
(800) 835-5237
thehenryford.org

Motown Museum
Detroit
(313) 875-2264
motownmuseum.com

People Mover
Detroit
(313) 224-2160
thepeoplemover.com

River Raisin Battlefield
Monroe
(734) 243-7136
nps.gov

Walter P. Chrysler Museum
Auburn Hills
(888) 456-1924
wpchryslermuseum.org

Wright Museum of African American History
Detroit
(313) 494-5800
thewright.org

Automobile in American Life, an ode to the motor car culture that is the social history of 20th-century America. Families and children love Greenfield Village.

The complex is located at 20900 Oakwood Blvd. and reached by following signs from Southfield Freeway. Admission is $17 for adults and $12.50 for children for the museum, $24 for adults and $17.50 for children for the village, and $35 for adults and $25.50 for children for a combination ticket that provides a 1-day admission to each attraction.

For a more intimate view of the auto barons themselves, visit one of the many mansions that auto money built and historical societies have since preserved. *Fairlane,* the Henry Ford estate, is a 56-room mansion located nearby on the *University of Michigan–Dearborn campus.* Built in 1915 at what was then an astronomical $1.8 million, the home is an extension of Ford's ingenuity wrapped up in his love for functionalism. It often hosted such dignitaries as Edison, President Herbert Hoover, and Charles Lindbergh. Underground are the massive turbines and generators that were designed by Ford and his friend Edison in the 6-level powerhouse that made the estate self-sufficient in power, heat, light, and even ice.

From the outside the house looks modest compared with other historic mansions. But inside you'll find such luxuries as a central vacuum cleaner, a 65-extension phone system, and a 1-lane bowling alley. On April 7, 1947, the Rouge River flooded and knocked out the powerhouse. That night, without heat, light, or phone service, Ford suffered a cerebral hemorrhage and died by candlelight.

trivia

Michigan's largest city has the distinction of lying north of the Canadian border. Visitors are often surprised when they learn that to reach Windsor, Ontario, they have to drive south on the Ambassador Bridge or through the Detroit-Windsor Tunnel.

To reach U of M–Dearborn, head west of Southfield Expressway on Michigan Avenue and then north on Greenfield Road, where signs point the way to the small campus. Although the grounds of Fairlane (313-593-5590; henryfordestate.org) remain open to the public from Mon to Fri 8 a.m. to 6 p.m., the estate is now closed. The University of Michigan–Dearborn and the Edsel & Eleanor Ford House in Grosse Pointe Shores, Michigan, have agreed to unite the Henry Ford Estate and Ford House in what they say will become a national model of sustainability. The university is in the process of transferring ownership of the Henry Ford Estate to the Ford House. The estate is closed for restoration work and no date has been set for re-opening.

The ultimate experience for many car buffs is the *Ford Rouge Factory Tour.* The massive industrial complex is located at the confluence of the Rouge and Detroit Rivers just south of Detroit and began by producing tractors, not cars, in 1921. At its peak in the 1930s, more than 100,000 people worked at the Rouge and a new car rolled off the line every 49 seconds. The Rouge was so big that 1,500 tons of ironwere smelted daily and every month 3,500 mop heads had to be replaced to keep the complex clean.

Today the Ford Rouge Center is still Ford Motor Company's largest single industrial complex, employing 6,000 workers. It is also one of the world's most advanced and flexible manufacturing facilities, capable of building up to 9 different models on 3 vehicle platforms, and features a 10.4-acre "living roof" where thousands of tiny sedum plants help decrease energy consumption and improve air and water quality.

The tour is offered through The Henry Ford (313-982-6001, 800-835-5237; thehenryford.org) with buses leaving the museum complex in Dearborn every 20 minutes from 9:20 a.m. to 3 p.m. Mon through Sat. It begins with 2 video presentations; the first a historic look at the Rouge, the second a stunning 360-degree IMAX view of how automobiles are made. A trip to an 80-foot-high observation deck of the living roof follows, but for most visitors the best is at the end. From an elevated walkway, the 2-hour tour concludes with a view of the assembly line below and workers putting the final touches on F-150 pickup trucks. The noise and heat of a car factory are not soon forgotten. Because production varies by vehicle demand, the assembly line is not always operating but visitors can still see the assembly line. Check out the website for non-production times. Tickets for the Ford Rouge Factory Tour are $15 for adults and $11 for children.

Movie stars and fresh air—you do remember drive-in theaters, don't you? At the **Ford Drive-in** in Dearborn, it's hard to forget them. Contrary to the popular belief that drive-ins are cinematic dinosaurs of the be-bop era, this motorized movieland in the hometown of Henry Ford is still packing them in.

Ford bills itself as the "largest drive-in theater in the world" because it features 5 theaters—that's right, 5 separate screens, each showing a different movie. Always a double feature, patrons get 2 films for the price of 1.

Ford Drive-in (313-846-6910 or 313-864-4372; forddrivein.com) is reached from I-94 by taking exit 210 and heading north on Wyoming Avenue. Some of the screens are entered from Wyoming Avenue and some from Ford Road. In-car heaters are available.

To most people Detroit is Motor City, but to music lovers it will always be Motown, the birthplace of the famous record company that Berry Gordy Jr. founded in 1958. Gordy started out with $800 and a small recording studio that was built in the back of his Grand Boulevard home. From Studio A emerged the distinct "Motown Sound" and such performers as Marvin

TOP ANNUAL EVENTS

JULY

Ann Arbor Street Art Fairs
Ann Arbor
artfair.org

Michigan Elvisfest
Ypsilanti
(734) 480-3974
mielvisfest.com

Port Huron to Mackinac Island Yacht Race (Boat Night)
Port Huron
(800) 852-4242

AUGUST

Woodward Dream Cruise
Birmingham
woodwarddreamcruise.com

LABOR DAY WEEKEND

Arts, Beats & Eats
Pontiac, Labor Day
(248) 334-4600
artsbeatseats.com

Detroit International Jazz Festival
Downtown Detroit
(313) 447-1248
detroitjazzfest.com

Gaye, Smokey Robinson and the Miracles, Gladys Knight and the Pips, the Supremes, the Jackson 5, and a very talented blind singer named Steveland Morris Hardaway, known now as Stevie Wonder. Eventually the famous "Hitsville USA" sign was hung on the front of the home, and Motown expanded into seven additional houses along the street before setting up its Woodward office.

The company continued recording in Studio A until 1972, when it moved its operation to Los Angeles. What remains today at Hitsville USA is *Motown Museum,* a state historic site. The museum is two adjoining houses filled with gold record awards, old album covers, publicity photos, and even some old Temptations costumes that are viewed to the beat of Motown hits played continuously in every room. For most visitors the intriguing part is Studio A and its control booth, looking as it did many years ago when Motown was a struggling recording company.

Motown Museum (313-875-2264; motownmuseum.com) is located at 2648 W. Grand Blvd., 2 blocks west of the exit off the Lodge Freeway. The museum is open Tues through Sat 10 a.m. to 6 p.m. and Mon as well in July and Aug. Admission is $10 for adults, $8 for children.

Although Detroit has its mansions and its auto barons, it is known primarily as a blue-collar town, an assembly-line haven that has made it as ethnically diverse as any city in the country. Detroiters love their heritage, ethnic foods, music, and the traditions of an old way of life. The ethnic pride and the love of traditional foods can best be seen at the **Eastern Market** (313-833-9300; detroiteasternmarket.com), a farmers' market that, at 43 acres, is said to be the largest of its kind (open to retailers rather than wholesalers) in the country and certainly one of the oldest in the Midwest. It dates back to 1841. Two areas, one open-air, the other enclosed, and both decorated with huge murals on the outside, are the heart of the market with more than 250 independent vendors and merchants. On Sat from 5 a.m. to 5 p.m. they overflow with shoppers, farmers, and vendors bartering for the freshest fruit, vegetables, flowers, meats, and cheeses to be found in the city. Everything from the farm is on sale here, from homemade bratwurst to live rabbits, and the market makes for an enjoyable stroll, even if you don't intend to buy anything. Ringing the market are butcher shops, fish markets, and stores specializing in spices, nuts, and foods imported from around the world.

To reach the Eastern Market, head downtown on I-75 and exit east on Mack Avenue. The market is 2 blocks east of the expressway, near Russell Avenue.

Restaurants also reflect the ethnically diverse, hardworking Detroiters who at nightfall put aside their jobs and enjoy themselves immensely with good food served in large portions at very reasonable prices. Coney Island hot dogs and baseball are a summer tradition in the Motor City. Begin with the Detroit Tigers, an American League club that moved into its new stadium, Comerica Park, in 2000; after the ninth inning, head over to **Lafayette Coney Island,** Detroit's premier hot-dog place. Located where Lafayette and Michigan Avenues merge near Kennedy Square downtown, the porcelain white eatery with its male waiters is an institution in Detroit. The fare is Coney dogs (with loads of chopped onions, chili, and mustard), loose burgers (loose hamburger in a hot-dog bun), and bean soup served on Formica counters and tables with paper napkins and truck-stop china. Yet arrive at midnight and you'll see patrons dressed in tuxedos enjoying a late-night hot dog after the symphony, seated next to a couple of rabid baseball fans with a team pennant. Lafayette Coney Island (313-964-8198) is

Dueling Coney Islands

In Michigan a chili dog is called a "Coney Island" in reference to the birthplace of the hot dog. The hot dog itself may be East Coast but the Coney Island is a Detroit tradition that dates back more than 90 years.

It began in 1917 when Constantine "Gust" Keros, a Greek immigrant to Detroit, opened *American Coney Island* on Lafayette Avenue. Keros sold his New York–style hot dogs for a nickel and was so successful that he enticed his brother, William, to immigrate from Greece and help with the family business. In 1924, the storefront next door became available and William Keros jumped at the opportunity to start his own shop, *Lafayette Coney Island.* The competition between the two brothers was friendly but fierce and soon both began slathering their hot dogs with chili to attract customers, leading to Detroit's unique version of a Coney Island. Or so the story goes.

What can't be debated is these two hot dog restaurants, still owned by third generation family members, have been slugging it out for the heart and soul of Detroiters ever since. They are both open 24 hours a day, 7 days a week, serving up a hot dog, covered with a "secret family chili sauce recipe," chopped onions, and yellow mustard and served in a steamed bun. Your order is called out, usually in a thick accent, by a waiter standing next to your table and arrives almost instantaneously with the toppings piled so high on the hot dog most of your plate is covered with chili and onions. All this for about $3.

In 1989, American Coney Island (313-961-7758; 114 W. Lafayette Blvd.; americanconeyisland.com) moved into an adjacent corner building but Lafayette Coney Island (313-964-8198; 118 W. Lafayette Blvd.) is still located in the same storefront where the Formica tables, cramped interior, and truck-stop china has changed little since the day it opened. Passion for the Coney Island hot dog is so strong in Detroit that most people have pledged an allegiance to one eatery or the other. Me? I'm a Lafayette Coney Island connoisseur to the point where despite having lived most of my life in southeast Michigan, I have never set foot in American Coney Island much less eaten one of their hot dogs.

But I hear they're good.

open 24 hours daily with hot dogs and loose burgers priced at around $2. They only accept cash.

A few blocks over at Monroe Street is lively Greektown, where a dozen restaurants, nightclubs, and Greek bakeries make it the liveliest spot in downtown Detroit. My favorite restaurant is *Pegasus Tavernas*

(313-964-6800; pegasustavernas.com), where you can enjoy the Detroit tradition of saganaki—flaming Greek kasseri cheese served to the cry of "Opa!" The best comfort food in Detroit is **Southern Fires** (313-393-4930; southernfiresrestaurant.com) at 575 Bellevue St. It's the place for fried catfish, collard greens, sweet potato pie, even fried corn. Detroit's Polish community is centered around the city of Hamtramck, where Pope John Paul II once performed mass. At the **Polish Village Cafe** (313-874-5726; thepolishvillagecafe.com) at Yehmans Street and Joseph Campau Avenue, you can dig into stuffed cabbage, pork goulash, and pierogi for less than $8. Great barbecue is easy to find throughout the city but it's hard to pass up the smoked meats and baby back ribs and pulled pork served at **Slows Bar BQ** (313-962-9828; slowsbarbq.com) at 2138 Michigan Ave. in the Corktown District of Detroit.

It may not be "off the beaten path," but Detroit's Central Automated Transit System is definitely above the city streets. Better known as the **People Mover,** the mass transit project was opened in 1987 after several years of controversial delays and cost overruns. The 2.9-mile elevated track circles the downtown heart of Detroit. Its automated cars stop every 3 minutes at 13 stations, each decorated with beautiful mosaics and other artwork. The ride costs only 75 cents and lasts 15 minutes, but it gives an excellent overall view of the city from a superb vantage point. The best stretch comes when the cars wind around Cobo Hall and passengers see a panorama of the Detroit River and the skyline of Windsor, the Canadian city to the south. The People Mover (313-224-2160; thepeoplemover.com) operates from 6:30 a.m. to midnight Mon to Thurs, until 2 a.m. Fri and Sat, and noon to midnight Sun.

The Detroit River, which connects Lake St. Clair with Lake Erie, was the

trivia

Detroit is the birthplace of Vernors, a fizzy ginger drink that many from the Motor City claim was the country's first soft drink, dating back to the 1860s. Pharmacist James Vernor was experimenting with ginger drinks at his drugstore on Woodward Avenue when in 1862 he enlisted in the Union Army. Before shipping out for the Civil War, Vernor stored one of his concoctions in an oak cask. When he returned four years later, he discovered to his utter amazement a carbonated drink with delectable taste. For years the Vernons factory on Woodward Avenue was a Detroit icon before it closed when the brand was sold to Cadbury Schweppes Americas Beverages of Texas.

avenue that the city's first residents—the French in 1701—used to arrive in Southeast Michigan. The river remains a focal point of activities for Detroiters, with several parks lining its banks and one—Belle Isle—located in the middle of it. Reached by a bridge at E. Jefferson and Grand Boulevard, the island park features the **Dossin Great Lakes Museum,** which traces the maritime history of Detroit and the Great Lakes in several rooms of displays and hands-on exhibits. Within the museum is the famed hydroplane racer, *Miss Pepsi,* the massive bow anchor of the doomed freighter, *Edmund Fitzgerald,* and, from the golden age of steamers of the 1940s, the restored smoking lounge of the SS *City of Detroit III.* Children will love Michigan's largest collection of model ships or stepping up to the steering wheel in the preserved pilothouse of a Great Lakes freighter that actually looks out on the Detroit River.

The **Dossin Great Lakes Museum** (313-833-5538) is open 11 a.m. to 4 p.m. on Sat and Sun. Opened April 2013, a new exhibit titled "Built by the River" traces the settlement that became Detroit. Early history examines Detroit's place at the center of the fur trade, and how its geographic placement made it a strategic spot for the French, British, and American armed forces. Later, its location on the river made Detroit a center of industrial development, manufacturing capital, and marine transportation. The river also serves as an international border and was a factor in Detroit's participation in the Underground Railroad as well as witnessing smuggling activity during the Prohibition era. Today it serves as the busiest international river crossing on the continent. Admission is free.

If the day is nice, you can spend an afternoon at Hart Plaza at the foot of Woodward Avenue overlooking the Detroit River and Windsor. For an even better view of the waterfront, **Diamond Jack River Tours** (313-843-9376; diamondjack.com) offers 2-hour cruises on the Detroit River that depart from Rivard Plaza at the foot of Rivard Street and Atwater Street. The cruises are offered June through Labor Day and are $17 for adults and $13 for children.

trivia

Michigan's first public whipping post stood at Woodward and Jefferson Avenues in Detroit from 1818 to 1831. At the intersection now is the giant sculptural fist. The controversial statue honors Joe Louis, Detroit's famous son who became world heavyweight boxing champion in 1937.

Detroit's Cultural Center, clustered around Woodward Avenue and Kirby Street, is dominated by the **Detroit Institute of Arts** (313-833-7900; dia.org). Thanks to auto baron wealth accumulated in the early 1900s and a $158 million renovation and expansion in 2008, the DIA is the fifth largest art museum in the country and its collection of more than 60,000 pieces is considered one of the best. It is known for its Italian Renaissance, Dutch-Flemish, and German expressionist art, but the most viewed work is probably Diego Rivera's mural, *Detroit Industry*, which fills a room and reflects the city's blue-collar work ethic. Hours are 9 a.m. to 4 p.m. Wed through Thurs, 9 a.m. to 10 p.m. Fri, and 10 a.m. to 5 p.m. Sat and Sun. Admission is $8 for adults and $4 for children. Admission is free on Ford Free Sundays, the second Sunday of each month, sponsored by the Ford Motor Company Fund.

Within easy walking distance of the DIA at E. Warren Avenue and Brush Street is the **Wright Museum of African American History** (313-494-5800; thewright.org), the largest such museum in the country; its collection ranges from art to clubs and golf shoes used by Tiger Woods. The museum's popular permanent exhibit is entitled "And Still We Rise." The impressive, $8 million exhibit uses multimedia displays to trace the 400-year history and culture of African Americans. Hours are 9 a.m. to 5 p.m. Tues through Sat and 1 to 5 p.m. Sun. Admission is $8 for adults and $5 for children.

Also located in the Cultural Center is the **Michigan Science Center** (313-577-8400; mi-sci.org) at 5020 John R St. The center was founded in the

Detroit's Cool Jazz

There's nothing like spending an evening in night clubs listening to local jazz and blues that have always been the foundation of the Detroit music scene. A list of clubs with the type of music they feature can be found in *Metro Times* (metrotimes.com), a free entertainment newspaper.

One of the better-known clubs for jazz is **Baker's Keyboard Lounge** (313-345-6300; officialbakerskeyboardlounge.com) at 20510 Livernois Ave. For blues head to **Nancy Whiskey** (313-962-4247; nancywhiskeydetroit.com) at 2644 Harrison St., or **Bert's Jazz Marketplace** (313-567-2030) at 2727 Russell St., a night club in the Eastern Market District with sticky menus, small wobbly tables, satisfying soul food, and excellent blues and jazz.

early 1970s as the Detroit Science Center and was among the first in the country to feature an IMAX Dome Theater. The Michigan Science Center now runs this Midtown Detroit gem as an entirely new nonprofit organization after purchasing the assets (building, land, and exhibits) of the former Detroit Science Center. Today the museum features 110,000 square feet of scientific exploration with hundreds of hands-on exhibits and 3 live stages where participants have a "hair-raising" good time, along with multiple hands-on lab areas for future scientists. You can still see a more-real-than-life movie in the Chrysler IMAX Dome Theater or gaze at the universe in the Dassault Systemes Planetarium. The Michigan Science Center is often home to large traveling exhibits, and even features a discovery space called Kids Town for the youngest explorers. Hours vary so check the center's schedule. Admission is $12.95 for adults and $9.95 for children.

In 1882 the Plymouth Iron Windmill Company began to manufacture and give away small BB guns to farmers to encourage them to purchase one of its windmills. Within four years, the northwest corner of Wayne County was well "windmilled," but the company kept producing the air rifles. Eventually Plymouth Iron Windmill Company became Daisy Manufacturing Company, and this small town was known as the "air rifle capital of the world" until the operations were moved to Arkansas in 1958.

You can learn about the start of Daisy air rifles and see a collection of the earliest models at the *Plymouth Historical Museum.* The museum also has many other displays, including an impressive Abraham Lincoln exhibit that contains a rare book belonging to Lincoln as a boy and a life mask the president made in 1860. But it is the display of Daisy air rifles that brings back fond memories of tin cans in the backyard to so many of us.

To reach the Plymouth Historical Museum at 155 S. Main St. (734-455-8940; plymouthhistory.org) from I-275, get off at exit 28, head west on Ann Arbor Road, and then turn north on Main Street. Hours are 1 to 4 p.m. Wed, Fri, Sat, and Sun. Admission is $5 for adults and $2 for children.

Monroe County

General George Armstrong Custer may have staged his ill-fated "last stand" at the Little Bighorn River in Montana, but he grew up in *Monroe,* Michigan. Custer was actually born in Rumley, Ohio, but spent most of his youth, until he entered a military academy at the age of 16, living with his half sister in this city along Lake Erie. Even after he became a noted brigadier general during the Civil War, Custer continued to return to Monroe, and in 1864 he married Elizabeth Bacon, his boyhood sweetheart, here.

Custer's intriguing life can be traced at the *Monroe County Historical Museum,* which features the largest collection of the general's personal artifacts in the country. The Custer exhibit room occupies a fourth of the museum floor, and focuses on his youth in Monroe and his distinguished Civil War career, rather than his well-known days on the western plains. There is an overcoat of buffalo hide that he wore during a winter campaign in 1868 and a buckskin suit that is impressive with its beadwork and porcupine quills. Custer was an avid outdoorsman and also a fine taxidermist. It comes as a surprise to many that Custer enjoyed mounting the game animals he hunted, and housed in the museum along with his favorite Remington buffalo rifle are many mounted game animals.

The museum also has displays on Monroe's early history, which dates back to French missionaries in 1634. But it is the life and tragic death of General Custer that most people find fascinating. The Monroe County Historical Museum (734-240-7780; co .monroe.mi.us/government/depart- ments_offices/museum/index.html) is at 126 S. Monroe St. in the heart of the city and is open Wed through Sun from 10 a.m. to 5 p.m. During the summer through Sept, it is open daily. Admission is $4 for adults, $2 for childen.

Unless you are a military buff, you might not realize that the Massacre of the River Raisin was among the largest battles in the War of 1812 and produced more American casualties than any other conflict. But you will because in 2009 the *River Raisin Battlefield* was dedicated as one of the country's newest National Park

trivia

The center of the University of Michigan campus is the Diag, a parklike opening that extends from State Street to S. University Avenue. The bronze seal in the center was donated by the Class of 1953, and legend has it that any freshman who steps on it before taking his or her first exam at U of M will fail the test.

Nearby on the west side of State Street is the Michigan Union. It was on the steps of this imposing building that John F. Kennedy first announced his vision of the Peace Corps in 1960 while campaigning for the White House.

units. At the battlefield and in its fine visitor center you will retrace what many historians believe was the turning point in the conflict with Great Britain.

After the disastrous opening months of the War of 1812 in which Mackinac Island, Chicago, and Detroit had fallen, two of them without even a shot fired, an elderly Revolutionary War veteran, General James Winchester, was sent to Michigan with almost 1,000 men. The large American force set up camp on an open field on the north side of the river. But in the pre-dawn darkness of January 22, almost 600 British regulars with six cannons and 800 Indians attacked. The fighting raged for 20 minutes and then for Winchester's army turned into a panicked flight for Ohio. Of the 400 Americans who ran, 220 were killed, another 147, including Winchester himself, were captured, and only 33 managed to escape to safety. The next day Indians returned to plunder the homes, scalp the wounded, and toss the bodies into burning homes. More than 60 unarmed Americans were killed, and a nation was horrified. Soon, "Remember the Raisin!" became a battle cry that led US troops to victory in the old Northwest.

All this history has been carefully preserved and clearly presented at the battlefield visitor center. Its most impressive display is a 14-minute fiber-optic map presentation. On 2 wall-size maps, the story of the River Raisin is retold with the Americans, British, and Indians, as colorful lights, maneuvering and taking up positions in front of you. The visitor center (734-243-7136; riverraisinbattlefield.org) is reached from I-75 by taking exit 14 and heading west on Elm Street. The center is open 10 a.m. to 5 p.m. Fri through Tues from Memorial Day through Labor Day. Winter hours are Mon through Fri 10 a.m. to 4 p.m., Sat and Sun 9 a.m. to 5 p.m. There is no admission charge.

Washtenaw County

Trendy *Ann Arbor,* the cultural capital of Southeast Michigan (and some say the entire state), is the site of the University of Michigan, the "Harvard of the West." The university dominates the city, its buildings and campus entwined in the town's landscape. It provides many of Ann Arbor's top attractions, such as the *Kelsey Museum of Archaeology* at 434 S. State St. (734-764-9304; lsa.umich.edu/kelsey), a renowned collection of art and artifacts, including mummies, from Egyptian, Greek, Roman, and classical

Mediterranean cultures. On Saturdays in the fall, Ann Arbor is U of M football; the largest stadium crowds in the country (112,000) gather to cheer on the Wolverines.

But there is another side to this college town, one that children will appreciate, and it begins at the *Ann Arbor Hands-On Museum.* This is no stuffy hall with an endless row of glass-enclosed displays. The entire museum is devoted to participatory exhibits—more than 250 in 9 galleries on 4 floors—and the concept that kids learn by doing. Housed in the classic Central Fire House, the museum was dedicated on September 28, 1982, the 100th anniversary of the building. Inside, the exhibits range from our world—watching dozens of caterpillars feeding on apple leaves and busily spinning their cocoons—to outer space—viewing images from NASA's Hubble Space Telescope that are updated daily. All are fun. The bubble capsule is where participants step into a ring of soap film and slowly raise a cylinder bubble around them until it pops. No stuffy science here, yet exhibits are accompanied by an explanation that is appreciated mostly by the parents. The Ann Arbor Hands-On Museum (734-995-5439; aahom.org) is recommended for children 8 years of age and older. It is at Huron Street and Fifth Avenue, which can be reached by following Business US 23 (Main Street) from M 14 north of the city or from I-94 by exiting to US 23 and then to Washtenaw Avenue. Hours are Mon 10 a.m. to 5 p.m., Tues 9 a.m. to 5 p.m., Wed 10 a.m. to 5 p.m., Thurs 10 a.m. to 8 p.m., Fri and Sat 10 a.m. to 5 p.m., and Sun noon to 5 p.m. Admission is $10 for adults or children.

Big Leaguers in Motown

Motown is also a diehard sports town, and its fans have plenty of big-league action to choose from in Southeast Michigan. The Detroit Pistons play men's basketball at the *Palace of Auburn Hills* (tickets: 248-377-0100; palacenet.com). The Detroit Red Wings, the 2008 and 2009 Stanley Cup winners, play at Joe Louis Arena (313-983-6606; redwings.nhl.com). The *Detroit Tigers* (313-471-2000; detroittigers.com), who reached the World Series in 2006, play baseball in impressive Comerica Park, while next door the *Detroit Lions* (800-616-7627; detroitlions.com) play football at Ford Field or they try to. In 2008 the Lions became the first NFL team to go winless in a 16-game season. But Detroiters still love them.

There are no mountains in Southeast Michigan, but that doesn't stop the region from being a mecca for mountain biking. In large part because of cycle-crazy Ann Arbor, the trails at *Pinckney Recreation Area* have been transformed into a playground for off-road cycling. It's estimated that more than 120,000 mountain bikers from Ohio, Indiana, and Illinois as well as Michigan visit the park annually to ride the challenging 17.5-mile Potawatomi Trail, the 5-mile Crooked Lake Trail, or the 2-mile Silver Lake Trail.

The trailhead for all trails is in the park's Silver Lake Day-Use Area, reached from US 23 by taking exit 49 and heading west on N. Territorial Road to Dexter-Townhall Road, then heading north on Dexter-Townhall Road past the park headquarters (734-426-4913) to the day-use area. In Pinckney mountain bikes can be rented at the *Village Cyclery* (734-878-0117; pinckneyvillagecyclery.com) at 109 E. Main St.

Oakland County

It's 4 p.m. in *Birmingham* and you're sipping tea from fine china in a setting that includes fresh-cut flowers, silver platters of cakes and other tempting edibles, a fire in a fireplace of imported Italian marble, and a tuxedo-clad piano player, er, excuse me, pianist.

Must be tea at the Townsend. The afternoon ritual, in all its elegance, takes place throughout the week in the *Townsend Hotel,* the most affluent hotel in this ritzy suburb of Detroit. Built in 1988, the hotel has 87 rooms and 52 suites on 3 floors, and among its guests have been entertainers such as Madonna, Michael Jackson, Paul McCartney, and New Kids on the Block. (Remember them?) Just about anybody who plays in Detroit stays at the Townsend.

Have afternoon tea here, and who knows? Maybe you'll see Billy Idol stroll in. It has happened before. From Woodward Avenue in downtown Birmingham, turn west onto Townsend Street, and the hotel is reached in 3 blocks. Afternoon tea is offered 7 days a week from 1 to 5 p.m. The cost is $36 for adults and reservations are required. Deluxe Tea at $60 includes champagne punch, soup or salad, fresh fruit, and torte of the day. Contact the Townsend Hotel (248-642-7900; townsendhotel.com) for reservations.

In 1904, George Booth, founder of Booth Newspapers and the publisher of the *Detroit News*, and his wife purchased a run-down farm in Bloomfield

Hills with a vision of establishing an educational community that would inspire creativity and excellence. A century later *Cranbrook Schools* have evolved into one of the country's leading centers for art and education as the home to 1,600 students from 17 states and 34 countries. Cranbrook graduates range from presidential candidate Mitt Romney and actress Selma Blair to Sun Microsystems founder Scott McNealy and Michael Kinsley, the first editor of the online magazine *Slate*.

But visitors are also welcomed to the school's impressive 315-acre campus that was designated a National Historic Landmark in 1989. An afternoon can be spent viewing the *Cranbrook Art Museum,* featuring the work of local, national, and international artists as well as 20 temporary exhibitions a year, or wandering through the 40-acre *Cranbrook House and Gardens,* the home of founders George and Ellen Booth. Kids will be amazed by the displays at the *Cranbrook Institute of Science,* the home of the only T. *Rex* skeleton in Michigan and the Bat Zone that is filled with live bats and other nocturnal creatures.

trivia

The country's first shopping mall, Northland, was built in Southfield in Oakland County in 1954.

Cranbrook (248-645-3323; cranbrook.edu) is located at 39221 Woodward Ave. in Bloomfield Hills. Cranbrook Art Museum (248-645-3323) is open Wed through Sun from 11 a.m. to 5 p.m. and admission is $8 for adults. Cranbrook Institute of Science (248-645-3200) is open 10 a.m. to 5 p.m. Tues through Thurs, 10 a.m. to 10 p.m. Fri and Sat, and noon to 4 p.m. on Sun. Admission is $12.50 for adults and $9.50 for children. Cranbrook House and Garden tours (248-645-3147) are offered at various times from July through Oct and are $10 for adults.

The newest museum in Southeast Michigan focuses on one of the state's most popular attractions: classic cars. In 1999 the *Walter P. Chrysler Museum,* with its collection of 75 cars, opened on the grounds of DaimlerChrysler's huge Auburn Hills complex. The sleek $10 billion center is the first on-site museum built by a North American auto company.

Inside are interactive displays, a video wall, life-size dioramas, and timelines that detail the history of the car company that Walter Chrysler founded in 1924. But the main attraction here is the cars themselves. Just

SOUTHEAST MICHIGAN DRIVE-INS

The 1950s are alive and well at *Eddie's Drive-in* (586-469-2345), a landmark burger place at 36111 Jefferson Ave. in Harrison Township. It's a nightly show in the summer when hip cats and cool chicks show off their hot rods while carhops on roller skates serve you shakes and fries to the be-bop music of that golden era. Eddie's is open from Apr to mid-Oct.

With its strong car culture you'd expect many other surviving drive-ins offering curbside service throughout Southeast Michigan and there are. Here a few of the best serving foot-longs, sandwiches called Hammy Sammy, and shakes made with real ice cream:

BERKLEY

A&W
4100 12 Mile Rd.
(248) 547-7126
cruisinaw.com

LIVONIA

Daly Drive-in
31500 Plymouth Rd.
(734) 427-4474
dalyrestaurants.com

YPSILANTI

Bill's Drive-in
1292 E. Michigan Ave.
(734) 485-2831

Chick Inn Drive-in
501 Holmes Rd.
(734) 483-3639

inside the front door is a massive 75-foot stainless steel pylon that holds aloft a 1941 Thunderbolt and a red 1989 Viper concept car. Called "The Tower," the display slowly rotates to give visitors a full view of the impressive cars. Other vehicles on exhibit include rare DeSoto, Hudson, Nash, and Rambler models, as well as trucks and concept cars.

To reach the museum (888-456-1924; chryslerheritage.com) depart I-75 at exit 78 and head east on Chrysler Drive into the DaimlerChrysler complex. Signs will direct you to the museum. Hours are 10 a.m. to 5 p.m. Tues through Sat and noon to 5 p.m. Sun. Admission is $8 for adults and $4 for children.

The urban sprawl of Southeast Michigan runs its course to Pontiac, but from there the terrain changes quickly to the rolling hills, lakes, and woods of northern Oakland. A drive of less than an hour from the heart of Detroit can remove you from the city and bring you to the porch steps of a rustic

Visiting the North Pole in Michigan

Our timing was perfect; on the March day we visited the Arctic Ring of Life exhibit at the *Detroit Zoo,* the temperature was in the mid-teens.

At Glacier Overlook we had our hands buried in our pockets and our backs against the wind when suddenly a polar bear appeared, strolled across the pack ice, and then belly flopped into water that was littered with small icebergs.

It looked—and felt—as if we were at the North Pole.

Which is exactly what the officials at the Detroit Zoo were hoping to achieve when they unveiled "the world's largest polar bear exhibit" in 2001.

The $14.9-million Arctic Ring of Life covers 4.2 acres and is designed to simulate a trek through the three environments found north of the Arctic Circle: tundra, open sea, and pack ice.

A one-way path first winds through the tundra, where you can see arctic foxes prance around or a pair of snowy owls blink back at you. From there you descend into the open sea via the Polar Passage.

This passage is a showstopper, a 70-foot-long, acrylic tunnel that takes you through the exhibit's 300,000-gallon sea environment. On one side are a half dozen seals lazily swimming and eyeing you through the transparent walls. On the other side it's possible to watch the powerful elegance of an 800-pound polar bear underwater. It's a fascinating experience watching seals swim over your head.

From the tunnel you venture into the pack ice environment by first entering an ice cave with a howling winter gale and icy walls that are covered with polar bear prints.

From the cave you reemerge outside and follow the path as it leads you past a handful of viewing points of the pack ice where polar bears can be seen swimming among the icebergs in the open water.

The Detroit Zoo (248-541-5717; detroitzoo.org) is open from 9 a.m. to 5 p.m. daily in the summer with shorter hours the rest of the year. Admission is $14 for adults and $9 for children.

To reach the zoo from I-696, exit north on Woodward Avenue just west of I-75. There are entrances to the zoo on both Woodward Avenue and Ten Mile Road.

cabin on a small pond in a wooded area where white-tailed deer often pass by. **Roston Cabin** in Holly Recreation Area makes a weekend spent in the woods as comfortable and warm as sitting around the fireplace at night. The cabin is snug and tight, but still rustic and secluded enough to make it seem like an adventure in the woods—even though the car is parked right outside.

Built by the Roston family as a weekend cottage in 1938–39, the cabin was obtained by the park, which began renting it out in 1984. It's a classic cabin built with walls of logs, polished planked floors, and red-checkered curtains on the windows. There is electricity, and the kitchen features an electric stove and refrigerator as well as a table, benches, and a wood stove. The sleeping room is larger, with a set of bunks and an easy chair facing a fieldstone fireplace. Overlooking the cozy room is a loft, the warmest part of the cabin at night, with 4 more mattresses. Outside you'll find a vault toilet, woodshed, a hand pump for water, and a barbecue grill.

It's necessary to reserve the cabin in advance by calling the park headquarters, and, surprisingly, the most popular time to rent it is during the winter when families arrive to cross-country ski on the unplowed park roads around the lakes. The overnight rate for the cabin is $50 Sun through Thurs and $80 Fri and Sat. Reservations can be made through the **Michigan Campground Central Reservation System** (800-447-2757; midnrreservations.com). The recreation area is reached by taking Grange Hall Road (exit 101) east off I-75.

Many people exit I-75 at Grange Hall Road and head west to explore the historical town of **Holly.** Established in the early 1800s, Holly was a sleepy little hamlet until 1855, when the Detroit-Milwaukee Railroad reached the town, bringing immediate growth and prosperity with the 25 trains that passed through daily. Martha Street, near the tracks, was the site of the Holly Hotel, many saloons, and frequent brawls. In 1880 an uproar between local rowdies and a traveling circus left so many beaten and bruised that the street became known as **Battle Alley.** The most famous moment in Battle Alley's history was on August 28, 1908, when Carry Nation, the notorious "Kansas Saloon Smasher," arrived in Holly at the request of the local Prohibition committee. The next day Nation, with umbrella in hand and her pro-temperance supporters a step behind her, invaded the saloons, smashing whiskey bottles, clubbing patrons, and preaching about the sins of "demon rum." Nation created the biggest flurry at the hotel, where she entered the "Dispensing Room" and attacked the painting of a nude over the bar.

Battle Alley and its hundred-year-old Victorian buildings have been restored as a string of about 10 specialty shops that include antiques markets both along the alley and on nearby streets.

The Holly Hotel, which was built in 1891 and suffered through two devastating fires, the second in 1978, has since been completely restored, including the painting of the nude. It is now listed on the National Register of Historic Places but no longer provides lodging. Instead, the hotel is a fine restaurant, known for both its classic and its creative cuisine, all set in a Victorian tradition that reflects its birth during the railroad era. The main dining room, with its pedestal tables, soft glow of gas lamps, and red velvet wingback chairs, is the stage for such entrees as medallions of beef with morel mushroom sauce, filet of beef Wellington, and Great Lakes white fish with Asiago and garlic panko gratin.

The Holly Hotel (248-634-5208; hollyhotel.com) is open for afternoon tea at 2 p.m. Mon through Sat and for dinner from 4 to 10 p.m. daily. A Sunday brunch is served from 10:30 a.m. to 2:30 p.m. for $19 for adults, $9 children. Dinner prices range from $23 to $33, and reservations are recommended.

Macomb County

In the fall one of the favorite activities in Southeast Michigan is a trip to a *cider mill.* Parents pack the kids in the car and head out to the edge of the county where a river turns an old wooden waterwheel. The wheel is the source of power for the mill, which crushes apples to extract the dark brown juice and refine it into cider, truly one of Michigan's culinary delights. After viewing the operation, visitors can purchase jugs of cider, cinnamon doughnuts, and sticky caramel apples and then retreat to a place along the river. Here they enjoy a feast in the midst of brilliant fall colors, in the warmth of an Indian summer, and with the fragrance of crushed apples floating by.

Cider mills ring the metropolitan Detroit area, but one of the oldest and most colorful lies right on the border of Oakland and Macomb Counties west of Rochester on Avon Road (Twenty-Three Mile Road). *Yates Cider Mill* was built in 1863 along the banks of the Clinton River and began its long history as a gristmill. It has been a water-powered operation ever since, but in 1876 it began making cider, and today the waterwheel still powers the apple elevator, grinders, and press as well as generating electricity for the lights inside. The mill can produce 300 gallons of cider per hour, all of which is needed in the fall to meet the demand of visitors who enjoy their treat around the huge red barn or across the street on the banks of the Clinton River. Yates Cider Mill (248-651-8300; yatescidermill.com) is open daily from 9 a.m. to 7 p.m. Sept through Nov, and from noon to 5 p.m. Sat and Sun Dec until May.

You won't find much apple cider to sip, but an equally interesting mill in Macomb County is the focal point at *Wolcott Mill Metropark.* Built in 1847 on the North Branch of the Clinton River, Wolcott Mill was a grist and feed operation for more than a century, commercially milling as late as 1967. Today the mill's grain-grinding machinery is still turning for visitors while exhibits and interpreters provide a glimpse of a bygone era.

The 2,380-acre park also includes several other historical buildings, a short nature trail, and a farm learning center where children can have contact with barnyard animals. Wolcott Mill Metropark (586-749-5997) is southeast of Romeo, with the mill entrance off Kunstman Road just north of Twenty-Nine Mile Road. Building hours for the park are 9 a.m. to 5 p.m. daily, with longer weekend hours during the summer and fall. There is a vehicle fee to enter the park.

St. Clair County

This county is often referred to as the Bluewater region of Michigan because it is bounded by Lake St. Clair to the south, Lake Huron to the north, and the St. Clair River to the east. M 29 circles the north side of Lake St. Clair and then follows the river to *Port Huron,* passing small towns and many bait shops, marinas, and shoreline taverns advertising walleye and perch fish fries. The most charming town on the water is *St. Clair,* 15 miles south of Port Huron and a major shipbuilding center in the early 1900s. The city has renovated its downtown section, centering it on *Palmer Park,* which residents claim has one of the longest boardwalks in the world facing freshwater. The favorite activity on the 1,500-foot riverwalk is watching the Great Lakes freighters that glide by exceptionally close, giving land-bound viewers a good look at the massive boats and their crews. The second favorite activity is walleye fishing. The *St. Clair River* is renowned for this fish, and anglers can be seen throughout the summer tossing a line from the riverwalk, trying to entice the walleye with minnows or night crawlers.

Above the walkway is a wide, grassy bank filled with sunbathers, kids playing, and, in mid-June, the arts and crafts booths of the *St. Clair Art Fair,* a popular festival along the river. Call the *St. Clair Art Association* (810-329-9576; stclairart.org) for the exact dates and times. The riverwalk ends to the north at the *St. Clair Inn* (810-329-2222; stclairinn.com), a historic hotel that was built in 1926 and today features outdoor dining in a courtyard overlooking the river.

trivia

The first underground railroad tunnel in the world was opened between Port Huron and Sarnia, Ontario, in 1891. It is 11,725 feet long with 2,290 feet underground.

Port Huron, a city of 30,000, is the site of the *Bluewater Bridge,* the international crossing between Michigan and Sarnia, Ontario. It is also recognized throughout the state as the start of the *Port Huron–Mackinac Sailboat Race* in late July. On the eve of the event, known as *Boat Night* (boatnight.com), the downtown area of Water, Lapeer, and Quay Streets, which borders the docks on the Black River, becomes congested with block parties. Sailors, local people, and tourists mingle in a festival that spreads throughout the streets, the yacht clubs, and even onto the sailboats themselves.

Port Huron has several museums, and one of the most interesting honors its favorite son; the *Thomas Edison Depot Museum* (810-982-0891) is located under the Bluewater Bridge at 510 Thomas Edison Parkway. The museum is housed in the historic Fort Gratiot Depot, built in 1858, where Edison picked up the Grand Trunk Railroad train, on which he sold candy and newspapers as a youth. Exhibits portray Edison's younger days and what led him to become the greatest inventor of our times. Outside the depot, a restored baggage car contains Edison's mobile print shop, which he used to publish the *Weekly Herald,* the world's first newspaper to be printed on a moving train. Edison sold the newspaper on the train for 2 cents a copy and eventually had a circulation of more than 400.

Edison in Port Huron

Port Huron's most famous resident was not its happiest one. *Thomas Edison* moved to the city with his family when he was 7 years old but quit school after only three days when a teacher wrote that the future inventor was "addled." His mother taught him at home, and Edison, already fascinated with science and chemistry, turned the family basement into his personal laboratory.

To pay for the chemicals and equipment, he took a job selling candy and newspapers on the Grand Trunk Railroad's commute to Detroit and back. The Port Huron Depot that he worked out of is now the Thomas Edison Depot Museum.

But Edison left the town as a teen to seek telegraph work and eventually his fortune out east at Menlo Park, New Jersey. "I do not think that any living human being will ever see me there again," he wrote to his father when he was 30 years old and already a well-known inventor. "I don't want you to stay in that hole of a Port Huron, which contains the most despicable remnants of the human race that can be found on earth."

Historians said that over time, Edison softened his views on Port Huron and later in life did return several times, mostly to attend family funerals.

The museum is open 11 a.m. to 5 p.m. daily from Memorial Day to Labor Day, and Thurs through Mon from May throu Oct. Admission is $7 for adults and $5 for children.

A short walk from the depot museum is the *Port Huron Museum* (810-982-0891; phmuseum.org) at 1115 Sixth St. The museum combines an art gallery with collections of natural history and artifacts from Port Huron's past. Included are bones and displays of the prehistoric mammoths that roamed Michigan's Thumb 10,000 years ago and memorabilia of Thomas Edison's boyhood home, which was located in the city. A popular attraction is the reconstructed pilothouse of a Great Lakes freighter. All the furnishings were taken from various ships, and visitors can work the wheel, signal the alarm horn, and ring the engine bell. All around the pilothouse is a huge mural that gives the impression you are guiding the vessel into Lake Huron. The museum, housed in a 1904 Carnegie library, is open 11 a.m. to 5 p.m. daily. Admission is $7 for adults and $5 for children.

Places to Stay in Southeast Michigan

ANN ARBOR

Bell Tower Hotel
300 S. Thayer St.
(800) 562-3559
belltowerhotel.com

Vitosha Guest Haus Inn
1917 Washtenaw Ave.
(734) 741-4969
a2vitosha.com

Weber's Inn
3050 Jackson Rd.
(734) 769-2500
webersinn.com

AUBURN HILLS

Courtyard by Marriott
2550 Aimee Ln.
(248) 373-4100
marriott.com

DEARBORN

Dearborn Inn
20301 Oakwood Blvd.
(313) 271-2700
marriott.com

The Henry
300 Town Center Dr.
(313) 441-2000
behenry.com

DETROIT

Atheneum Hotel
1000 Brush St.
(313) 962-2323
atheneumsuites.com

Book Cadillac Detroit
1114 Washington Blvd.
(313) 442-1600
bookcadillacwestin.com

The Inn At 97 Winder
97 Winder St.
(800) 925-1538
theinnat97winder.com

Roberts Riverwalk Hotel
1000 River Place
(313) 259-9500
detroitriverwalkhotel.com

MONROE

The Lotus Bed & Breakfast
324 Washington St.
(734) 735-1077

MOUNT CLEMENS

Concorde Inn
44315 Gratiot Ave.
(586) 493-7300
concordeinn.com

PORT HURON

Fairfield Inn
1635 Yeager St.
(810) 982-8500
marriott.com

ROCHESTER

Royal Park Hotel
600 E. University Dr.
(248) 453-8732
royalparkhotel.net

TROY

Drury Inn
575 W. Big Beaver Rd.
(248) 528-3330

Places to Eat in Southeast Michigan

ANN ARBOR

Arbor Brewing Co.
114 E. Washington Ave.
(734) 213-1393
arborbrewing.com
Brewpub

Gandy Dancer
401 Depot St.
(734) 769-0592
muer.com/gandy-dancer
Seafood

Prickly Pear Southwest Cafe
328 S. Main St.
(734) 930-0047
pricklypearcafe.com
Tex-Mex

Zingerman's Delicatessen
422 Detroit St.
(734) 663-3354
zingermansdeli.com
Deli

SELECTED SOUTHEAST MICHIGAN TOURISM BUREAUS

Ann Arbor Area Convention and Visitors Bureau
120 W. Huron St.
Ann Arbor 48104
(800) 888-9487
visitannarbor.org

Blue Water Area Convention and Visitors Bureau
(Port Huron and St. Clair)
405 Water St., Suite 100
Port Huron 48060
(800) 852-4242
bluewater.org

Metropolitan Detroit Convention and Visitors Bureau
211 W. Fort St.
Detroit 48226
(800) 338-7648
visitdetroit.com

Monroe County Tourism Bureau
106 W. Front St.
Monroe 48161
(800) 252-3011
monroeinfo.com

Ypsilanti Area Visitors and Convention Bureau
106 W. Michigan Ave.
Ypsilanti 48197
(800) 265-9045
visitypsinow.com

CLARKSTON

Union
54 S. Main St.
(248) 620-6100
clarkstonunion.com
American

DEARBORN

Big Fish
700 Town Center Dr.
(313) 336-6350
muer.com/big-fish
Seafood

Shatila Bakery and Cafe
14300 W. Warren Ave.
(313) 582-1952
shatila.com
Middle East

DETROIT

Dakota Inn Rathskeller
17324 John R St.
(313) 867-9722
dakota-inn.com
German

Elwood Bar & Grill
300 E. Adams St.
(313) 962-2337
elwoodgrill.com
American

Fishbone's Rhythm Kitchen Cafe
400 Monroe St.
(313) 965-4600
fishbonesusa.com
Cajun

Hockeytown Cafe
2301 Woodward Ave.
(313) 965-9500
hockeytowncafe.com
Sports Bar

Roma Cafe
3401 Riopelle St.
(313) 831-5940
romacafe.com
Italian

OTHER ATTRACTIONS

Cranbrook Institute of Science
Bloomfield Hills
science.cranbrook.edu

Eddy Discovery Center
Chelsea

Fox Theatre
Detroit

Holocaust Memorial Center
Farmington Hills
holocaustcenter.org

Meadowbrook Hall
Rochester
meadowbrookhall.org

U of M Exhibit Museum of Natural History
Ann Arbor
isa.umich.edu/exhibitmuseum

U of M Museum of Art
Ann Arbor
umma.umich.edu/

Yankee Air Museum
Belleville
yankeeairmuseum.org

Traffic Jam and Snug
511 W. Canfield St.
(313) 831-9470
trafficjamdetroit.com
Brewpub

The Whitney
4421 Woodward Ave.
(313) 832-5700
thewhitney.com
Fine Dining

Xochimilco
3409 Bagley St.
(313) 843-0179
Mexican

FARMINGTON

Bone Yard Bar-B-Que
31006 Orchard Lake Rd.
(248) 851-7000
theboneyardbbq.com
Barbecue

FERNDALE

Howe's Bayou
22848 Woodward Ave.
(248) 691-7145
howesbayouferndale.net
Cajun

MADISON HEIGHTS

The Breakfast Club
30600 John Rd.
(248) 307-9090
Breakfast

MONROE

Bolles Harbor Cafe
13986 Laplaisance Rd.
(734) 457-2233
bollesharborcafemonroe
.com
Cafe

NORTHVILLE

Genitti's Hole-in-the-Wall
108 E. Main St.
(248) 349-0522
genittis.com
Italian

OAK PARK

Bread Basket Deli
26052 Greenfield Rd.
(248) 968-0022
breadbasketdelis.com
Deli

ROYAL OAK

**BD's Mongolian
Barbecue**
430 S. Main St.
(248) 398-7755
gomongo.com
Asian/Barbecue

Inn Season Cafe
500 E. Fourth St.
(248) 547-7916
theinnseasoncafe.com
Vegetarian

SOUTHFIELD

Sweet Lorraine's Cafe
29101 Greenfield Rd.
(248) 559-5985
sweetlorraines.com
American

TROY

Melting Pot
888 W. Big Beaver Rd.
(248) 362-2221
meltingpot.com/troy/
welcome
Fondue

WATERFORD

Lion's Den
4444 Highland Rd.
(248) 674-2251
lionsdenrestaurant.com
American

WEST BLOOMFIELD

The Lark
6430 Farmington Rd.
(248) 661-4466
thelark.com
Country Inn

THE THUMB

Within the mitten that is the Lower Peninsula of Michigan, there is a special area known as "the Thumb." The state's most recognized appendage is shaped by Saginaw Bay to the west and Lake Huron to the east. The bodies of water not only outline the peninsula but also have wrapped it in rural isolation, the Thumb's trademark and the reason it is called "the getaway close to home."

Home is likely to be one of three of the state's largest urban areas: Detroit, Flint, or Saginaw, all less than a two-hour drive from the four counties that compose the region. Yet the Thumb is a world away. In this place where interstate highways give way to country roads and indistinguishable suburbs turn into distinct villages, the bustle and heartbeat of the city is replaced by the rural charm of the country.

You don't have nightclubs in the Thumb or dominating skylines or symphony orchestras. But you have more than 90 miles of lakeshore to view, small museums to discover, and an easy way of life whose rural pace will soothe the soul and rest a weary urban mind.

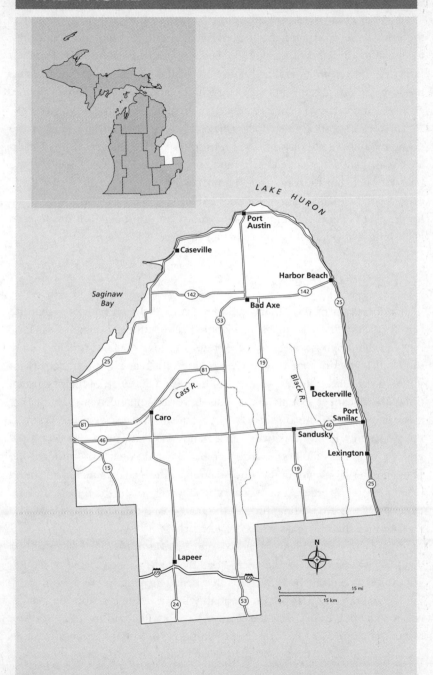

THE THUMB

LAKE HURON

Port
Austin

Caseville

Harbor Beach

Saginaw
Bay

142   142   25

Bad Axe

53

81

Cass R.

Black R.

25

19

Deckerville

Caro   Port
Sanilac

81   46   Sandusky

46   Lexington

15

19

25

N

Lapeer

69   69

0   15 mi
0   15 km

24   53

Lumber companies opened up the Thumb in the early 1800s, but after the trees were gone and the loggers went north, the region slipped into the small-town realm of agriculture. Today the area is still predominantly a farm belt, and from its rich soil come corn, sugar beets, grains, beans, and the lush grass that supports vast dairy herds and livestock. Huron County produces more navy beans per acre than anyplace else in the world.

In recent years tourist dollars have become a significant part of the economy, but the region will never turn into one of the strips of motels and ice-cream stands that characterize much of the Lake Michigan shoreline, the heart of Michigan tourism. The Thumb lies on the other side of the state, away from the mainstream of summer traffic. And many travelers, who come for the fine beaches, country markets, and picturesque lighthouses, leave it cherishing that out-of-the-way character the most.

Lapeer County

A misconception of the Thumb held by many Michigan natives is that the region is flat, without so much as a ripple between the shoreline of Saginaw Bay and the lapping waters of Lake Huron. A drive through Lapeer County dispels that notion immediately. The rolling hills that are the trademark of northern Oakland County continue north through the heart of the peninsula. In southern Lapeer County these hills have an enhancement that makes them unique in Michigan: the distinct white rail fences of horse country. Follow County Road 62 between M 24 and M 53 and dip south along the gravel crossroads of Blood, Garder, or Barber, and you'll pass through one of the greatest concentrations of horse farms in the state. Come in late spring when the grass is green, a new coat of whitewash covers the fences, and the mares and foals are trotting through the fields—and this area could easily be mistaken for the bluegrass region of Kentucky.

The heart of Michigan's horse country is ***Metamora,*** a village of 500 that lies just east of M 24 and is crowned by the towering steeple of the Pilgrim Church (built in 1878). Settlers first began arriving in the area in 1838, but Metamora earned a spot on the map when it became a stop for a stagecoach route that turned into the Detroit–Bay City Railroad in 1872. North of Metamora along M 24 is ***Lapeer,*** a town of 6,270. Settlers began arriving in the area in 1828 and borrowed their village name from *la pierre*, the French

AUTHOR'S TOP TEN PICKS

**Be Good to Your
Mother-in-Law Bridge**
Croswell
(810) 679- 2299

Bird Creek County Park
Port Austin
(989) 269-6404

Farm Restaurant
Port Austin
(989) 874-5700
thefarmrestaurant.com

Frank Murphy Museum
Harbor Beach
(989) 479-6477

Huron City Museums
Huron City
(989) 428-4123
huroncitymuseums.org

Pioneer Log Cabin Village
Bad Axe
(800) 358-4862

Pointe Aux Barques Lighthouse
Huron City
(989) 428-4749
pointeauxbarqueslighthouse.org

Port Crescent State Park
Port Austin
(989) 738-8663

**Sanilac County Historical Village
and Museum**
Port Sanilac
(810) 622-9946
sanilaccountymuseum.org

Sanilac Historical Site
New Greenleaf
(517) 373-3559

translation of the Indian name for the Flint River, which lies nearby. Lapeer became the county seat in 1831, and eight years later the county courthouse was built on the town common.

Lapeer is still the center of government, and the ***Lapeer County Courthouse*** still stands at the corner of Court and Nepessing Streets. It is an impressive building featuring a Greek Revival style with 4 fluted Doric columns. It's topped by a 3-tiered tower and a Roman dome and is noted as the "oldest courthouse still being used in Michigan today," even though the county has long since built a newer, all-brick building across the street. The old courthouse keeps its title because every summer, the judge, the jury, and a handful of history buffs move to the other side of the street to hear a few cases in the second-floor courtroom of this landmark structure.

The first floor is now the ***Lapeer Historical Society Museum*** (810-245-5808), and for a small admission fee, visitors can wander through the turn-of-the-20th-century judge's chambers or the first sheriff's office in the county. The Courthouse Museum is open from 10 a.m. to 3 p.m. Wed and Sat.

More history and a lot of country charm can be found just up the road from Lapeer at the ***Past Tense Country Store*** (810-664-5559; pasttensec-ountry.com). The store is only minutes from downtown Lapeer and can be reached by driving north on M 24 and then turning east on County Road 7 (Daley Road). The first intersection on Daley is Farnsworth Road, and visible to the south from this intersection is one of the most impressive houses in the region. The huge, 23-room home was built by the Farnsworth family, who were part of the first wave of settlers to farm the county. There are several buildings on the old farm, including the original barn that Lucie Hiner renovated into the Past Tense Country Store in 1971.

The store is an intriguing place, worth browsing through even if you are not in a buying mood. It is part country store, part antiques shop, and part museum. Walk in on a chilly day and the rush of warm air from the wood-burning stove greets you. Then you'll notice the hundred-year-old

TOP ANNUAL EVENTS

JUNE

Log Cabin Day
Bad Axe
(989) 550-2733

Michigan Sugar Festival
Sebewaing
(989) 883-2150
sebewaingchamber.com

JULY

Farmer's Festival
Pigeon
(989) 453-7400

Maritime Festival
Harbor Beach
(989) 479- 3363
harborbeach.com

Swinging Bridge Festival
Croswell
(810) 679-2299
croswellswingingbridgefestival.com

AUGUST

Cheeseburger in Caseville Festival
Caseville
(800) 606-1347

Fish Sandwich Festival
Bay Port
(989) 551-9929

German barrel piano and the classic red Texaco gasoline pump next to it. The store itself is 4 rooms, each stocked to the rafters with such items as handmade baskets, dried flowers, candles, knickknacks, and children's toys, including one of the most amazing teddy bear collections you'll ever see outside a museum. Upstairs are numerous pieces of antique furniture, while one room is devoted to Christmas, with an old sled in the middle and walls covered with ornaments.

Above every shelf of merchandise, Hiner draws you back into the rural history of Lapeer with small artifacts she has saved. Above the wall of hard candy, a requirement in every country store, are rows of cleaning products and cans of food, all from an era long gone. Some you'll recognize, like Oxydol, Quaker Oats, or Calumet Baking Powder, though the packaging hardly resembles the modern-day counterparts. Many you will not (Quick Arrow Soup Chips or Red Moon Early Peas), for they have long since vanished from supermarkets.

Hiner and her family live in the Farnsworth house and operate the store, which is open Mon through Sat from 10 a.m. to 6 p.m. and Sun from 11 a.m. to 6 p.m.

Sanilac County

M 25, the state road that leads out of Port Huron, follows the shoreline of Sanilac County and continues along the entire coast of the Thumb, ending in Bay City. While the road does not offer a watery view at every bend, there are more than enough panoramas of Lake Huron and shoreline parks to make it one of the more scenic drives in the Lower Peninsula.

Heading north on M 25, the first town you reach in Sanilac County is **Lexington,** which was incorporated in 1855 and boomed at the turn of the 20th century. Back then the bustling town of 2,400 was a common stop for Great Lakes shipping and boasted an organ factory, a brewery, a flour mill, and 6 saloons. In 1913 the great storm that swept across Lake Huron destroyed the town's docks and virtually isolated it. Lexington slipped into a standstill until the automobile and roads revived it in the 1940s, and today the town of almost 800 has worked harder than any other community in the Thumb to promote its future by preserving its past.

Lexington's streets are lined with turn-of-the-20th-century homes and buildings, including 4 listed on the National Register of Historic Places. One of them is the **Charles H. Moore Public Library** (lexingtonlibrary .net) at Main and Huron Streets next to the village hall. The brick building was built in 1859 as the Devine Law Office but somehow passed into the hands of Moore, a local seaman who died in 1901, leaving the building to his three daughters. When a dispute erupted in 1903 as to where to put the town library, the daughters offered the former law office as a permanent site.

It has been the library ever since and today holds nearly 12,000 books, including a rare-book collection. Librarians will tell you that as many people wander through just to view the renovated interior as to check out a book. The wood trim and stained-glass windows have been fully restored inside, as has the graceful wooden banister that leads you past a picture of the "old seaman" to the upstairs. It's hard to imagine a more pleasant place to read than the sunlit room of the second floor, which features desks, tables, and office chairs that were originally used by the law firm.

The Moore Library (810-359-8267) is open Mon from 10 a.m. to 7 p.m., Tues, Wed, and Fri from 10 a.m. to 5 p.m., Thurs 1 to 7 p.m., and Sat from 10 a.m. to 1 p.m.

Moore was also responsible for another building in Lexington that is now a National Historic Site. When the seaman built his home in the 1880s, he located it just a block from the lake where he plied his trade. The huge Queen Anne–style home at Simons and Washington Streets was constructed from white pine that loggers were shipping out of the port of Lexington. In 1901, Mary, the youngest daughter, used the house as a backdrop for her marriage to Albert E. Sleeper, a newly elected state senator. When Sleeper's political career led to his election as governor in 1917, the house became an important summer retreat for the couple, who were eager to escape the busy public life in Lansing.

Today the home at 7277 Simons St. is still used as a summer retreat as the **Captain's Quarters Inn** (810-359-2196; cqilex.com), Lexington's first bed-and-breakfast. Guests spend summer evenings much the way the governor and his wife did—on the wraparound porch in wicker rockers (there are 7 now instead of 2), enjoying the cool breezes off Lake Huron. Rooms range from $115 to $160 per night.

Port Sanilac Lighthouse

Port Sanilac's most distinctive landmark is its lighthouse, a redbrick house and whitewashed tower overlooking the town harbor and the watery horizon of Lake Huron. Built in 1886, the 80-foot tower was originally a kerosene-fueled continuous white light. In 1889 it was changed to red, and in 1926 the lighthouse was wired for electricity and changed to a flashing light with a range of 12 to 15 miles. Although the lighthouse is not open to visitors, it's a photographer's delight thanks to its contrasting colors.

The Port Sanilac Lighthouse is on Lake Street, 1 block east of M 25.

From Lexington M 25 continues north along Lake Huron and in 11 miles reaches the next lakeside town, **Port Sanilac.** Like Lexington, Port Sanilac's early history and wealth can be seen in the old homes that border its streets. One is the Loop-Harrison House, a huge Victorian mansion just south of town on M 25 that now serves as the **Sanilac County Historical Village and Museum.** The home was built in 1872 by Dr. Joseph Loop, who arrived in Sanilac in 1854 and began a practice that covered a 40-mile radius. The home and its extensive furnishings passed down through three generations of the family until Captain Stanley Harrison, grandson of the good doctor, donated it to the Sanilac Historical Society in 1964.

The Historical Society has kept the home intact, and visitors can wander through 2 floors of rooms that have remained virtually the same since the 1870s, right down to the original carpet, the cooking utensils in the kitchen, and the doctor's instruments in his office. The village includes 7 buildings ranging from the Platt's General Store and a 157-year-old one-room schoolhouse to a pioneer log cabin from 1883, a church from the turn of the century, and what is probably the state's last remaining historic Barn Theater. At 228 S. Ridge

trivia

Michigan's oldest continuously operating hardware store is Raymond Hardware at 29 S. Ridge St. (810-622-9991; raymondhardware.com) in downtown Port Sanilac. Founded in 1850 by Uri Raymond, the high-roofed building is a classic hardware store that sells "anything and everything."

Bark Shanty Point

Port Sanilac dates back to the summer of 1830 when a group of lumbermen arrived to peel the bark from the hemlocks in the area for tanning leather. Their accommodations were in a hastily built shanty that was covered in bark. The crude shelter was left standing on the shore after the men departed in the fall, and it quickly became a landmark to sailors who referred to the spot as Bark Shanty Point. Eventually a settlement emerged, and in 1857 the residents decided that the name of a famous Wyandot Indian chief was a little more digni-fied for their community than Bark Shanty Point.

St., the Sanilac County Historical Village and Museum (810-622-9946; sanilac-countymuseum.org) is open June through Aug from 11 a.m. to 4 p.m. Wed through Fri and noon to 4 p.m. Sat and Sun. Admission is $5 for adults and $2 for students.

Closer to town on M 25 is another impressive home that has become the *Raymond House Inn,* Port Sanilac's bed-and-breakfast at 111 S. Ridge St. The home was built in 1871 by Uri Raymond, one of the founding fathers of the town, who established what is now Michigan's oldest con-tinuously operating hardware store just up the street. The exterior of this Victorian-style home makes it hard to miss with its redbrick facade, high peaked roofs, and white gingerbread trim. Inside, high ceilings, classic moldings, winding staircases, and large rooms add to the inn's turn-of-the-20th-century charm.

This house is charming and massive at more than 6,000 square feet. It includes 7 guest rooms on 3 floors, 5 with private bathrooms, and even an art gallery and gift shop. The inn is open year-round, and nightly rates range from $65 to $115. For reservations call Raymond House Inn at (810) 622-8800 or (800) 622-7229, or go to theraymondhouseinn.com.

The stretch of M 25 from Port Sanilac to Forestville is especially scenic and passes three roadside parks on high bluffs from which you can scramble to the Lake Huron shoreline below. For those who want to explore the cen-ter of the Thumb, the Bay City–Forestville Road, the only intersection in tiny Forestville, provides a good excuse to turn off M 25. Head west, through the hamlets of Charleston and Minden, and look for the petroglyphs sign at the corner of Bay City–Forestville and Germania Roads. *Sanilac Historical Site* is located just south on Germania and is marked by a large Department of Natural Resources sign. Situated in the wooded heart of the Thumb, the park features a large slab of stone with petroglyphs, Indian carvings that archaeologists believe to be between 300 and 1,000 years old and the only ones in the Lower Peninsula. The department has erected a large pavilion over the rock, which contains dozens of carvings. The most prominent one features a bowman with a single long line depicting his arm and arrow. A short trail leads from the parking lot a few hundred yards inland to the pavilion and then continues beyond as a 1.5-mile interpretive trail.

There is no entrance fee. The park and the trail system are open year-round. But the petroglyphs pavilion is only open late May through early Sept on Wed through Sun from 10 a.m. to 5 p.m. Contact the *Michigan Department of Natural Resources* (989-856-4411; michigan.gov/sanilacpetroglyphs).

Another reason to head inland in summer and fall is to pick berries—sweet, juicy, and back-breakingly close to the ground. Next to the town of Croswell is the *Croswell Berry Farm* (810-679-3273) at 33 Black River Rd. This farm features strawberries in early July, then extends the picking season with blueberries, and finishes up the year with raspberries that are harvested as late as November. The last person goes out in the field at 3 p.m. Hours are 8 a.m. to 4 p.m. Mon through Sat, 9 a.m. to 4 p.m. Sun.

One final reason to head inland to Croswell is to get some advice for keeping your marriage intact from a bridge that Dear Abby would

Kayaking at the Tip of the Thumb

You don't have to travel to Alaska or even northern Michigan to join a guided kayak adventure. You don't have to go any farther than the Tip of the Thumb where **Port Austin Kayak** (989-550-6651; portaustinkayak.com) rents kayaks and offers guided paddles throughout the summer. The cost of a guided tour is the price of a 3-hour rental ($22) plus $75 for the guide for up to 8 people. The cost for the guide is the same whether there is 1 person or 8. The outfitter also teams up with House of Yoga of Port Austin to offer a weekend of kayak and yoga on the shores of Lake Huron. Included in the 3-day retreat is unlimited use of kayaks and bikes, 2 guided kayak tours, and 3 yoga sessions. Cost is $150 per person and you go home totally relaxed.

appreciate. In the middle of this Sanilac County village is the ***Be Good to Your Mother-in-Law Bridge,*** which was first constructed in 1905 and has been rebuilt three times since then with David Weis, a local businessman, assisting in the effort.

Best known in town for offering sage advice to newlyweds, it was Weis who hung a sign at one end of the bridge that advises them to be good to their mothers-in-law and at the other end one that admonishes them to love one another. It's such good advice that the bridge has become something of a ritual with both newlyweds and longtime married couples, who are photographed under the black-and-white sign and then walk hand in hand across the structure.

They hold hands partly out of devotion to each other and partly to keep their balance. The 139-foot suspension footbridge is held up by 4 thick cables that make you bounce with each step across. The wooden slats sway, jiggle, and dip toward the Black River, coming within 8 feet of its murky surface. Some people are even more nervous about crossing the 4-foot-wide swinging bridge than strolling up to the altar.

Small tree-lined parks are at each end of the bridge, while a short walk away on Wells Street is the ***Croswell Museum,*** a former railroad depot that features a horse-drawn hearse, local artifacts, and plenty of fading photographs of the town's beloved swinging bridge. The parks and bridge are open daily from dawn to dusk. The Croswell Museum is open Sat and Sun from 1 to 5 p.m.

Huron County

The country charm of M 25 continues into Huron County as it winds north toward Port Austin on the Tip of the Thumb. Along the way it passes several museums, including two in ***Harbor Beach,*** a quiet rural town of 2,000 residents.

Frank Murphy Museum preserves the birthplace of Governor Frank Murphy, best known for refusing to use the National Guard to end the 1937 Flint Sit-Down Strike at General Motors. By pushing for collective bargaining, Murphy, in effect, paved the way for the United Auto Workers and unionization of the auto industry. Murphy also served as mayor of Detroit, US attorney general, and a US Supreme Court justice from 1940 to his death in 1949. The house is packed with historical artifacts relating to one of Michigan's most influential residents.

Frank Murphy Museum is at 142 S. Huron Ave. next door to the Harbor Beach Visitor Center (989-479-6477) in downtown Harbor Beach. Tours are offered Memorial Day through Labor Day, Tues through Fri noon to 4 p.m., Sat and Sun 10 a.m. to 4 p.m. Adults $2, children $1. Just north of town on M 25 at the Harbor Beach Marina is *Grice House Museum*. The Gothic-style home was built in 1875 and still contains 19th-century furnishings along with displays on the early history of Harbor Beach. Outside there is a one-room schoolhouse and a barn full of farm tools from days gone by. Both museums are open from Memorial Day to Labor Day noon to 4 p.m. Tues through Fri and 10 a.m. to 4 p.m. Sat and Sun. There is a small admission for either one.

Another small museum along M 25 is at *Lighthouse County Park,* 15 miles north of Harbor Beach. The museum is on the first floor of the classic *Pointe Aux Barques Lighthouse* (pointeauxbarqueslighthouse .org), which was built in 1857 and is still used by the US Coast Guard. The lighthouse actually overlooks 2 parks; the county park around it features 74 campsites with electricity for recreational vehicles, a swimming beach, a boat launch, and a picnic area. Out in Lake Huron is an underwater park, the Thumb Area Bottomland Preserve, which the state set up in 1985 to protect the 9 known shipwrecks that lie offshore. Many of the relics that are gathered from the wrecks are stored in the Lighthouse Museum, which is open daily from 10 a.m. to 4 p.m. during the summer. There is no admission charge for the park (989-428-4749) or the museum.

The Fires of 1881

What began as small fires in the middle of a hot, dry summer turned into the Thumb's worst disaster when on September 5, 1881, a gale swept in from the southwest. The high winds turned the fires into an inferno that raged for three days and burned more than a million acres in Sanilac and Huron Counties alone.

The fire put a sudden end to the logging era in the region while killing 125 people and leaving thousands more destitute. Aid to victims was the first disaster relief effort by the new American Red Cross. Its prompt response quickly won the support of the country.

Where Lighthouse Road loops back to M 25 is the Thumb's most impressive attraction, **Huron City Museums.** The town was founded in the mid-1850s by lumberman Langdon Hubbard, who needed a port for his 29,000-acre tract of timberland, which included most of northern Huron County. It quickly became the largest town in the county, with several hundred residents and two sawmills that produced 80,000 feet of lumber a day. After the Great Fire of 1881 that swept across the Thumb devastated Hubbard's logging efforts, he sold his land to immigrant farmers (after opening a bank to lend them the money), and for a while Huron City hung on as a farming community.

By the early 1900s, Huron City had withered away to a ghost town when it experienced a revival—a religious awakening, you might say. One of Hubbard's daughters had married William Lyon Phelps, a Yale professor and an ordained minister, and each summer the couple returned to Huron City and stayed at Seven Gables, the rambling Hubbard home. Eventually Dr. Phelps began preaching in the nearby church on Sunday. Local people soon discovered the magic of his oratory: simple solutions and relief from the problems of everyday life. The church, which originally held 250, was quickly enlarged to 1,000 in the 1920s as people throughout Michigan heard of the preacher and began finding their way to Huron City for his Sunday afternoon service.

trivia

A historical marker at a rest area along M 25 is dedicated to the Storm of November 1913, another deadly disaster in the history of the Thumb. The devastating storm blew in with little warning, sinking more than 40 ships, killing 235 sailors, and destroying almost every dock along Michigan's Lake Huron shoreline.

Dr. Phelps died in 1937, but Huron City survived when the granddaughter of the founder preserved the community as a museum town. Twelve buildings are on the site, nine of them furnished and open to the public. They include a country store, a church, a lifesaving station, a settler's cabin, the old inn, a barn with antique farm equipment, and the Phelps Museum, which was built in honor of the minister in the early 1950s. Huron City Museums (989-428-4123; huroncitymuseums.com) is open July and Aug from 10 a.m. to 4 p.m. on Fri and Sat. Where Lake Huron and Saginaw Bay

Grindstone Capital of the World

Where M 25 begins to curve around the top of the Thumb, you can take Pointe Aux Barques Road to Grindstone City. Amazingly, this tiny village was once the world's leading producer of natural-sandstone grinding wheels. Sandstone was first quarried in 1834 by Captain Aaron G. Peer, who shipped it to Detroit, where it was used to pave the intersection of Woodward and Jefferson Avenues. Two years later the first grindstone wheel was turned out, and for nearly a century Grindstone City grindstones were shipped all over the world. Today you can still see many of the huge grindstones, some 6 feet in diameter, on the beach and around the village's boat harbor.

meet is Port Austin, the town at the Tip of the Thumb. M 25 winds through the center of Port Austin and near its two busiest spots in the summer, the city marina and, just east of the marina's breakwall, delightful Bird Creek County Park. This 7-acre park includes a beautiful sandy beach and a half-mile boardwalk where people fish during the day and gather nightly to watch the sunset over Saginaw Bay.

In keeping with the restored atmosphere of Port Austin, there is the **Bank 1884 Restaurant** for, unquestionably, the finest dining in town. Built in 1884 as the Winsorsnover Bank on the corner of Lake and State streets, the red-washed, brick building ceased being a place of financial business in 1957. In 1982 extensive renovation of the historic building began and two years later it reopened as a restaurant. The interior features stained glass over the classic stand-up bar, a teller's cage on the first floor, and walls of oversize photographs depicting early Huron County. The changing menu usually has prime rib of beef au jus and that Michigan summertime favorite: lightly battered lake perch. Hours vary, so check the website. Prices for entrees range from $19 to $25, and reservations (989-738-5353; thebank1884. com) are strongly recommended for the weekends.

West of Port Austin, M 25 begins to follow the shoreline of Saginaw Bay and is especially scenic in its 19-mile stretch to Caseville. It passes many views of the bay and its islands, numerous roadside parks, and the finest beaches in the Thumb. One of the parks is **Port Crescent State Park**, popular with sunbathers and swimmers for the long stretches of sandy shoreline. The park also offers opportunities and facilities for camping, hiking, and fishing, and it contains the Thumb's only set of dunes, a unique place for beachcombers to explore. There is an entrance fee to Port Crescent State Park (989-738-8663; michigandnr.com) and a $27 charge to camp overnight.

Even more than for sand and sun, Saginaw Bay has always been known as an angler's destination for yellow perch. Visitors, especially families, can still enjoy good fishing even without a boat or knowledge of where to go by joining a perch party boat. The large charter boats hold about 20 and usually depart twice a day for half-day fishing trips. In Caseville, *Miss Caseville* (989-856-2650; bella-caseville.com/misspa) offers party-boat charters that depart Wed through Sun when there are at least 8 anglers. The fee is $39 per person. You need to bring your own pole; the boat provides the bait and takes you where the perch are biting. Perch fishing is easy, and on a good day you may need a bucket to bring home your catch.

trivia

Huron County accounts for more than 90 percent of the country's production of navy beans.

To enjoy your perch without having to put a minnow on your hook, stay on M 25 as it curves southwest toward Bay Port. From the 1880s until the late 1940s, this sleepy village was known as the "largest freshwater fishing port in the world," as tons of perch, whitefish, walleye, and herring were shipped as far away as New York City in refrigerated railroad cars. Today it honors its fishing past on the first Sunday in August with its annual *Bay Port Fish Sandwich Festival.* The small festival includes arts and crafts, petting zoo, fireworks, and lots of sandwiches—close to 8,000 are served during the event.

A small commercial fishery is still operating in Bay Port, a place to go for fresh walleye, perch, whitefish, and herring. From the center of town, head for the waterfront docks of the *Bay Port Fish Company* (989-656-2121; bayportfish.com) at 1008 First St. for the catch of the day or to watch fishermen work on the boats or nets in the evening from Apr through Nov, depending on the weather. The company, which is open from 9 a.m. to 3 p.m. daily, sells whitefish, perch, salmon, catfish, walleye, and smoked fish.

In the heart of Huron County is *Bad Axe,* the county seat and a city of 4,000 residents. The town's most interesting attraction is *Pioneer Log Cabin Village* (989-269-8325 or 800-358-4862). This unique outdoor museum

Dining Down on the Farm

You're in the heart of the Thumb, might as well head to a farmhouse for a hearty home-cooked meal of country goodness and straight-from-the-fields freshness. There are two wonderful restaurants in Huron County that make you feel like your aunt still lives on a farm, if for no other reason than they're surrounded by corn-fields and faded red barns.

The first is just outside of Port Austin, a short drive in the country to a converted farmhouse at 699 Port Crescent Rd. What else could you possibly name this place but *The Farm Restaurant* (989-874-5700; thefarmrestaurant.com)?

The restaurant was originally the Old Homestead and was known for fried chicken and homemade pies when Jeff and Pam Gabriel purchased it in 1993. The owner and chef is now Mary Gabriel-Roth. Favorites include farmers' style Hungarian meatballs with smoky paprika–sour cream brown sauce, served with roasted garlic mashed potatoes and seasonal vegetables; and chicken schnitzel, panko-crusted chicken breast with lemon caper sauce, roasted garlic mashed potatoes, creamed cabbage, and seasonal vegetables.

The dessert menu is also impressive and many diners opt for the warm seasonal cobbler topped with vanilla ice cream. There are just some things people expect when eating dinner at a farmhouse.

Hours vary, so check the Farm schedule. Entrees range in price from $17 to $28.

More wholesome cooking can be found 3 miles south of Harbor Beach on M 25 at *Williams Inn* (989-479-3361) where a huge sign outside says LET'S EAT HERE! Let's, because this farmhouse restaurant with its green awning is too inviting to pass up.

In the huge enclosed porch of Williams Inn, diners can feast on such traditional favorites as country fried steak, grilled ham steaks topped with a sweet pine-apple ring, or roast beef, slow roasted to be extra tender and juicy. But the best time to come is on Sunday morning for the inn's breakfast buffet, when you can load your plate up with 3 types of homemade sausage, ham, eggs, waffles, hash browns and thick-cut potatoes, and hot-from-the-oven biscuits that can be topped with sausage gravy.

The only thing better than the selection is the price: $6 for adults and $3.25 for children.

During the summer Williams Inn is open from 8:30 a.m. to 8 p.m. Mon through Thurs, 7 a.m. to 10 p.m. Fri and Sat, and 7 a.m. to 8 p.m. on Sun.

One Bad Axe

Rudolph Papst is credited by many with giving Bad Axe its name. While surveying for a new road across the heart of Huron County in 1861, he discovered a "bad axe" near his campsite one night and labeled the spot Bad Axe Corners on his map.

In 1872 county supervisors wanted the government moved from Port Austin to a more central location in the county and chose Bad Axe Corners, which in reality was little more than a junction in a dense forest. But 5 acres were quickly cleared, and in 1873 a courthouse was built. Since then Bad Axe has grown to be Huron County's largest city while its residents have resisted several attempts to give it a more dignified name.

features a home, blacksmith shop, chapel, general store, barn, and one-room schoolhouse. All the buildings are log cabins that were built in Huron Cabin and moved to Bad Axe. The cabins are fully furnished to reflect the pioneer lifestyle of the 19th century and often are staffed during the summer by guides in period costumes.

The village is located in Bad Axe City Park at 210 S. Hanselman St. and is open Sun from 2 to 5 p.m. from May through Sept. There is no admission fee.

Places to Stay in Michigan's Thumb

BAD AXE

Franklin Inn
1070 E. Huron St.
(989) 269-9951 or
(800) 645-0211
franklininnbadaxe.com

CASEVILLE

Bella Vista Inn
6024 Port Austin Rd.
(989) 856-2650
bella-caseville.com

Crew's Lakeside Resort
4750 Port Austin Rd.
(989) 856-2786
crewslakesideresort.com

The Lodge at Oak Pointe
5857 Port Austin Rd.
(989) 856-3055
oakpointelodge.com

HARBOR BEACH

State Street Inn
646 State St.
(989) 479-3388
thestatestreetinn.com/

Train Station Motel
2044 N. M 25
(989) 479-3215

LEXINGTON

Captain's Quarters Inn
7277 Simons St.
(810) 359- 2190
cqilex.com

Inn the Garden Bed and Breakfast
7156 Huron Ave.
(810) 359-8966
inngarden.com

Lex-on-the-Lake Lodges
5795 Main St.
(810) 359-7910

PORT AUSTIN

Breakers-on-the-Bay
1404 Port Austin Rd.
(989) 738-5101
breakersonthebay.com

Krebs Cottages
3478 Port Austin Rd.
(989) 856-2876
krebscottages.com

Lakeside Motor Lodge
8654 Lake St.
(989) 738-5201

PORT SANILAC

Raymond House Inn
111 S. Ridge St.
(810) 622-8800
theraymondhouseinn.com

Places to Eat in Michigan's Thumb

BAD AXE

Franklin Inn
1070 E. Huron St.
(989) 269-9951 or
(800) 645-0211
franklininnbadaxe.com
American

CASEVILLE

Hersel's on the Bay
6024 Port Austin
(989) 856-2500
bella-caseville.com
Fine Dining

HARBOR BEACH

Williams Inn
1724 S. Lakeshore Rd.
(989) 479-3361
American

METAMORA

White Horse Inn
1 E. High St.
(810) 678-2150
American

PORT AUSTIN

Bank 1884
Lake and State Streets
(989) 738-5353
thebank1884.com
Fine Dining

Farm Restaurant
699 Port Crescent
(989) 874-5700
thefarmrestaurant.com
American

OTHER ATTRACTIONS

Luckhard Museum
Sebewaing

Pigeon Historical Museum
Pigeon

Sleeper State Park
Caseville

SELECTED CHAMBERS OF COMMERCE & TOURISM BUREAUS

Bad Axe Chamber of Commerce
P.O. Box 87
Bad Axe 48413
(969) 269-6936
badaxemich.com

Caseville Chamber of Commerce
6632 Main St.
Caseville 48725
(800) 606-1347
casevillechamber.com

Harbor Beach Chamber of Commerce
146 S. Huron Ave.
Harbor Beach 48441
(989) 479-6477
harborbeachchamber.com

Huron County Visitors Bureau
250 E. Huron Ave.
Bad Axe 48413
(800) 358-4862
huroncounty.com

Port Austin Chamber of Commerce
2 W. Spring St.
Port Austin 48467
(989) 738-7600
portaustinarea.com

Lighthouse Cafe
44 W. Spring St.
(989) 738-5239
thelighthouse-cafe.com
American

PORT HOPE

Four Seasons Cafe
4411 Main St.
(989) 428-3200
Cafe

PORT SANILAC

Mary's Diner
14 N. Ridge St.
(810) 622-9377
American

THE HEARTLAND

By the 1830s "Michigan Fever" had become an epidemic. Scores of pioneer families from the East Coast floated through the Erie Canal, made their way to Detroit, and then took to the newly completed Detroit-Chicago Road, which cut across the southern half of the Lower Peninsula. They soon discovered the rolling prairies of Michigan, where the soil was very rich and the land very cheap—the federal government was selling it for only $1.25 an acre.

From this onrush of settlers between 1825 and 1855, some of the state's largest cities emerged: Kalamazoo, Lansing, Battle Creek, Jackson, and Grand Rapids, all in this central region. But the Heartland of Michigan, the only area without direct links to the Great Lakes, is still an agricultural breadbasket. It is faded red barns and rolling fields of oats, the birthplace of Kellogg's Corn Flakes, and the home of a village antiques dealer who scours area farms for the furniture and knickknacks that fill her store.

The vibrant cities, each with a distinct downtown that never sleeps, are popular destinations for travelers who can zip from one to the next on interstate highways six lanes wide. But the unique nature of this region is found by

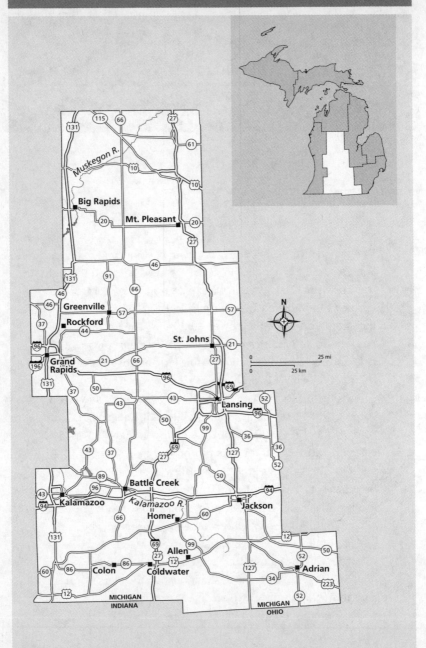

rambling along its two-lane county roads, which take you past the horse-drawn carriages of Amish country, down main streets of small villages, and along roadside stands loaded with the summer's harvest. In these out-of-the-way places, you can sample the fruits of Michigan's Heartland.

Lenawee County

At the northern edge of Lenawee County are the famed *Irish Hills,* an area of green rolling hills with intermittent lakes and ponds. US 12 cuts through the middle of this popular area and has become an avenue of manufactured tourist attractions: miniature golf courses and Go Kart tracks, a dinosaur amusement park, another park called Stagecoach Stop USA, motels, gift shops, and even an international speedway that holds Indy car races. So

AUTHOR'S TOP TEN PICKS

Abbott's Magic Manufacturing Company
Colon
(269) 432-3235
abbottmagic.com

Air Zoo
Kalamazoo
(866) 524-7966
airzoo.org

Antiquing in Allen
Allen
(517) 869-2788

Frederik Meijer Gardens
Grand Rapids
(888) 957-1580
meijergardens.org

Gerald R. Ford Museum
Grand Rapids
(616) 254-0400
fordlibrarymuseum.gov

Gilmore Car Museum
Hickory Corners
(269) 671-5089
gilmorecarmuseum.org

Hidden Lake Gardens
Tipton
(517) 431-2060
msu.edu

Michigan Library and Historical Center
Lansing
(517) 373-3559

State Capitol Tours
Lansing
(517) 373-2353

Van Andel Museum Center
Grand Rapids
(616) 456-3977
grmuseum.org

TOP ANNUAL EVENTS

MARCH

Clare Irish Festival
Clare
(989) 386-2442

MAY

Alma Highland Festival and Games
Alma
(989) 463-8979
almahighlandfestival.com

JUNE

World's Longest Breakfast Table
Battle Creek
(800) 397-2240
bcfestivals.com

JULY

Common Ground Festival
Lansing
(577) 267-1502
commongroundfest.com

AUGUST

Abbott's Magical Get-Together
Colon
(269) 432-3235
magicgettogether.com

Civil War Muster
Jackson
(517) 788-4320
civilwarmuster.org

Great Lakes Folk Festival
East Lansing
greatlakesfolkfest.net

SEPTEMBER

Celebration on the Grand
Grand Rapids
(616) 730-2191
celebrationonthegrand.org

Historic Homes Tour
Marshall
(800) 877-5163
marshallmi.org

Michigan Wine and Harvest Festival
Kalamazoo and Paw Paw
(269) 655-1111
wineandharvestfestival.com

overwhelming are these modern-day sights that it's easy to pass by one of the most interesting attractions and probably the only one that is free, *Walker Tavern.*

Located in *Cambridge Junction Historic State Park,* the white clapboard tavern overlooks US 12, and rightfully so. The highway was originally an Indian trail and then became a stagecoach route known as the Detroit-Chicago Road. The stagecoach era lasted from 1835 to 1855, and on these rickety wagons, passengers traveled 50 miles a day with the hope of reaching Chicago in five days. The string of frontier taverns along the way was a crucial part of the system. They provided not only overnight accommodations (two or three travelers would share a bed for 25 cents a night) but also meals for the weary passengers who had just spent the day bouncing along the rough dirt road.

By the 1830s Walker Tavern had a reputation as a fine place to dine. Proprietor Sylvester Walker ran not only the inn but a small farm as well, while his wife, Lucy, performed miracles baking in the stone fireplace. A typical supper at Walker Tavern might include stewed chicken, biscuits, corn bread, and applesauce cake or pumpkin pie. The tavern still stands on its original site, and the pub, sitting room, and kitchen have been renovated. Next to the tavern is a reconstructed wheelwright shop, featuring the tools used to build and repair the fragile wooden wheels as well as the covered wagons and carriages of the era. Visitors begin the self-guided walking tour at the Interpretive Center with a film in its theater and an exhibit on the settling of Michigan.

Cambridge Junction Historic State Park (517-467-4401; michigan.gov/ walkertavern) is at US 12 and M 50, 25 miles south of Jackson. The tavern complex is open from 10 a.m. to 5 p.m. Tues through Sun from Memorial Day through Labor Day.

Also located in the Irish Hills is Lenawee County's other outstanding attraction, **Hidden Lake Gardens.** Glaciers were responsible for the rolling terrain of the gardens, and when the ice sheet finally melted away, it left a topography of prominent knolls, ridges, valleys, and funnel-like depressions. Harry A. Fee was responsible for preserving it. The Adrian businessman fell in love with the scenic land formations and in 1926 purchased 226 acres, including its namesake lake. He began developing the landscape and supervising its early plantings before giving the gardens to Michigan State University in 1945. The visitor center was added in 1966, the plant conservatory four years later, and today Hidden Lake Gardens covers 670 acres with 6 miles of picturesque, winding, one-way roads, 5 miles of hiking trails to its remote corners, and more than 2,500 introduced species of plants.

Upon entering the gardens most people head for the visitor center, which includes an orientation and information area, a gift shop, and a walk-through exhibit concourse. Next door is the plant conservatory, where 8,000 square feet of glass houses plants from around the world. Along with the kumquats and vanilla plants in the tropical house and the old-man cacti in the arid dome, there is the 80- by 36-foot temperate house used to display unusual houseplants and seasonal flowers. From the conservatory visitors can follow a winding drive around Hidden Lake and then ascend through a unique forest carpeted in ivy before topping out at Gobblers Knob with a view of the surrounding ridges and hardwood trees below. The network of one-way roads also leads visitors past a glacial pothole, through an oak upland forest, and around an open meadow, and ends, of course, at a picnic area.

The entrance to the gardens (517-431-2060; hiddenlakegardens.msu .edu) is located on M 50, 2 miles west of Tipton or 7 miles west of Tecumseh. The gardens, visitor center, and plant conservatory are open daily from 9 a.m. to 7 p.m. Apr through Oct and 9 a.m. to 4 p.m. Nov through Mar. Admission is $3 per person. The first Monday of every month is free unless it is a holiday such as Labor Day.

There are many mansions-turned-restaurants in Michigan, but few evoke an aura of gracious living and fine dining the way the **Hathaway House** does. A National Historic Site, the home was built by David Carpenter, who arrived in Blissfield in 1836 as a 21-year-old with $25. Seventeen years later, Carpenter was a wealthy merchant, and he decided to build a home that would reflect his position as one of the county's most prominent residents. The 18-room Hathaway House resembles a southern mansion. Inside guests are seated in 6 distinctively decorated rooms that were previously the east and west parlors, the card room, and the library, among others. In this restaurant you can still run your hand along the original cherry banister of the sweeping staircase, be warmed during the winter by one of 5 fireplaces, and admire the classic woodwork.

trivia

Adrian's *Croswell Opera House* at 129 E. Maumee St. is the third oldest continuously operated theater in the country. The Opera House (517-263-6868; croswell .org) dates back to 1866 and today still features live theater productions.

Afterward you can drop in at the Main Street Stable. What used to be the carriage house in the back of Carpenter's mansion is now a lively little pub that still features a rustic interior of hand-hewn beams, wooden benches, and lanterns hanging from the ceiling.

The Hathaway House (517-486-2141 or 888-937-4284; hathawayhouse .com) is reached from US 23 by taking exit 5 and heading 10 miles west on US 223. Hours are 5 to 9 p.m. Thurs through Sat. Brunch is served on Sun from 11 a.m. to 2 p.m. and dinner from 11 a.m. to 7 p.m. Dinner entrees range from $22 to $30.

Hillsdale County

In 1827 a surveying crew from the Detroit-Chicago Road was working in the fertile prairie of the St. Joseph Valley when one crew member, Captain Moses Allen, fell in love with the area. His homestead led to a small hamlet of homes and shops known as Allen's Prairie, the first white settlement west of Tecumseh. This is the birthplace of Hillsdale County, but today *Allen* is better known as the Antiques Capital of Michigan.

It began as a weekend flea market in the late 1960s and soon drew crowds of antiques hunters from several states to the junction of US 12 and M 49. Eventually some of the antiques dealers who rented the summer stalls began to set up permanent businesses in Allen. Today this quaint village of fewer than 300 residents supports a dozen antiques malls, shops, and auction houses scattered in the downtown area and to the west along US 12. Some of the shops are in old homes or weathered barns that are packed with large furniture and other odds and ends. One of the malls is so large it houses more than 400 dealers.

The most interesting mall is *Preston's Antique Gaslight Village,* west of town on US 12. Preston's is a collection of almost 20 historic buildings assembled in a quaint 5-acre village that includes an 1860 farmhouse, a 1920s two-story Sears catalog house, a one-room school, and a Methodist church from 1871. Many now house antiques dealers and craft shops—and someday they all will. Preston's (517-869-2928) is open from 10 a.m. to 6 p.m. Fri, Sat, and Sun.

If you are heading south to Allen, swing through the picturesque village of *Litchfield* 14 miles to the north at the other end of M 49. Near the center of town is the Litchfield Town Hall, and featured in the huge storefront display windows is the *Litchfield Community Hand Tool Collection.* In one window are 75 tools from the turn of the 20th century, in the other another 63, all numbered to correspond to a list taped on the window and in surprisingly good condition. In the 3 smaller windows on the second floor, more tools are hung in display as the town's collection continues to grow and grow. Someday it might have to use all these tools to build a museum for them.

The **Tristate Corner** in Hillsdale County is hardly a major tourist attraction. But there is enough interest in this geographical oddity that

trivia

Somerset Center's **McCourtie Park,** located in the northeast corner of Hillsdale County, was once the Prohibition-era playground of cement mogul William McCourtie and features 17 sculpted cement bridges across a winding stream.

the Hillsdale County Historical Association maintains a stone monument dedicated to where three states— Michigan, Indiana, and Ohio—come together, the only such spot in the Midwest that doesn't involve a river.

The monument is actually in Michigan, but it explains exactly where the corner is (130 feet to the south) because when you reach this obscure spot, a farm field on a county dirt road, you want to make sure you're standing in all three states at the same time.

It's not as famous as Four Corners, the spot where Arizona, New Mexico, Colorado, and Utah come together, but on the other hand, as the locals say, it won't burn two weeks of your vacation to visit.

From Camden, in the southwest corner of Hillsdale County, head south on M 49 and then west on Territorial Road. In less than 3 miles, turn south on Cope Road and look for the stone monument on the left-hand side of the road.

St. Joseph County

Michigan is known for many things, but to the average tourist, magicians and magic are not generally among them. Yet Harry Houdini died in Michigan, and the state has deep roots in the art of illusion and the related conjuring culture. One of the most famous American magicians in the 1920s, Harry Blackstone, toured the country with his act. At one time he passed through the village of **Colon** and then returned in 1926 and purchased property. Blackstone toured in the winter but spent his summers in Colon creating new illusions and rehearsing his show. One summer Australian magician Percy Abbott came to Colon to visit Blackstone and fell in love with a local girl and the quiet area. Abbott, eager to end his days of traveling, moved to Michigan and formed a partnership with Blackstone to begin a magic-apparatus manufacturing company.

The partnership went sour after only eight months, but the Australian magician went ahead with his plans and in 1933 set up *Abbott's Magic Manufacturing Company.* Today this sleepy farming village is the home of the world's largest magic company, an interesting stop even if you've never done a card trick. The walls inside are plastered with posters and photographs of magicians, for all the famous performers, from Doug Henning to David Copperfield, have done business with this company. A display room in the factory, an all-black brick building, has cases and shelves filled with a portion of the 2,000 tricks and gadgets Abbott's Magic builds. And there is always a resident magician on hand to show you how they work.

A year after beginning his company, Abbott also instituted an open house for magicians as a sales incentive, and that quickly evolved into Colon's annual festival, Magica Get-Together. Every August more than a thousand amateur and professional magicians flood the village for a series of shows at the high school auditorium. Abbott's Magic Manufacturing Company (269-432-3235; abbottmagic.com) is at 124 St. Joseph St., 1 block off M 86, and is open from 9 a.m. to 5 p.m. Mon through Fri and 9 a.m. to 4 p.m. on Sat.

trivia

The longest of Michigan's handful of remaining covered bridges is just north of Centreville along Covered Bridge Road. Built in 1887, the *Langley Covered Bridge* is 282 feet long and uses three spans to cross the St. Joseph River.

More magic memorabilia can be viewed at the *Colon Community Museum* (269-432-2462), which is housed in an 1893 church at 219 N. Blackstone Rd. Although many artifacts deal with the town's first pioneer families, one area is devoted to the personal items and photographs of Blackstone and Abbott. The museum is open Tues, Thurs, and Sun from 2 to 4:30 p.m. from Memorial Day to Labor Day and the rest of the year by appointment.

Jackson County

The Lower Peninsula lacks the waterfalls that grace the countryside in the Upper Peninsula, but in Jackson there are the **Cascades.** Billed as the largest constructed waterfalls in North America, the Cascades were a creation of "Captain" William Sparks, a well-known Jackson industrialist and philanthropist. They date to the early 1930s, when Sparks was developing a 450-acre park as a gift to the city and wanted it to showcase something different, something no other Michigan city had.

What he developed were the Cascades, a series of 18 waterfalls with water dancing down the side of a hill from one to the next. Six fountains, varying in height and patterns, supply more than 3,000 gallons per minute, while 1,200 colored lights turn the attraction into a nightly event of constantly changing light, color, and music. The total length of the falls is 500

Michigan's Oldest Restaurant & Hotel

Detroit's Roma Cafe (313-831-5940; romacafe.com) near the Eastern Market is the oldest restaurant in the state. The cafe began as a boardinghouse in 1890, offering a bed and meals to farmers who arrived to sell their produce and goods at the market. By the 1920s the boarding portion of the business was closed but the restaurant remained, serving fine Italian meals at the corner of Riopelle and Erskine Streets for 119 years.

Michigan's oldest hotel is the *National House Inn* (269-781-7374; nationalhouse-inn.com) overlooking Marshall's picturesque Fountain Circle at 102 Parkview. The inn was built in 1835 with bricks that were molded and fired on the site, making it the oldest brick building in Calhoun County. It was located two dusty days and nights by stagecoach from Detroit and served as a welcome halfway stop for early travelers on the way to Chicago.

When the Michigan Central Railroad arrived in Marshall in 1844, the inn catered to railroad passengers then closed its doors as a hotel in 1878, the victim of dining cars and Pullman sleepers. At that time the building was converted to a factory for producing windmills and farm wagons. But it returned to being a place of fine lodging when in 1976 the National House Inn was restored as a bed-and-breakfast with 16 rooms as part of a community bicentennial project. Today it is listed as a state historical site and on the National Register of Historic Places.

feet, and energetic viewers climb the 129 steps that run along each side of the Cascades, dodging the spray along the way. Others prefer to sit in the amphitheater seats to watch the water and light show that takes place nightly from 8 p.m. to 11 p.m. Memorial Day to Labor Day.

The Cascades (517-788-4320, co.jackson.mi.us/departments/parks/cascades_falls) can be reached from I-94 by taking exit 138 and heading south for 3 miles. Signs point the way to the falls. Admission is $4 per adult and $6 per adult on nights when there is a fireworks show. Children are free.

Ten miles southwest of Jackson is the Victorian town of Concord, the proper setting for the *Mann House,* a Michigan historical museum. The three-story house was built in 1883 by Daniel and Ellen Mann, two of the earliest settlers in the area. They raised two daughters, Jessie and Mary Ida, who continued to live in the house and maintained the original furnishings, most dating to the 1870s. The younger daughter died in 1969 but bequeathed the historic house and all its contents to the people of Michigan through the Michigan Historical Commission.

The house can be toured today, and its 8 rooms are a well-preserved trip back to life in the 1880s. The table is set in the dining room; a chess game waits to be played in the parlor; toys, books, and knickknacks fill the children's rooms. As soon as you walk through the wrought-iron gate at the street, you enter an era gone by. The Mann House (517-524-8943; michigan.gov/mannhouse) is at 205 Hanover St. in Concord and is open from 9 a.m. to 4 p.m. Mon through Sat from Memorial Day to Labor Day. There is no admission fee.

Deer hunting is not just an outdoor sport in Michigan, it's a passion. Every November more than 750,000 hunters participate in the 16-day firearm deer season. Add in the people who participate in the archery and muzzleloading deer seasons, and the number tops a million.

These hunters' shrine is the *Michigan Whitetail Hall of Fame Museum,* just off I-94 near Jackson.

trivia

The Republican Party was born on the corner of Second and Franklin Streets in Jackson. The hall where the founders had originally planned to meet on July 6, 1854, was too small for the 1,500 people who arrived to form a new political party. So the crowd walked 8 blocks to an oak grove and met there "under the oaks."

The Parlour

Late one night, when the *Parlour* is humming with people, ice-cream dishes clanging, and waitresses hustling orders from the kitchen, a woman screams and no one takes notice. It's her first trip to the landmark ice-cream parlor, and a waitress has just placed in front of her the largest Black Cow she has ever seen. The fountain glass itself is 12 inches high, and still the rich mixture of root beer and ice cream is cascading over the top, because at the Parlour, they put 5 scoops of vanilla—count 'em, 5—in their Black Cow.

"Oh my goodness," said the woman, in a near state of calorie shock. "All I asked for was a root beer float, and look what they brought me."

If you're a die-hard ice-cream lover, then the Parlour is heaven on earth, or at the very least a parfait paradise. Operated by the Jackson Dairy, this hot fudge haven is basically 4 U-shaped lunch counters plus a handful of booths for those of us who like to pig out anonymously. Everybody else has to sit across from total strangers and indulge in 5 scoops of cherry ripple drowning in a sea of marshmallow syrup. Then again, maybe it's better they are strangers.

Or else, who cares? When you enter the Parlour, you have momentarily forgotten about your waistband if you ever thought about it to begin with. The most popular item is the Deluxe Pecan Combo: 3 scoops of ice cream smothered in hot fudge and hot caramel, sprinkled with pecans, and buried in real whipped cream. You don't eat this sundae, you attack it, using your spoon like a shovel to remove large portions from the sides before it avalanches onto your place mat.

The Parlour (517-783-1581) is at Wildwood Avenue and 1401 Daniel Road in Jackson and reached from I-94 by taking exit 137. Head south on Lawrence and then east on Wildwood Avenue.

At this unusual "hall of fame," you can feed live deer, or, if you are around on June 1, see newborn fawns. Inside the hall is a gallery of more than 100 trophy racks including 50 Boone and Crockett world-record buck racks and Michigan's record buck. This is the stuff that deer hunters dream about while sitting in their blinds every November.

The Michigan Whitetail Hall of Fame (517-937-0533) is at 4220 Willis Rd. and reached by taking exit 150 at Grass Lake and following the signs. Hours are 11 a.m. to 7 p.m. daily, winter hours 11 a.m. to 6 p.m. Admission is $5 for adults and $1 for children.

Calhoun County

Homer is a small town in the southeast corner of the county, and its most impressive structure is a century-old gristmill on the banks of the Kalamazoo River. The US government once wanted to turn the mill's black walnut beams into propellers for World War I airplanes. Another historic building in town, though considerably smaller, is a fun place to have breakfast on the Fourth of July: the **Homer Fire Museum.** The redbrick structure with its arched windows and decorative cornice was built in 1876, 5 years after Homer was incorporated as a village. It has always been the classic fire hall on the main street, but in its early days it also served as a jail, town hall, and place for public meetings and local theater performances. It's the oldest building in town, and when Homer residents decided to replace it, they preserved the old fire hall by attaching the new fire station to it.

In 1983 it was set up as a museum, with suits and equipment donated by former firefighters. By far the most impressive item on display had always been there, a horse-pulled steam pumper built in 1887. Homer bought it

Sojourner Truth Museum Exhibit

The **Kimball House Museum** is a restored 1886 Victorian home furnished with antiques and devoted to the history of Battle Creek. But by far the most interesting exhibit is dedicated to **Sojourner Truth.** This famous antislavery reformer was born into slavery in Hurley, New York, in 1797 but was freed when the state emancipated slaves in 1829. A mystic who believed she heard God's voice, Truth began to preach in the streets of New York City in 1829 and then along the Eastern Seaboard after embracing the abolitionist movement in 1843. She added women's rights to her causes a few years later, and in 1864 she was received by President Abraham Lincoln at the White House.

Eventually Truth relocated to Battle Creek but continued to stump the country on speaking tours, advocating women's rights. Illiterate all her life, Truth was nevertheless a charismatic speaker who drew large crowds to her lectures and quickly became Battle Creek's first nationally known figure.

The second-floor exhibit at the Kimball House Museum features a handful of Truth's mementos, including her crude attempt to write her name. The museum is at 196 Capital Ave., 3 blocks north of Michigan Avenue. The museum (269-966-4157) is open 1 to 4 p.m. Sun from May through Dec.

from Union City in 1904 for $1,200 and placed it in the fire hall, where it has been ever since. The museum does not have regular hours, but those who are passing through can go to the Homer City Offices (517-568-4321) next to the fire station, and an employee will open up the museum for you. There is no admission fee.

Battle Creek is best known as the Cereal Bowl of America, dating back to 1876 when Dr. John Harvey Kellogg joined the staff of the Battle Creek Sanitarium. A Seventh-day Adventist at the time, Kellogg spent 25

Strange as it Sounds

It looked so plain when the woman behind the counter handed it to me, wrapped in waxed paper and placed in a brown paper bag. But there it is: a buttered turkey sandwich, slices of moist meat on a bun, topped with mayonnaise. It's the kind of sandwich you'd make after Thanksgiving dinner with the leftover rolls and that platter of turkey still sitting in the kitchen.

But here at a place they call **Turkeyville, USA,** you don't have to wait until Uncle Harry and the kids go home. You can order one year-round because this simple sandwich—turkey, butter, mayonnaise on soft white bread—is the foundation of a multimillion-dollar company. Cornwell's Turkeyville, USA has been called "the oldest, best-known, and possibly largest all-turkey specialty restaurant in North America."

The Cornwells have done to the turkey what the Zehner family has done to the chicken in Frankenmuth: turned a meal into a tourist attraction. Today the restaurant is an entertainment complex serving an average of 1,000 people a day, grossing more than $2 million annually, and feeding more than 400 busloads a summer—and pretty much does it all on the backs of 15,000, 30-pound toms a year. In 1985, when a photo of founders Wayne and Marjorie Cornwell was featured in *People* magazine with an item proclaiming their buttered bun "the world's best turkey sandwich," people around here knew the Cornwells had hit the big time.

After you've had your fill of turkey, you can wander into Cornwell's Ice Cream Parlour or the huge gift shop. Also among the attractions is a dinner theater, plus craft shows, bazaars, and other events throughout the year.

From I-94, take I-69 north to exit 42 and then head west on N. Drive North, also known as Turkeyville Road. The restaurant is reached in a half mile. Cornwell's Turkeyville, USA (800-228-4315; turkeyville.com) is open from 11 a.m. to 7 p.m. daily year-round.

years developing the sanitarium into an institution recognized around the world for its "health building and training" based on the church's principles of a vegetarian diet, abstinence from alcohol and tobacco, and a regimen of exercise. Along the way he found a way to process grains into appetizing breakfast food as an alternative to the standard breakfast of eggs and meat. Cornflakes and other cereals quickly revolutionized the eating habits of people everywhere, and by the early 1900s more than 40 cereal manufacturers were based in Battle Creek, including Kellogg's.

The best place to learn about Dr. Kellogg and the birth of cereal is at the *Dr. John Harvey Kellogg Discovery Center,* one of 8 buildings within *Historic Adventist Village.* On the second floor of the center are interactive exhibits focused on the health treatments and practices that made the Battle Creek Sanitarium world famous a century ago. The rest of the re-created 19th-century village is devoted to the history of the Seventh-day Adventist Church and includes a log cabin, one-room schoolhouse, and the houses of the Adventist pioneers who settled in the west end of Battle Creek in 1855.

The Historic Adventist Village (269-965-3000; adventistheritage.org) is just west of Battle Creek at 480 W. Van Buren St.; it is open from Apr 1 to Nov 1, Sun through Fri from 10 a.m. to 4 p.m., and 2 to 4 p.m. on Sat. In the winter, the village is open only on Sat from 2 to 4 p.m. Call for an appointment in the winter. Admission by donation.

Not every attraction in Battle Creek is wrapped around sugar-frosted flakes. Just south of the city in a wooded area along Harper Creek is *Binder Park Zoo,* one of Michigan's most unusual displays of fauna and flora. Instead of a series of cages and animal houses in the middle of a city, Binder Park is a walk through the woods along boardwalks, brick walkways, and wood-chip trails, passing animal exhibits that have been designed around the existing flora and terrain.

The most impressive is Wild Africa, where you can view gazelles, zebras, or one of the largest giraffe herds in the country. In other areas you will see giant tortoises, Chinese red pandas, snow leopards, or wallabies from Australia, but the section kids love the most is Binder's zoo within a zoo. Miller Children's Zoo is the largest animal-contact area in the state and provides children an opportunity to feed and touch dozens of animals, including donkeys, rabbits, pygmy goats, draft horses, and pigs. Constructed around these contact stations are intriguing play areas. There's the Pig Pen, with models of pigs that children can play on; the dinosaur area, with a 100-foot-long brontosaurus and a fossil-find pit; a giant spiderweb to climb; and a farm area with a silo slide and cow climber.

Binder Park Zoo (269-979-1351; binderparkzoo.org) is reached from I-94 by taking exit 100 south along Beadle Lake Road and following the signs to the entrance at 7400 Division Dr. The zoo is open from mid-Apr to mid-Oct from 9 a.m. to 5 p.m. Mon through Fri, 9 a.m. to 6 p.m. Sat, and 11 a.m. to 6 p.m. Sun. Admission is $12.95 for adults and $10.95 for children.

Battle Creek is also home to one of the most unusual county parks in Michigan. The focus of *Historic Bridge Park* is the preservation of turn-of-the-century truss bridges, making it the first of its kind in the country. Truss bridges that need to be replaced elsewhere are relocated over Dickinson Creek within the park and then restored for their historic and aesthetic value. There are currently 5 metal truss bridges and a stone arch bridge in the park but eventually there will be up to 15, providing walkers, picnickers, and cyclists a unique way to cross the stream.

After being closed for over a year due to an oil spill from a broken Enbridge pipeline upstream from the park, Historic Bridge Park reopened on June 5, 2102, following a cleanup and renovations. Enbridge also paid for improved restroom facilities, parking lots, and a new playground, as well as an improved stairway up to the Charlotte Highway Bridge. Enbridge has funded an endowment for maintenance of the new park features.

To reach the park from I-94, depart at exit 104 and head south on 11 Mile Road. Turn right on F Drive North and left on Wattles Road where the entrance is posted. Historic Bridge Park (269-781-9841; historicbridges.org) is open year-round from 8 a.m. to 8 p.m. and there are no entry fees.

Kalamazoo County

Is it a museum or a theme park? You decide—but what can't be debated is the fact that the *Air Zoo* has been gradually expanded until today it's the tenth largest non-government aviation museum in the nation. Officially the Air Zoo is dedicated to the aircraft of World War II and the role they played in the Allies' success. It's a "living museum" that not only displays many planes in its hangars at the southeast corner of the Kalamazoo/Battle Creek

International Airport but also restores them to working condition. Inside there are more than 80 planes and historical crafts on display, including a Curtiss P-40 "Flying Tiger" and 3 Grumman cats: "Wildcat," "Hellcat," and "Bearcat," thus the reason for the Air Zoo's name.

But at the Air Zoo you can also join a space walk and discover how walking in space is different from walking on earth, fly a bi-plane complete with wind in your hair, experience weightlessness just like an astronaut on a Zero Gravity ride, or view a WWII bombing mission in a unique 4-dimensional, 180-degree theater (3-D film plus live actors). The Air Zoo (866-524-7966; airzoo.org) is at 6151 Portage Rd. and is open Mon through Sat 9 a.m. to 5 p.m. and noon to 5 p.m. on Sun. General admission is $8 and an unlimited ride pass is an additional $7 per person.

Also on the edge of Kalamazoo is the *Celery Flats Interpretive Center.* This is a truly unique facility that teaches the history of the efforts of Dutch immigrants to convert wetlands into one of the most productive celery-growing areas in the world. From the 1890s through the 1930s, fields of green-tipped celery covered Portage, Comstock, and Kalamazoo; the celery was touted as "fresh as dew from Kalamazoo."

trivia

The city of Kalamazoo dates back to 1829 when Titus Bronson arrived and founded a settlement that was first called Bronson. The only known speech Abraham Lincoln gave in Michigan was in Kalamazoo.

The historic area offers an 1856 one-room schoolhouse, a 1931 grain elevator, and historical displays on celery, as well as an opportunity to rent canoes to explore the surrounding wetlands. Celery Flats (269-329-4522; portagemi.gov) is open from June through Aug from 10 a.m. to 3 p.m. Mon through Fri; Sat and Sun, noon to 5 p.m. From I-94 take exit 76A and head south 2.5 miles on S. Westedge Avenue and then east 0.5 mile on Garden Lane. Admission is $3 for adults and $2 for children.

Barry County

In 1962 Donald Gilmore, the son-in-law of Dr. W. E. Upjohn, founder of one of the nation's leading pharmaceutical firms, was restoring a 1920

Pierce-Arrow touring car in the driveway of his Gull Lake summer home. The project dragged on into the fall, and by the time it was finished, Gilmore had to erect a tent around the car and light a kerosene heater. This was no way to work on a classic car. So Gilmore purchased three farms north of his home and then scouted the countryside for old wooden barns, which he had dismantled and moved.

The wooden structures held his growing collection, and in 1966 Gilmore opened his barn doors to the public on 90 acres of rolling farmland. The Classic Car Club of America added its collection to what had become the Hickory Corners Museum in 1984, and today the *Gilmore Car Museum* forms a complex of 22 barns displaying 200 vintage automobiles in mint condition. The car that attracts the most attention is a 1929 Duesenberg. Some visitors, however, are fascinated with Rolls-Royces, and the museum contains 15 of them, including 8 in one barn, ranging from a 1910 Silver Ghost to a 1938 Phantom III.

There is also a 1927 Bugatti Grand Sport Roadster, the "Gnome-Mobile" from the Disney movie of the same name, as well as other transportation displays, including a replica of the Wright Brothers' Kitty Hawk flier. Those intrigued by hood ornaments can view a collection of more than 1,500—the largest such collection in North America—that captures everything from a windblown angel to an archer taking aim at the road ahead. They come from as far away as the former Soviet Union and include leaded-glass ornaments from France.

Dedicated in May 2012, the *Automotive Heritage Center* is a state-of-the-art $5 million, 32,000-square-foot attraction. Fashioned after an early 1900s factory, the center is the museum's largest expansion to date. The center connects to one of the museum's historic barns, which leads to 5 additional exhibit galleries as well as the vintage Franklin Auto Dealership.

The center features a large exhibit gallery, a multimedia theater, and an expansive research library and archives, as well as educational and interactive areas, a museum store, offices, and artifact storage facility.

The complex (269-671-5089; gilmorecarmuseum.org) is located at M 43 and Hickory Road, 7 miles north of Richland. From I-94, take exit 80 and head north to M 43. The museum is open year-round from 9 a.m. to 5 p.m. Mon through Fri and 9 a.m. to 6 p.m. Sat and Sun. Admission is $10 for adults and $8 for children ages 7 to 15.

Nearby is the **Kellogg Farm**. Founded in 1984 by Michigan State University, this experimental dairy is a working farm that combines research and teaching. It's also a popular spot for urban folks to visit and learn what it's like down on the farm. There is a visitor center with educational exhibits and a viewing area of the robotic milking parlor where cows are milked daily.

The Kellogg Farm (269-671-2507) is reached from I-94 by taking exit 85 and heading north 7 miles on Thirty-fifth Street. Turn east on M 89 and in 3 miles north on Fortieth Street to reach the posted entrance. Hours are 8 a.m. to 5 p.m. and 8 a.m. to 8 p.m. on Daylight Saving Time. The visitor center is open 8 a.m. to noon Mon through Fri. There is no admission charge.

Ingham County

One of the best urban park developments in Michigan is **Lansing's River Trail** (lansingrivertrail.org). The 6-mile-long park is a greenbelt that stretches on both sides of the Grand River from Kalamazoo Avenue just north of I-496 to North Street, 3 miles downstream. A riverwalk, made of long sections of boardwalk near or on the river, runs along the entire east side of the park, with bridges that lead to more walkways on the west side. Interesting attractions are found throughout the park, and you could easily spend an entire day walking from one to the next.

At the south end at 240 Museum Dr. is the **R. E. Olds Transportation Museum** (517-372-0422; rcoldsmuseum.org), dedicated to the history of transportation in Lansing, where at one time or another 15 makes of automobile were manufactured. More than 50 vehicles, from the first Oldsmobile, built in 1897, to an Indy 500 pace car, fill the old City Bus Garage along with old motoring apparel and other memorabilia. The museum is open Tues through Sat from 10 a.m. to 5 p.m. and Sun from noon to 5 p.m. Admission is $6 for adults, $4 for children, and $12 for families.

Right next door at 200 Museum Dr. you'll find the **Impression 5 Museum** (517-485-8116; impression5.org), which is described as an "exploratorium" for children and their parents, stressing hands-on exhibits. The 240 exhibits on several floors range from a music room, filled with unusual instruments to be played, to a bubble room where children can be totally encased in a bubble. Impression 5 is open 10 a.m. to 5 p.m. Tues to Sat and noon to 5 p.m. Sun. Admission is $5 for adults or children.

Planet Walk

For most children one of the most enjoyable aspects of the River Trail is the Planet Walk, a cleverly simple but thoroughly enjoyable trek through our solar system. It is also very enlightening. Most maps of our solar system have condensed the distances to fit the sun and the orbiting planets on the same page. You learn the names of the planets, but distances in the universe, the 93 million miles from the sun to Earth or the 3.7 billion miles to Pluto (recently downgraded to a dwarf planet), are simply too large for children to comprehend from textbooks.

That's the idea behind the Planet Walk. The one-way walk of 2 miles is strung out along River Front Park, beginning and ending at two of Lansing's most enjoyable attractions: the Impression 5 Museum and Potter Park Zoo. In between it's a 45- to 60-minute walk from the sun to Pluto, a hike in which every step represents a million miles.

Not only are the distances properly scaled but so are the size and mass of the sun and each planet. The sun, located near the entrance to the Impression 5 Museum, is a 20-inch golden sphere looking like an over-inflated basketball.

From there it's a few quick steps to reach Mercury, the size of a pencil eraser. The first 4 planets are reached within a few hundred feet. But the rest are spread out, and it's probably three-quarters of a mile between Saturn and Uranus alone.

Continuing north along the east side, you'll walk under Michigan Avenue and past views of the state capitol, around Sun Bowl Amphitheater and the city's **Farmers' Market** (open Tues, Thurs, and Sat), and eventually reach the **Brenke River Sculpture and Fish Ladder.** The structure is a swirl of steps and stone benches leading down to the fish ladder that curves its way around scenic North Lansing Dam. Come mid-September you can watch salmon and steelhead trout leap from one water ledge of the ladder to the next on the way to their spawning grounds.

There are two great ways to explore Lansing's River Trail and the Grand River: by land and by water.

You can rent bicycles, tandems, even child trailers for the back of the bike at **Riverfront Cycle** (517-482-8585; riverfrontcycle.com) located near the trail at 507 E. Shiawassee St. The bike shop is open Mon through Fri, 10 a.m. to 6 p.m., and 10 a.m. to 5 p.m. Sat.

You can also cruise the Grand River aboard the triple-deck **Michigan Princess** (517-627-2154; michiganprincess.com) on a variety of outings, including dinner cruises, color tours, and evening trips that feature music, dancing, or a murder mystery theater. Located at 2995 W. Main St., the paddle-wheeler is operated year-round, thanks to heated cabins, with most tours priced between $15 and $45 per adult.

For a closer look at Michigan's most famous government building, join a *State Capitol Tour* and be prepared for the building's stunning interior. In 1992 a major renovation of the century-old capitol was completed at a cost of more than $45 million. When the building was originally dedicated on January 1, 1879, it was one of the first state capitols to emulate the dome and wings of the US Capitol in Washington, DC, and today it is considered by most as an outstanding example of Victorian craftsmanship. All tours begin in the rotunda, where visitors stand on the floor of glass tiles imported from England and stare at the stars in the top of the dome 172 feet above. In between are portraits of governors on the second level and, on the main floor, flags carried by Michigan regiments during battles from as long ago as the Civil War. Tours also include a look into the restored state Senate and House of Representative chambers as well as other offices and rooms, each accompanied by bits and pieces of Michigan's history.

To reach the state capitol from I-96, follow I-496 through Lansing and take the Walnut exit to 115 W. Allegan St. State capitol signs point the way to the building and parking nearby. Capitol Tour Guide Service (517-373-2353) offers the tours every half hour Mon through Fri from 9 a.m. to 4 p.m. Visits by groups of more than 10 must be scheduled in advance. There is no charge for tours.

Almost as impressive as the state capitol is the *Michigan Library and Historical Center,* which opened in 1988. Nationally recognized for its architectural design, the 312,000-square-foot center houses the Michigan Historical Museum, the State Archives, and the Library of Michigan, the second largest state library in the country.

Most people, however, visit the center to see the museum. The Michigan Historical Museum features 12 permanent galleries displaying facades of a lumber baron's mansion and the state's first territorial capitol, a walk-through copper mine tunnel, and an impressive woodland diorama. Other rooms feature a working sawmill, historic cars, a stake fort, and many other

Chocolate Cheese & Other Attractions at MSU

You don't have to be enrolled at Michigan State University to enjoy its campus. In fact it's better if you're not . . . who needs to pay tuition?

MSU is loaded with attractions that are open to the public and many of them will be of interest to adults, such as the *Eli and Edythe Broad Art Museum* (517-884-3900; broadmuseum.msu.edu), newly opened in 2012, or the *Wharton Center for Performing Arts* (800-942-7866; whartoncenter.com). But most are geared for children, and families can have a great time at MSU.

In the heart of the campus is the *Michigan State University Museum* (517-355-2370; museum.msu.edu) where you can explore 3 floors devoted to natural history, from mounted skeletons of the great Jurassic dinosaurs Allosaurus and Stegosaurus to Habitat Hall where life-sized dioramas depict the environments of North America—forests, grasslands, deserts, tropics, and tundra. The MSU Museum is open from 9 a.m. to 5 p.m. Mon through Fri, 10 a.m. to 5 p.m. Sat, and 1 to 5 p.m. Sun.

The *Michigan 4H Children's Garden* (517-355-5191; 4hgardencowplex.com) is designed especially for children with its maze entrance, Magic Bubble Fountain, and pizza garden and is open from sunup to sundown daily. Things get icky at *Michigan State University Bug House* (517-355-4662; ent.msu.edu/bughouse) as kids will learn that a cricket's ears are on its knees and a fly has taste buds on its feet. They will also be able to view an extensive collection of pinned bugs or have the opportunity to get up close and personal with a whole room of creepy crawlers. The Bug House is located in room 147 of the Natural Science building and is open for drop-in visits Mon from 5:30 to 7:30 p.m.

But the best place to visit, whether you're a kid or not, is the *Michigan State University Dairy Store* (517-355-8466; dairystore.msu.edu) in Anthony Hall on Farm Lane. At the store there is an observation deck to watch workers process milk and cream and a multimedia presentation about how the MSU Dairy Plant makes cheese and ice cream. Or you can skip all that and just order a double dip of some the creamiest ice cream you'll ever taste. There are 32 flavors to choose from. Even better, try the store's most unusual offering: chocolate cheese. The dessert cheese is made of cocoa, sugar, and peanuts that are mixed into cheddar and other cheeses. Its fudge-like taste and consistency has MSU alumni ordering it online from around the country long after they graduate.

The MSU Dairy Store is open 9 a.m. to 8 p.m. Mon through Fri and noon to 8 p.m. Sat and Sun. Everything, from the Bug House to the museum, is free unless you're tempted to order a scoop of Badger Cherry Cheesecake or Final Four Fudge Dribble.

exhibits relating to the history of the Great Lakes State. To view the museum and the capitol is a full day for most families.

The Michigan Library and Historical Center (517-373-3559; michigan .gov/museum) is at 702 W. Kalamazoo St., within easy walking distance of the capitol. Hours are 9 a.m. to 4:30 p.m. Mon through Fri, 10 a.m. to 4 p.m. Sat, and 1 to 5 p.m. Sun. There is no admission charge.

Ionia County

When autumn arrives in Michigan and the leaves begin turning shades of red, yellow, and orange, many people instinctively head north to view the fall colors. But the southern portions of the state also enjoy their share of autumn brilliance, and one of the best drives is a 15-mile route that is lined by hardwood forests and rolling farm fields and crosses three covered bridges, including the oldest one in Michigan, *White's Covered Bridge.*

Nestled in a wooded area and spanning the Flat River, White's Covered Bridge was built in 1867 by J. N. Brazee for $1,700 and has faithfully served the public ever since. It is a classic covered bridge, its trusses hand-hewn and secured with wooden pegs and hand-cut square nails. The bridge is 14 feet wide and 116 feet long, and you can still drive a car across it; most travelers park on the other side and return on foot for a closer inspection. The bridge is reached by driving to the hamlet of Smyrna in Ionia County (5 miles southwest of Belding) and then heading south on White's Bridge Road.

Continue south on White's Bridge Road for 4 miles, and turn west (left) onto Potters Road for a short distance to Fallasburg Bridge Road, which will lead you over another covered bridge in Fallasburg County Park just inside Kent County. Brazee and his construction company also built the *Fallasburg Covered Bridge.* Its design is similar to White's bridge, and it was built with the same high standards that have allowed both these structures to exist for more than a century. Above both entrances

trivia

Grand Rapids entered the national furniture market with exhibits at the Philadelphia Centennial Exposition in 1876. Today the city still accounts for 40 percent of the business and office furniture market.

The Roadside Table

For those who like obscure historical sites, Ionia County has one of the best in the state. Located at Morrison Lake Road and Grand River Avenue, south of the town of Saranac, is the place known simply as the Roadside Table. It was at this very spot that in 1929 county engineer Allen Williams used a stack of leftover guardrail planks to build a table, the first public picnic table ever placed on a highway right-of-way. Today, of course, there are roadside tables and rest areas in all 50 states, and the only sights more common on our nation's highways are billboards and McDonald's restaurants. Along the road, the site is marked only by a small white historical site sign, but a green state historic site plaque detailing the story has been erected next to the tables. The state still maintains the tables and garbage barrels, even though most of the traffic now flows along I-94 to the south.

to the Fallasburg Bridge is a stern warning: $5 FINE FOR RIDING OR DRIVING ON THIS BRIDGE FASTER THAN A WALK. The county park is a pleasant stretch of picnic tables and grills on the grassy slopes of the Flat River.

From the park, take Lincoln Lake Avenue south into the town of Lowell and head west on M 21 along the Grand River until you finally cross it into the town of Ada, where signs will point the way to the *Ada Covered Bridge.* The original bridge that crossed the Thornapple River was built in 1867 by Will Holmes but was destroyed by fire in 1980. The residents of Ada immediately opened their hearts (and their wallets), and the bridge was quickly rebuilt and restored. The Ada Bridge is open to pedestrian traffic only.

Kent County

The favorite son of *Grand Rapids* is Gerald R. Ford, a local congressman who eventually became the 38th president of the United States. In 1981 the *Gerald R. Ford Museum* opened, and today the center, dedicated to Ford's life and his days in office, is one of the city's top attractions. More than 2 million visitors have passed through the center, which features 2 floors of exhibits and displays that underwent a $5.3-million makeover in 1997.

The museum still features a full-scale reproduction of the Oval Office as it appeared in Ford's administration and a Watergate gallery that includes a 6-minute, multiscreen history of the 1972 break-in along with the actual burglary tools, but now has several new galleries that feature hands-on and computerized exhibits. Among them is a TelePrompTer that allows you to give a Ford speech and an interactive Cabinet Room that allows you to take part in Presidential decision making. President Ford died in 2006 and his Presidential Burial Site is also on the museum grounds and open to the public.

The Gerald R. Ford Museum (616-254-0400; fordlibrarymuseum.gov) is at 303 Pearl St. NW on the west bank of the Grand River, and is reached by exiting US 131 at Pearl Street. Hours are 9 a.m. to 5 p.m. daily. Admission is $7 for adults and $3 for children.

Long before the presidential seal was stamped on this portion of Kent County, Grand Rapids was known as the City of Furniture. In 1853 it was a small frontier town surrounded by forests with a seemingly endless supply of lumber and situated on the banks of the Grand River, which provided power for the mills. In this setting William "Deacon" Haldane opened a cabinet shop and soon was building not only cupboards but also cradles, coffins, and tables and chairs. By the end of the decade, there were several shops, and soon "Grand Rapids–Made Furniture" became the standard of excellence.

As impressive as the Ford Museum is, it now has a rival practically next door. In 1994 the ***Van Andel Museum Center*** opened to the public, replacing the old Grand Rapids Public Museum. The $40-million structure is on the Grand River, and overlooking the water is its centerpiece, a glass pavilion housing a working 1928 carousel with hand-carved horses and a Wurlitzer organ. Rides are $1, and it's debatable who has more fun—children or their parents.

Other exhibits in the 3-story building include a replica of a Union Depot waiting room, a 76-foot finback whale suspended from the ceiling, an entire street from Grand Rapids in the 1890s, a high-tech planetarium, and many interactive and hands-on exhibits that focus on natural science and the unique western Michigan environment.

The Van Andel Museum Center (616-456-3977; grmuseum.org) is at 272 Pearl, just east of the Pearl exit off US 131. Hours are 9 a.m. to 8 p.m. Tues, 9 a.m. to 5 p.m. Wed through Sat, and noon to 5 p.m. Sun. There is an admission fee of $8 for adults and $3 for children ages 3 to 18.

Sculpture Park Features "Bigger Than Life" Art

Frederik Meijer once said, "All art is bigger than life." So he created a huge unusual open-air museum for his outstanding art collection. This is the same Fred Meijer of supermarket fame. Meijer Inc. is one of the nation's largest family-owned retailers. But Meijer wasn't born into the lap of luxury. The son of Dutch immigrants, Meijer grew up on a farm in the small community of Greenville, 25 miles northeast of Grand Rapids. Money was tight and Meijer did whatever odd jobs he could find. For a while, he sold eggs at 10 cents a dozen from a pony and cart.

Even in the hardest of times, Meijer says his parents made sure their children learned about culture. Meijer children took music lessons and Frederik played the violin for 15 years—even if finding money for music lessons was often difficult. When his dad opened the family's first grocery story on June 30, 1934, the 14-year-old Meijer was there as a bag boy. Throughout his years at Greenville High School, Meijer put in about 40 hours a week at the family business. He never went to college but continued working with his father until Hendrik died in 1964 at age 80.

In 1951, Meijer and his wife Lena moved to Grand Rapids but kept close ties to their hometown of Greenville. Then in 1983, the Meijers sponsored a project that would change their lives forever. That year, the Meijers funded the creation of a public work by Detroit sculptor Marshall Fredericks based on the classic Danish children's tale, *The Ugly Duckling* by Hans Christian Andersen. Meijer fell in love with the art of sculpture and began buying works by Fredericks. Before long, he had a wealth of sculptures in storage.

When he was approached in 1990 by the West Michigan Horticultural Society to help create a new botanical garden, Meijer saw a natural fit. He could combine his wife's love of gardens and flowers with his own desire to build and share a significant sculpture collection. That's how the **Frederik Meijer Gardens & Sculpture Park** was born. In his initial gift, Meijer donated 70 acres of land, operational and

When the state began stocking salmon in the Great Lakes in the 1960s, the fish would spawn up the Grand River but had problems getting beyond the Sixth Street Dam in Grand Rapids. The solution was the **Fish Ladder Sculpture,** a unique sculptured viewing area designed by local artist Joseph Kinnebrew. Located at 560 Front Ave. Northwest, just on the north side of I-196, the ladder is a series of 7 small ledges on the west bank of the river that let the salmon easily leap around the dam. The rest of the sculpture is foundation support, and more than 60 sculptures from his extensive collection. The Frederik Meijer Gardens opened on April 20, 1995. Now 132 acres, the gardens feature the largest tropical conservatory in Michigan, indoor specialty gardens, outdoor gardens, nature trails, boardwalk, and indoor sculpture galleries for changing exhibitions. Then came the 30-acre sculpture garden in 2002.

Sculptures are set among trees, streams, waterfalls, hills, and meadows offering views from many different vantage points. The park has a 16-foot waterfall with winding stream and landscaped natural areas called Nature's Niches, the Meditation Garden, the Gallery, the Meadow, the Hollow, the Commons, and the Wedding Garden. Each is uniquely different and all are connected by more than 1.5 miles of sculptured pathway.

The sculpture garden has more than two dozen pieces in bronze, iron, stainless steel, marble, industrial porcelain, and painted aluminum. It features modern as well as abstract and non-objective styles. Each sculpture setting was designed to blend harmoniously with the natural setting. In many instances, the artists themselves were involved in the placement and in the development of the site.

You can see works by giants like Rodin and Aristide Maillol, Jacques Lipchitz, Louise Nevelson, and Henry Moore. Of course, one of the biggest headliners of the Sculpture Park is the 24-foot bronze monument, *The American Horse*, created by Nina Akamu in homage to Leonardo da Vinci. At the turn of the 16th century, the legendary Italian Renaissance artist whose great works include *The Last Supper* and the *Mona Lisa* was commissioned to create the world's largest horse sculpture. A full-scale clay model was as far as da Vinci's plans got. The model was destroyed when invading French troops used it for target practice.

Da Vinci's 500-year-old dream became reality when the 15-ton statue was unveiled in Grand Rapids. Its twin resides in Milan, Italy. At three stories tall, it is the largest equine sculpture in the world. Stand at its feet and look up at one huge uplifted hoof to appreciate its immense size. Contact Frederik Meijer Gardens and Sculpture Park at (888) 957-1580 or visit meijergardens.org.

a platform above the ladder that provides a close view of the large fish as they jump completely out of the water from one ledge to the next.

The first salmon begin arriving in early September, and the run is over in October. Local people say the third week of September is when you'll see the major portion of the spawning run. Spectators won't be the only ones there, however, as the river will be filled with anglers trying to interest the fish in a lure, a spectacle in itself.

Hot Dog Hall of Fame (No Kidding!)

To travelers passing through Rockford, the **Corner Bar** appears from the outside to be just that, a small-town tavern on the corner of Main Street and Northland. Once you step inside, though, you soon realize that this pub, decorated in brass nameplates, sports memorabilia, and newspaper clippings, is packed with history and hot-dog legends. For starters, the Corner Bar is the oldest brick building in Rockford. Built in 1873, it survived several fires, including the Great Main Street Fire of 1896, and today is exceeded in age only by a wood-frame house behind the railroad depot.

At one time the building was a dry-goods store, then a hardware store, and finally, at the turn of the 20th century, its most enduring business moved in. It became a saloon noted for its hot dogs. People came from all around to enjoy hot dogs served in steamed buns and topped with special sauce, a good heaping of relish, and chopped onions. Among the patrons one night in 1967 were several members of the Detroit Lions football team who amazed their waitress when they challenged each other to eat 12 hot dogs apiece. By the following year owner Donald R. Berg had turned that 12-dog challenge into the Hot Dog Hall of Fame, Michigan's most unusual hall of fame, where 12 hot dogs at $2 apiece can immortalize your appetite with a brass nameplate on the wall. The present record of 43.5 hot dogs was set in March 2006 by Tim Janus. The bar (616-866-9866; rockfordcornerbar.com) is open from 11 a.m. to 10 p.m. Mon through Thurs, 11 a.m. to 11 p.m. Fri and Sat, and 11 a.m. to 9 p.m. Sun.

Fred Meijer, founder of the chain of Meijer's stores, is also responsible for *Frederik Meijer Gardens,* the largest tropical conservatory in the state. Meijer funded the project after members of West Michigan Horticultural Society pointed out to him that their side of the state had no large public gardens.

Opened in 1995, the 132-acre complex features plants from around the world, waterfalls, streams, and more than 60 bronze sculptures by Marshall Fredericks and other renowned artists. Along with the main conservatory are smaller garden areas including Arid Gardens, Victorian Garden, and Gardener's Corner where specialty plants are sold. Winding through the complex is the "magnificent mile," a system of barrier-free nature trails and boardwalks that overlook wetlands, ponds, and meadows.

The gardens (888-957-1580; meijergardens.org) are northeast of Grand Rapids. From I-96 take exit 38 and head north on E. Beltline Road and then east on Bradford Street to reach the gardens at 1000 E. Beltline Ave. Northeast. Hours are 9 a.m. to 5 p.m. Mon and Wed through Sat, 9 a.m. to 9 p.m. Tues, and 11 a.m. to 5 p.m. Sun. Admission is $12 for adults, $6 for children 5 to 13, and $4 for children 3 and 4.

Just 15 miles north of Grand Rapids is the small town of **Rockford,** which dates back to the 1840s when a dam and sawmill were built along the Rogue River. Soon a railroad line passed through Rockford, and the town became a trading center with warehouses, a train depot, mills, and a bean-processing plant built along the river. What connected them on land was an unnamed alley that eventually became known as Squires Street. In 1970, the bean plant was renovated into the Old Mill, a cider mill and restaurant. This led to more historical buildings being bought and turned into a strip of specialized shops and stores.

Today **Squires Street Square** is the heart of Rockford, a charming 3-block section of more than 40 shops and restaurants. You'll find stores in old warehouses, barns, a former shoe factory, a carriage house, even in railroad cars. The **Rockford Historical Museum** (616-866-2235; rockford museum.org) occupies the Power House at 11 E. Bridge St., which sits on the banks of the Rogue River and at one time was a generator plant for a local factory. The museum is open Thurs, Fri, and Sat from 1 to 4 p.m. in the summer. All the businesses are within walking distance of each other, and most are open Mon through Sat. Rockford can be reached from US 131 by taking exit 97 and following Ten Mile Road east a short way.

Places to Stay in Michigan's Heartland

BATTLE CREEK

Hampton Inn
1150 Riverside Dr.
(269) 979-5577

McCamly Plaza Hotel
50 Capital Ave. Southwest
(888) 622-2659
mccamlyplaza.com

COLDWATER

Chicago Pike Inn
215 E. Chicago St.
(800) 471-0501
chicagopikeinn.com

EAST LANSING

Kellogg Hotel
on the Michigan State campus
219 S. Harrison Rd.
(800) 875-5090
hfs.msu.edu/kellogg
kelloggcenter.com

Marriott East Lansing
300 M.A.C. Ave.
(517) 337-4440
marriott.com

SELECTED CHAMBERS OF COMMERCE AND TOURISM BUREAUS

Calhoun County Visitors Bureau
77 E. Michigan Ave., Suite 100
Battle Creek 49017
(800) 397-2240
battlecreekvisitors.org

Experience Grand Rapids
171 Monroe Ave. Northwest, Suite 700
Grand Rapids 49503
(800) 678-9859
experiencegr.com

**Greater Lansing
Convention and Visitors Bureau**
500 E. Michigan Ave., Suite 180
Lansing 48906
(888) 252-6746
lansing.org

**Jackson Convention and Visitors
Bureau**
141 S. Jackson St.
Jackson 49201
(571) 764-4440
experiencejackson.com

**Kalamazoo County
Convention and Visitors Bureau**
141 E. Michigan Ave., Suite 100
Kalamazoo 49007
(800) 888-0509
discoverkalamazoo.com

GRAND RAPIDS

Amway Grand Plaza Hotel
187 Monroe Ave. Northwest
(800) 253-3590
amwaygrand.com

Courtyard by Marriott
11 Monroe Ave. Northwest
(616) 242-6000
marriott.com

Holiday Inn Downtown
310 Pearl St. Northwest
(616) 235-7611
holidayinn.com

JONESVILLE

Munro House Bed & Breakfast
202 Maumee St.
(800) 320-3792
munrohouse.com

KALAMAZOO

Country Inn
1912 E. Kilgore Rd.
(800) 596-2375
countryinns.com

Hall House Bed & Breakfast
106 Thompson St.
(888) 761-2525
hallhouse.com

Radisson Plaza Hotel
100 W. Michigan Ave.
(888) 201-1718
radisson.com

Stuart Avenue Inn
229 Stuart Ave.
(800) 461-0621
stuartavenueinn.com

LANSING

Lexington Lansing Hotel
925 S. Creyts Rd.
(877) 322-5544
lexingtonlansing.com

Radisson Hotel
111 N. Grand Ave.
(517) 482-0188
radisson.com

Red Roof Inn
3615 Dunckel Rd.
(517) 332-2575
redroof.com

MARSHALL

Arbor Inn
15435 W. Michigan Ave.
(269) 781-7772
arborinnmarshall.com

National House Inn
102 S. Parkview Ave.
(269) 781-7374 or
(800) 424-0807
nationalhouseinn.com

STANTON

Clifford Lake Hotel
561 W. Clifford Lake Dr.
(989) 831-5151
cliffordlakeinn.net

**Places to Eat
in Michigan's
Heartland**

BATTLE CREEK

**Arcadia Brewing
Company**
103 W. Michigan Ave.
(269) 963-9690
arcadiaales.com
Brewpub

Clara's on the River
44 N. McCamly St.
(269) 963-0966
claras.com
Fine Dining

Pancake House
185 Capital Ave.
(269) 964-6790
pancakehousebc.com
Breakfast

EAST LANSING

Beggar's Banquet
218 Abbott Rd.
(517) 351-4573
beggarsbanquet.com
American

El Azteco
225 Ann St.
(517) 351-9111
elazteco.me
Mexican

Harpers
131 Albert St.
(517) 333-4040 ˙
harpersbrewpub.com
Brewpub

GRAND RAPIDS

Bistro Bella Vita
44 Grandville Ave. SW
(616) 222-4600
bistrobellavita.com
Italian

**The Cottage Bar &
Restaurant**
18 LaGrave Ave. SE
(616) 454-9088
cottagebar.biz
American

Cygnus 27
Amway Grand Plaza
187 Monroe Ave.
Northwest
(616) 774-2000
amwaygrand.com
Mediterranean

Mangiamo
1033 Lake Dr. Southeast
(616) 742-0600
thegilmorecollection.com
Italian

**Grand Rapids Brewing
Company**
1 Iona Ave. Southwest
(616) 458-7000
grbrewingcompany.com
Brewpub

JACKSON

Bella Notte Ristorante
137 W. Michigan Ave.
(517) 782-5727
bellanotteristorante.com
Italian

Crazy Cowboy
215 S. Mechanic St.
(517) 817-1910
thecrazycowboy.com
Mexican

JONESVILLE

Rosalie's Roadhouse
417 W. Chicago St.
(517) 849-2120
American

KALAMAZOO

Bell's Eccentric Cafe
355 E. Kalamazoo Ave.
(269) 382-2332
bellsbeer.com
Brewpub

Epic Bistro
359 S. Kalamazoo Mall
(269) 342-1300
millenniumrestaurants
.com/epic-bistro
American

OTHER ATTRACTIONS

Grand Rapids Art Museum
artmuseumgr.org

Grand Rapids Children's Museum
grcm.org

Honolulu House
Marshall

John Ball Zoological Gardens
Grand Rapids
johnballzoosociety.org

Kalamazoo Nature Center
Kalamazoo
naturecenter.org

Kalamazoo Valley Museum
Kalamazoo
kalamazoomuseum.org

Kellogg Bird Sanctuary
Augusta
kbsc.msu.edu

Kingman Museum of Natural History
Battle Creek
kingmanmuseum.org

Leila Arboretum
Battle Creek
lasgarden.org

Michigan Supreme Court Learning Center
Lansing
courts.michigan.gov

Michigan's Women's Historical Center & Hall of Fame
Lansing
michiganwomenshalloffame.org

Potter Park Zoo
Lansing
potterparkzoo.org

Theo & Stacy's
234 W. Michigan Ave.
(269) 388-5020
theoandstacys.com
Greek

LANSING

Clara's Lansing Station
637 E. Michigan Ave.
(517) 372-7120
claras.com
Fine Dining

Green Door Blues Bar & Grill
2005 E. Michigan Ave.
(517) 482-6376
greendoorlive.com
American

Mitchell's Fish Market
2975 Preyde Blvd.
(517) 482-3474
mitchellsfishmarket.com
Seafood

Nuthouse Sports Grill
420 E. Michigan Ave.
(517) 484-6887
nuthousesportsgrill.com
American

MARSHALL

Schuler's
115 S. Eagle St.
(616) 781-0600
schulersrestaurant.com
American

Williamston Red Cedar Grill
150 E. Grand River Ave.
(517) 655-3766
redcedargrill.com
Fine Dining

LAKE HURON

The Lake Huron shoreline, the eastern side of Michigan, is a region that has come full circle in its history and its appearance. The first inhabitants of the area were Indians who traveled lightly through the woods and lived off the land but rarely disfigured it. When Europeans arrived, they were awed by what was perceived as an endless forest, woods so thick with towering white pines that the sun rarely reached the forest floor.

All that changed in the mid-1800s. Lumbering companies that had exhausted the forests in Maine were looking for pine to cut for new settlements on the Great Plains, which were desperate for wood in their treeless region. Michigan met those needs as the greatest lumber-producing state in the nation between 1850 and 1910, with an estimated 700 logging camps and more than 2,000 mills. Massive log drives filled the Saginaw and Au Sable Rivers, which were avenues to the sawmill towns on Lake Huron. In mill towns like Saginaw and Bay City, sawmills lined the riverbanks, and huge mansions lined the streets as more wealth was made off Michigan's white pine than by miners in the Klondike Gold Rush.

LAKE HURON

Rogers City

Alpena

LAKE HURON

Fletcher Pond

Lewiston

Hubbard Lake

Au Sable R.

Mio

Tawas City

Au Gres

Standish

Wixom Lake

Sandford Lake

Midland

Bay City

Saginaw

Frankenmuth

Chesaning

Shiawassee R.

Flint

Owosso

N

0   30 mi

0   30 km

By the turn of the 20th century, all that was left were the stumps. The lumbering era had devastated the region, turning it into treeless areas that were wastelands of soil erosion. The Huron National Forest was established in 1909 along the Au Sable River, the first of many such preserves, in an effort to repair and manage the land. Lake Huron entered a new era in which terms such as reforestation, conservation, and renewable resources replaced the lumber lingo of log drives, river rats, and clear-cuts.

Almost a century later the northeastern portion of the Lower Peninsula is once again a forested region. The trees are of a different generation and often a different species, but the effect on visitors is the same as when the first Europeans wandered through. To walk quietly among the towering pines in a forest padded by needles while listening to the gentle rustling of a cold-water trout stream is as much an attraction in this part of the state as sandy beaches or a cottage on the lake.

Shiawassee County

In the early 1900s a young writer was tracking a grizzly bear he had shot in British Columbia when suddenly the wounded animal appeared and trapped the man on a narrow mountain ledge. As the author would write later, "Sudden death seemed the hunter's inevitable fate. Then the huge bruin turned away, leaving the hunter unharmed. But not unchanged—the man packed away his guns and never hunted for sport again."

Instead *James Oliver Curwood* used the experience in his best-selling novel *The Grizzly King,* which was published in 1916. In 1989, when the book served as the basis of the movie *The Bear,* **Owosso**'s favorite son—and one of its best-kept secrets—was finally exposed to the rest of the country. Curwood was born in the Shiawassee County town of Owosso in 1878 and returned with his family in 1891. After attending the University of Michigan for two years and working on a newspaper in Detroit, Curwood resigned to pursue literary work entirely in 1907.

He wrote 33 novels, most of them fast-paced tales set predominantly in northwest Canada, or "God's country," as the author called it. They were bestsellers worldwide and, between royalties and movie deals, made Curwood a millionaire and allowed him to build **Curwood Castle** along the banks of the Shiawassee River in Owosso in 1922. Built solely as a writing studio, the castle features a great room on the first floor, where the author entertained guests; a twisting staircase leads to his work area upstairs. Today the castle is a museum devoted to the author, featuring memorabilia from Curwood's life, including his original writing desk, which is used in the reception center.

The castle, a replica of a French chateau, is part of the city's historical area, which also includes the first cabin built in Owosso. The museum (989-725-0597) is at 224 Curwood Castle Dr., which is reached from M 52 south of the Shiawassee River. The castle is open from 1 to 5 p.m. daily except Mon. There is a small admission fee.

Another reason to make tracks to Owosso is to see the tracks and what steamed across them at the ***Steam Railroading Institute.*** The 7-acre museum is packed with railroad memorabilia and exhibits, but its star attraction is Père Marquette No. 1225, the steam locomotive that was built in 1941 and used to develop the train images for the movie *Polar Express*. Various excursions are offered throughout the year on this famous train with the most popular one staged during the holidays. On weekends from Thanksgiving to late Dec, the Père Marquette No. 1225 makes a special 4-hour North Pole Express trip, stopping at Santa's home, which has been conveniently set up at the Saginaw County Fairgrounds.

Also on-site is a gift shop with engineer caps, shirts, movie posters, and, of course, copies of the book *Polar Express*. The museum (989-725-9464; michigansteamtrain.com) is at 405 S. Washington St. and open from 10 a.m. to 4 p.m. Fri through Sun. Admission is $6 per person and the North Pole Express trip is $70 for adults and $40 for children.

More railroading lore is just a short drive south of Owosso at *Durand*. At the turn of the 20th century, Durand was what Detroit's Metro Airport or Chicago's O'Hare is today—the transportation hub of the Midwest. The

TOP ANNUAL EVENTS

FEBRUARY

Perchville USA
Tawas City
(800) 558-2927

JUNE

Bavarian Festival
Frankenmuth
(800) 386-3378
frankenmuthfestivals.com

Curwood Festival
Owosso
(989) 723-2161

River Roar
Bay City
(866) 287-7627

JULY

Auburn Corn Fest
Auburn
(866) 457-2582
auburnjaycees.org

Brown Trout Festival
Alpena
(800) 425-7362
alpenami-browntrout.com

Chesaning Showboat Festival
Chesaning
(800) 989-3056
chesaningshowboat.org

AUGUST

Nautical City Festival
Rogers City
(989) 734-2535
nauticalfestival.org

OCTOBER

Great Lakes Lighthouse Festival
Alpena
(586) 566-1603
lighthousefestival.org

first railroad, the Detroit-Milwaukee Line, arrived at the small town in 1865 because of Durand's central location, and by 1907 there were seven lines, promoting the construction of *Union Station*, a massive depot 239 feet long and costing $60,000 to build. It burned down two years later but was quickly rebuilt by Grand Trunk Railroad as the age of railroading and the town of Durand entered their golden eras. Almost half of the town's population of 2,500 worked for Grand Trunk, and more people changed trains in Durand than there were residents living there!

Union Station (989-288-3561; durandstation.org), often called the "most photographed depot in the country," was designated the Michigan Railroad History Museum and Information Center. Visitors can wander through the station and view a gallery of railroading artifacts, including handcars, engine lights, rolltop desks, and other furnishings of a 1900-era depot.

Durand can be reached from I-69 by heading south at exit 116. Union Station is on the south side of Main Street and its museum is open Tues and Wed 1 to 5 p.m., Thurs 9 a.m. to 5 p.m., Fri and Sat 10 a.m. to 5 p.m., Sun 1 to 5 p.m.

Genesee County

The heart of Genesee County is *Flint*, Michigan's fourth-largest city and the home of the Buick Division of General Motors.

The automobile industry and cars are a major part of Flint's livelihood, and both have been well preserved in the city's *Sloan Museum*. The most dramatic chapter in Flint's history is the Great Sit-Down Strike of 1937, which is retold in the museum's permanent 10,000-square-foot exhibit entitled Flint and the American Dream. The 44-day ordeal ended when General Motors agreed to sign its first contract with the United Auto Workers. It was a bitter struggle that led to the unionization of all American autoworkers and changed the course of history in Michigan, if not the entire country.

Sloan Museum, however, is probably best known for its classic car collection. More than 60 cars are on display in 2 buildings and range from the oldest production-model Chevrolet in existence and a 1910 Buick "Bug" raced by Louis Chevrolet to prototype vehicles that never made it into production.

The museum (810-237-3450; sloanmuseum.com) is in the Flint Cultural Central and is reached from I-475 by taking exit 8A. Head east on Longway Boulevard and follow the signs to the Cultural Central at 1221 E. Kearsley St. Hours are 10 a.m. to 5 p.m. Mon through Sat, Thurs 10 a.m. to 8 pm., and Sun noon to 5 p.m. Admission is $9 for adults and $6 for children.

Flint also has many interesting nonautomotive attractions, including its delightful *Flint Children's Museum*. Described by its staff as a "touchable discovery center," the museum was proposed in 1980, and after six years of collecting donated materials, the center opened in 1986. Unlike other hands-on museums in Ann Arbor and Lansing, the exhibits here are not complex demonstrations in science or physics. They're simply everyday items that children can touch, ride, climb, and make believe with.

Among the museum's 40 hands-on exhibits is Mr. Bones, who will take your kids on a bicycle ride to show them how their skeletons work. At Our Town, children shop for groceries or visit Fractions Pizza Parlor, while at Recycled Rhythms they can bang, toot, and hum on a variety of unconventional musical instruments. Most of the displays are recommended for children ages 3 to 10 years old, but the Tot Spot is a cleverly designed area with activities for even younger visitors.

> ## trivia
>
> The largest planetarium in Michigan is the *Longway Planetarium* (810-237-3400; sloanmuseum .com) in Flint, which features a 60-foot domed screen.

The museum (810-767-5437; flintchildrensmuseum.org) is located at 1602 W. University Ave. Take I-75 to I-475 and then exit 8A to head west on Robert T. Longway Road, which turns into Fifth Avenue. Turn south on Grand Traverse Street and then west on University Avenue. The center is open year-round from 9 a.m. to 5 p.m. Tues through Fri, 10 a.m. to 5 p.m. on Sat, and noon to 5 p.m. on Sun. Admission is $6 per person.

There are only two natural waterfalls in the Lower Peninsula, so many cities have created their own, including Flint. *Stepping Stone Falls* is an artificially created cascade of water over an intricate patchwork of steps and levels and one of the most picturesque spots in Genesee County. A scenic, winding path leads visitors to an overlook of the falls, and in the evening underwater lighting creates multicolored patterns on the rushing waters.

Stepping Stone Falls (800-648-7275) is located at the foot of Mott Lake at 5161 Branch Rd., across from the historic attraction of Crossroads Village. Hours are 8 a.m. to 11 p.m. Sun through Thurs and 8 a.m. to midnight Fri and Sat from May 1 through Sept 1. From Sept 2 through Dec 31, the falls are open 8 a.m. to 9:30 p.m. daily. Admission is free.

Departing from Stepping Stone Falls is the **Genesee Belle Paddle-wheel Riverboat,** a replica of the riverboats that once traveled down the Mississippi River. From May 25 to Sept 2, the *Genesee Belle* (810-736-7100; geneseecountyparks.org) takes passengers on a scenic 45-minute cruise through Mott Lake on Fri and Sun evening, departing at 7 p.m. Tickets are $2.50 for adults and $1.50 for children. A great—and affordable—way to beat the heat in the middle of summer.

Saginaw County

The only Michigan county without a natural lake, Saginaw County still has plenty of water, as the Saginaw, Tittabawassee, Bad, Cass, Shiawassee, and Flint Rivers make it the largest river basin in the state, with 160 miles of waterway. It was these natural avenues and the vast forests bordering them that allowed the area to boom with loggers and sawmills in the mid-1800s. By the early 1900s the trees and loggers were gone, but reminders of the immense wealth they produced are seen throughout the county in magnificent mansions, especially along Washington Boulevard in Saginaw. Among them at 1581 S. Washington Blvd. is **Montague Inn** (989-752-3939; montagueinn.com), an elegant Georgian mansion turned urban bed-and-breakfast with park-like grounds and cozy fireplaces. The rooms and suites at the inn range from $59 to $160 but even if you're not looking for lodging, its fine restaurant is worth departing I-75.

But to learn about the lumbering era, head to Saginaw's eclectic **Castle Museum** at 500 Federal Ave. Built in 1898, at the height of Saginaw's golden era as a lumbering center, the 60,000-square-foot castle wasn't the home of a rich lumber baron but a post office designed in the style of a French chateau. Today the Historical Society of Saginaw County occupies the castle and its collection includes a lumbering exhibit that retraces the half-century when Saginaw produced more lumber than anywhere in the country.

Castle Museum (989-752-2861; castlemuseum.org) is open Tues through Sat from 10 a.m. to 4:30 p.m. and Sun from 1 to 4:30 p.m. Admission is $1 for adults and 50 cents for children.

Also in Saginaw, near the Anderson Water Slide, an American creation, is the city's *Japanese Cultural Center and Tea House.* The house was actually built by Japanese artisans, who used no nails, only intricate traditional hand tools. Today the center is the only facility in the country where visitors can observe the classic formal tea ceremony.

The house is open from noon to 4 p.m. Tues through Sat. The symbolic tea ritual is performed and interpreted on the second Sat of each month, except for Dec, beginning at 2 p.m. There is a $3 fee. The house (989-759-1648; japaneseculturalcenter.org) and its tranquil gardens are located in Saginaw's Celebration Square, just north of M 46 at S. Washington Boulevard and Ezra Rust Drive.

Generally recognized as Michigan's number-one attraction is the German town of *Frankenmuth.* "Little Bavaria" is famous for home-style chicken dinners served at one of two huge restaurants, *Zehnder's* and the *Bavarian Inn,* which face each other on Main Street. The restaurants were founded by the Zehnder brothers, whose family arrived in Frankenmuth from Bavaria in 1846. Each restaurant is a sprawling complex of a dozen German-themed dining rooms, gift shops, bakeries, and candy shops. More than 700 tons of chicken are served annually in the restaurants along with

Chesaning Showboat

In 1937, after local businessman Harley Peet provided a $400 loan, the city of Chesaning launched its first "Showboat." At the time it was little more than a local talent show performed on the Shiawassee River with residents sitting in borrowed bleachers. Today the 6-day event, called the *Chesaning Showboat Festival,* is one of the top entertainment venues in the state. Each evening show still arrives on the showboat to a packed house but is now headlined by a nationally known entertainer. Artists appearing there have ranged from Adam Lambert to Sugarland and Grand Funk Railroad to Larry McCray. It's normally standing room only for the shows, which attract more than 40,000 visitors before the showboat takes its final trip back up the river. For dates and ticket information, contact the Chesaning Showboat Office (989-845-3056; chesaningshowboat.org).

The Polka Hotel

Frankenmuth is of German descent so you'll find both home-brewed ales and homegrown polka. The town's most favorite son and most famous accordionist is *Marv Herzog,* who was renowned for his Bavarian-American polka music. The bandleader performed for years throughout the country and even the world but always managed to return to his hometown for polka festivals, playing such favorites as "In Heaven There is No Beer" and "Red Raven Polka."

After Herzog died in 2002, his friend Bob Drury, owner of the Drury Hotel chain, built the hotel in Frankenmuth in honor of the late polka king. The 38-room *Marv Herzog Hotel* opened in 2007 on the banks of the Cass River within walking distance of a Zehnder's chicken dinner. Inside you'll find Herzog's accordion on display in the lobby along with his lederhosen and many awards while each guest room celebrates a year of his life with a collage of memorabilia.

Marv Herzog Hotel (877-400-4210; marvherzoghotel.com) is at 501 Main St. and rooms range from $125 to $149 per night.

buttery noodles, savory dressing, giblet gravy, salads, and homemade breads in an all-you-can-eat affair.

Chicken dinners are $19.95 per person at the restaurants, which stop seating at 9:30 p.m. daily. The Bavarian Inn (989-652-9985; bavarianinn.com) is at 713 S. Main St., and Zehnder's (800-863-7999; zehnders.com) is at 730 S. Main St.

What could be better with a chicken dinner than a mug of dark German beer? Frankenmuth is the home of the state's oldest brewery, *Frankenmuth Brewery,* which is located near the corner of Tuscola and Main Streets. It began making beer in 1862 as the Cass River Brewery and then became Geyer Brewing in 1874. The company was temporarily shut down in 1976 and again in 2007 but has such a loyal following in this German town that it has managed to reopen each time. A state historic site, Frankenmuth Brewery (989-262-8300; frankenmuthbrewery.com) now doubles as a brewery and a fine restaurant and offers informal tours of its beer-making facility year-round. After seeing how the beer is made, how can you not grab a table and order a pint . . . or even a pitcher?

You can enjoy a stein of the local brew in almost every restaurant and bar in town, but the most intriguing place is *Tiffany's* just north of

Zehnder's Restaurant on S. Main Street. The lumbermen's saloon is located on the first floor of the Hotel Goetz, which was built in 1895, when Frankenmuth was one of the leading logging communities in the Saginaw Valley. The tavern picks up its name from its 18 Tiffany chandeliers, made in the 1930s. It is also adorned by a beautiful wooden bar, the original tin ceiling, inlaid tile floor, and leaded stained glass. Tiffany's (989-652-6881; tiffanys-foodandspirits.com) is open from 11 a.m. to midnight on Fri and Sat, when there is live entertainment, and from 11 a.m. to 11 p.m. the rest of the week.

Christmas in July? Only in Frankenmuth, where *Bronner's Christmas Wonderland* is home of the world's largest year-round display of holiday ornaments, decorations, trimmings, and gifts. More than 50,000 items are stocked in the 230,000-square-foot building that houses the store's showroom, warehouse, and offices. The business can be traced back to 1945, when Wally Bronner operated Bronner's Displays and Signs out of his parents' home and was approached by Bay City officials to decorate the city streets for the upcoming holiday.

Bronner created and built lamppost panels for the city, leading to more requests by other towns and eventually to his present business providing Christmas decorations to businesses, communities, and private homes. The store is an amazing trip into the spirit of the holiday, especially its religious aspect. Inside you will find more than 500 kinds of nativity scenes, figures from 1 inch tall to life-size; 260 Christmas trees decorated in such themes as sports and wildlife; and more than 6,000 ornaments from around the world. There are music boxes, every model of Hummel figurine ever produced,

Shopping at Birch Run

In the early 1980s, Birch Run was a sleepy little village at the Frankenmuth exit of I-75. Today it's the discount shopping capital of Michigan, thanks to *Prime Outlets at Birch Run* (989-624-6226, premiumoutlets.com). The 170 stores form the largest manufacturers' mall in the state and include everything from Ann Taylor to Lane Bryant and Eddie Bauer to J. Crew. The mall is right off I-75, exit 136, and most shops are open from 10 a.m. to 9 p.m. Mon through Sat and 10 a.m. to 7 p.m. Sun. This place can be unbearably crowded on the weekends with travelers dropping in for a little shopping on their way up north. The best time to shop is the middle of the week from 3 to 6 p.m.

Shiawassee National Wildlife Refuge

When the fall migration peaks in late October or early November, more than 25,000 Canada geese and 30,000 ducks are often at the **Shiawassee National Wildlife Refuge.** The sight of so many birds gathered at one time is nothing short of spectacular, making this one of the great wildlife sightings in Michigan.

One of two federal wildlife refuges in Michigan, Shiawassee encompasses 9,042 acres on the doorstep of Saginaw and includes the confluence of four major rivers, the Flint, Cass, Shiawassee, and Tittabawassee. When combined with the Shiawassee River State Game Area, which borders it to the west, this goose management area exceeds 20,000 acres and is larger than any state park in the Lower Peninsula.

The Ferguson Bayou Trail, a 5-mile loop from the Curtis Road parking area, is the best trail to see birds any time of the year but especially during the fall migration. The trail is a network of gravel roads, two-tracks, and paths along the dikes that leads to an observation tower in the heart of the refuge. Most visitors walk to the tower, but the easiest way to explore the park is on a hybrid or mountain bike.

From the tower in the fall, small flocks of geese can be seen arriving by late afternoon. By evening it's practically pandemonium with hundreds of birds coming and going. Stick around for the sunset and your day will end with the most memorable sight at the refuge: flights of geese silhouetted against a red-orange sky.

The Shiawassee National Wildlife Refuge is 7 miles south of M 46 in Saginaw and reached from M 13 by turning west on Curtis Road. Within a mile is the refuge headquarters (989-777-5930) where trail maps and bird checklists are available. The Ferguson Bayou Trail is 3 miles beyond the headquarters near the end of Curtis Road.

and, in the store's Nutcracker Suite, 200 styles of wooden characters imported from Austria, Switzerland, and Germany.

You can't miss the store—outside it is surrounded by 15 acres of painted snowflakes, twinkling lights, and the same kind of lamppost Bronner designed more than 60 years ago for Bay City. Bronner's Christmas Wonderland (989-652-9931; bronners.com) is at the south end of town just off Main Street (M 83). It is open from June through Dec from 9 a.m. to 9 p.m. Mon through Sat and noon to 7 p.m. Sun. From Jan through May, hours are 9 a.m. to 5:30 p.m. Mon through Thurs and Sat, 9 a.m. to 9 p.m. Fri, and noon to 5:30 p.m. Sun.

Midland County

To most people the city of *Midland* is Dow Chemical Corporation, the place where Herbert Dow founded the company in 1897 that today gives us everything from Ziploc sandwich bags and Saran Wrap to much of the aspirin used in the country. The *H. H. Dow Museum* tells the story of the young chemist and features replicas of the gristmill and brine well that he built to launch his famous company as well as the 1890 lab where he perfected his bromine-extracting process.

The *Herbert H. Dow Historical Museum* (989-631-5930) is reached from downtown Midland by heading west on Main Street for 1.2 miles and then turning north on Cook Road to 3200 Cook Rd. Hours are 11 a.m. to 4 p.m. Thurs through Sat. Admission is $5 for adults and $3 for children.

Another interesting museum is the *Alden B. Dow Museum of Science and Art* in the Midland Center for the Arts. The science, history, and art museum reopened in 1994 after a $3-million face-lift and is 4 floors of hands-on displays and exhibits. Staff members estimate that 340 topics are covered in the new exhibits and that a person who pushed every button, viewed every screen, and took part in every interactive display would spend more than 20 hours in the hall.

A 500-pound life-size mastodon skeleton greets visitors, and from there the topics range from how an Olympic skater does a triple axel to viewing a replica of Midland's famed Frolic Theater (complete with the aroma of popcorn). The hall (989-631-5930; mcfta.org) is at Eastman Avenue and West Street and is open 10 a.m. to 4 p.m. Tues, Wed, Fri, and Sat and 10 a.m. to 8 p.m. Thurs. Admission is $8 for adults and $5 for children 12 and under.

Midland is also a city of parks, with 2,700 acres in 74 parks scattered throughout the community. The most famous of these is *Dow Gardens,* 110 acres of streams, waterfalls, small bridges, and beautifully manicured landscaping next to Discovery Square, home of the *Midland Center for the Arts.*

What began as Herbert Dow's backyard in 1899 was eventually extended and shaped in the 1970s by his son, Alden Dow, a noted architect and a student of Frank Lloyd Wright. It was the younger Dow who installed the "jungle walk" through a thicket, the sensory trail, and various waterfalls.

The gardens (989-631-2677; dowgardens.org) are just northwest of downtown Midland off Business US 10 (Eastman Road), next to the Midland Center for the Arts. Hours are 9 a.m. to 8:30 p.m. daily from mid-Apr to Labor Day with shorter hours the rest of the year. Admission is $5 for adults and $1 for children.

Another intriguing park is *Chippewassee,* site of the *Tridge,* the only three-way footbridge in the world, city officials proudly claim. The unusual bridge was built in 1981 over the confluence of the Tittabawassee and Chippewa Rivers, and its wooden spans connect three shorelines. In the middle they form a hub where benches overlook the merging currents of two rivers. The Tridge and the nearby riverfront area form the center of activity in downtown Midland. Tunes by the Tridge free concerts are presented June and July from 7 to 9 p.m. with a culminating Battle of the Bands the first Thursday in August.

During the third week of July, the annual Riverdays festival is held in downtown Midland for 4 days. Festivities include a milk jug raft race, pancake breakfast, children's activities, and concerts in the nearby park. Visitors can enjoy riding on an old-time ferry, called the *Princess Laura,* down the

Père Marquette Rail-Trail

Departing from the Tridge is the *Père Marquette Rail-Trail,* a perfectly paved path without so much as a ripple, much less a hill. Originally a line for the Flint and Père Marquette Railroad, the rail-trail extends from Midland to Clare, 32 miles.

It's open to a variety of nonmotorized users, including runners, walkers, and cyclists. But in the first 3 miles, from the Tridge to Dublin Road, the most popular form of transportation is in-line skates. The Père Marquette is well designed for that. At the street crossings are locator maps, benches, and, most important, large red posts to stop skaters from flying across the intersections.

This stretch is also very scenic. From the Tridge you skirt the Tittabawassee River for more than a mile, passing fishing docks, the historic Upper Bridge, and one of the original cement mile markers that told railroad engineers how far it was to Saginaw. The trail also passes the H. H. Dow Museum, which has installed interpretive displays along the way.

For more information call the Midland County Parks and Recreation Commission at (989) 832-6874.

river. Nearby, individuals can rent canoes and paddle the rivers themselves if they wish. Also located near the Tridge is the Midland Farmers' Market and its free 4-H Club petting zoo for children (open Sun in July from 1 to 4 p.m.).

Bay County

The shoreline of Saginaw Bay was the final destination for much of the lumber from the valley, with 32 sawmills clustered on the waterfront of Bay City. The city flourished on timber and shipbuilding, and a drive down Center Avenue shows where much of it went. The lumber barons seemed infatuated with building the most elaborate homes they could afford, and the restored mansions in this historic district overwhelm visitors. In the middle of this Victorian-era street at 321 Washington Ave. is the *Historical Museum of Bay County* (989-893-5733; bchsmuseum.org), which spins the story of Bay City's golden era through 3-dimensional exhibits. The newest exhibit is "Bay City: Seaport to the World" in the Kantzler Maritime Gallery, where kids can climb behind the wheel to steer the tug *Witch*. The museum is open from 10 a.m. to 5 p.m. Mon through Fri and noon to 4 p.m. Sat. There is no admission charge, but donations are welcomed.

More impressive than the grand homes, however, is the *Bay City City Hall*. Built in 1894, the Romanesque-style stone building dominates the city skyline with its 125-foot clock tower at the southeast corner. It was listed in the National Register of Historic Places, and in 1976 the building underwent major renovation that preserved the original woodwork and distinctive metal pillars in the huge lobby. Visitors are welcome to stroll throughout the massive structure and view the 31-foot Chmielewska Tapestry that hangs in the council chambers. Woven with hand-dyed yarns of 500 colors by a young artist from Poland, the tapestry depicts the historic buildings of the community. A climb of 68 steps up the clock tower brings you to a most impressive view of Bay City, the Saginaw River, and the surrounding countryside.

The city hall (989-895-9423) is located downtown at 301 Washington Ave. and is open from 8 a.m. to 5 p.m. Mon through Fri. Inquire at the personnel office in room 308 for a trip up to the clock tower. There is no admission fee.

City hall was closed October 2010 after a fire sparked by roof work caused massive water damage. City hall is scheduled to reopen in 2013 after considerable construction delay. For now, workers remain in an office at 700 W. Fourth St. while the commissioners hold city meetings at the Père Marquette Depot across the street at 1000 Adams St.

Another attraction in Bay City is the *Delta College Planetarium and Learning Center.* Opened in 1997 with funding from NASA, the center is a striking red-domed building that looks like a spaceship in the middle of Bay City. The planetarium uses state-of-the-art equipment to take visitors on simulated outer-space journeys, while the exhibit hall features displays on astronomy and space travel. Outside there is a sundial.

trivia

Bay and Saginaw Counties are the heart of Michigan's sugar beet industry and the home of Pioneer Sugar. The state's first sugar beet factory opened in Bay City in 1889 after Dr. Robert Kedzie of Michigan Agricultural College (now Michigan State University) encouraged local farmers to grow the crop the year before. Within a few short years, Saginaw Valley became the sugar bowl of Michigan.

The center is at 100 Center Ave. and Water Street and stages 2 to 3 shows daily. Contact the planetarium (989-667-2260; delta.edu/planet) for the times. Admission for most shows is $6 for adults and $4 for children.

The best way to escape from Bay City is aboard an *Appledore Schooner.* Departing from a dock in downtown Bay City, the pair of tall sailing ships begin in the Saginaw River but soon are unfurling their massive sails in Saginaw Bay for a variety of cruises. The 3-hour "Legends of the Saginaw Sails" day cruises include lunch onboard and a local historian immersing passengers in stories of Bay City's golden era of lumber and shipping. In the evening the Appledores offer dinner cruises and unusual "Stargaze Sails" that are hosted in conjunction with Delta College Planetarium.

Day cruises are at 11 a.m. on most Saturdays and Sundays in the summer and are $37 for adults and $27 for children. Dinner and Stargaze cruises are on Fri and Sat evening throughout the summer and range in price from $70 to $80 per adult. Many other cruises, including a fall color sail, are offered during the year. For a schedule of trips or to make a reservation, contact *BaySail–Appledore Tall Ships* (989-895-5193; baysail baycity.org).

Arenac County

Located out in the middle of Saginaw Bay, 10 miles from Au Gres, is **Big Charity Island,** a 300-acre sanctuary of forests, beaches, rare plants such as Pitcher's thistle, bald eagles, and a lighthouse that was built in 1857. Until recently the island, with its miles of sandy shoreline and nature trails, was inaccessible to everybody but boaters experienced in navigating the choppy and often stormy Saginaw Bay.

Now even landlubbers can visit the island through **Charity Island Transport, Inc.** (989-254-7719; charityisland.net). The Au Gres company offers an unusual dinner cruise to Big Charity Island that borders on being romantic. You board the *Northstar*, a 50-foot ferry, at the Northport Marina for the hour-long cruise to the island. Once on land you enjoy a hearty meal of Great Lakes perch and sirloin tip steak on the veranda of the restored lightkeeper's house served by the lightkeeper and his wife. The evening finishes off with a return cruise to Au Gres timed to coincide with the sunset. In 2012, Charity Island Excursions became licensed to sell adult beverages on its boats and at the lighthouse. Try some fine Michigan wines while you enjoy the scenery.

The dinner cruise is a 5-hour outing that takes place Fri, Sat, and Sun from the end of May to mid-Oct. The cost is $84 per person.

Iosco County

Perhaps the most famous river of the logging era was the **Au Sable,** which begins west of Grayling and ends at Lake Huron between the towns of Oscoda and Au Sable. In the 1890s it was assumed that forests were meant to be cut, and "driving the Au Sable" was a group of men known as "river rats" and "bank beavers," who floated logs down the Au Sable to sawmills on Lake Huron. A century later it's "downstaters," "flatlanders," and "fudgies" driving the river. Now, however, they're following the **Lumbermen's Monument Auto Tour,** an especially popular fall trip in Iosco County when tourists come to admire the color of the leaves rather than the size of the trunks.

Many motorists begin the 68-mile loop at the **Tawas Area Chamber of Commerce** (800-558-2927; tawas.com) where they pick up a free copy of the Lumbermen's Monument Auto Tour brochure. From Tawas City you head west on M 55 for a mile, then turn north (right) onto Wilber Road to reach Monument Road, which ends at River Road. A half-mile to the east (right) is the entrance to the *Lumbermen's Monument.*

The impressive bronze statue of three loggers was erected in 1931 and is now surrounded by trees very much like those they made a living cutting down. Even more impressive to many is the nearby interpretive area and museum, which give a good account of the logging era with displays and hands-on exhibits. They put the logger into perspective, a man viewed by many today as a colorful, Paul Bunyan–like character who ate apple pie and fry cakes for breakfast. In reality he provided cheap labor. In the middle of the winter, he made $2 for a 12-hour day spent pulling a saw while cold water sloshed in his boots. Little wonder that by the time most loggers turned 35 years old, they were too worn out or too sick to continue their trade. The museum and interpretive area, which include overlooks, outdoor displays, and a cook's raft on the Au Sable River known as a Wanigan, are open from 10 a.m. to 5 p.m. daily from May to mid-Oct.

The auto tour continues west along River Road and in 1.5 miles comes to *Canoer's Memorial Monument.* The stone monument, topped off by a pair of paddles, was originally built as a memorial to Jerry Curley, a 17-year-old who died in 1953 practicing for the annual Au Sable River Canoe Marathon. Today it stands in honor of all racers who attempt the annual 150-mile

Cruising in Iosco County

The best way to enjoy the fall colors in Iosco County is aboard the **River Queen,** a full-size paddlewheel riverboat that began operating on the Au Sable River in 1966. The *River Queen* departs from a dock on the Au Sable River 6 miles west of Oscoda and offers its 2-hour tours daily at noon and 3 p.m. from late June through late Aug and then at 1 p.m. through late Sept.

The tours most in demand are the weekend color tours from late Sept through mid-Oct at 10:30 a.m., 1 p.m., and 4 p.m. These are relaxing cruises along the Au Sable in which passengers enjoy the spectacular fall colors, beautiful scenery, and possibly even a few wildlife sightings such as bald eagles. Most trips are $14 per adult and $7 per child. Reservations are a must in the fall and can be made by contacting the *River Queen* office (989-739-7351; ausableriverqueen.net).

event from Grayling to Oscoda, often cited as the toughest canoe race in the country (ausablecanoemarathon .org). From the monument site there is another fine overview of the Au Sable River Valley, and for those who keep one eye on the sky, bald eagles can often be seen in this area.

Still heading west on River Road, you reach *Iargo Springs* in another mile. Iargo is the Chippewa Indian word for "many waters," and this was a favorite spot for members of the tribe traveling along the Saginaw-Mackinac Trail. It's almost 300 steps and 8 rest stops down to the springs but well worth the exertion of the climb back up. The area below is pleasant and tranquil as the springs gurgle out of the moss-laden bluffs into the Au Sable River under a canopy of towering pine trees.

trivia

One of the few remaining one-room log schools left in Michigan is the *Old Bailey School* along County Road F30 (Mikado-Glennie Road) near the hamlet of Mikado. Built in 1894, the school remained in use until 1941 and today is used by area residents for a strawberry shortcake social on the Fourth of July.

Alcona County

At Harrisville, US 23 swings away from Lake Huron and remains inland well into Alpena County. Taking its place along the water in northern Alcona County is Lakeshore Drive, the route to two interesting attractions. The first is *Cedar Brook Trout Farm,* reached 2.5 miles north of Harrisville immediately after turning off US 23. Because of the almost perfect conditions for raising rainbow and brook trout, Cedar Brook was established in the early 1950s as the first licensed trout farm in Michigan. The key to the farm's success is the cold-water springs that flow from the nearby sandy bluffs. The water is funneled into the 13 ponds and rearing tanks, and its year-round constant temperature (47 degrees) and high level of oxygen are ideal for trout. The constant flow allows owner Jerry Kahn to manage without pumps. He begins with eggs and raises the trout from frylings to rainbows that will measure well over 16 inches.

The bulk of Kahn's business is shipping thousands of trout in a tank truck to individuals and sportsmen's organizations for stocking their own lakes and rivers. He also lets travelers stop by and catch their own in two ponds, one stocked with rainbows, the other with brook trout. The water in the ponds is cold and clear, and below the surface you can easily see hundreds of fish swimming around. Throw some feed in the ponds (available from a coin-operated dispenser), and dozens of large fish rise to the surface in a feeding frenzy. Anglers are provided with cane poles, tackle, bait, and a warning that catching the trout is not as easy as it looks. No fishing license is needed.

trivia

Alcona County is the site of the only gold mine to operate in the Lower Peninsula. Prospectors went to the vicinity of Harrisville looking for silver or copper after hearing reports of Indians finding large quantities of the minerals in the area. What the miners found in 1912 wasn't copper or silver but gold nuggets. To avoid a gold rush, they kept the discovery secret for several months until a stock company was formed and a mine shaft sunk. Tons of Alcona black dirt was processed for gold, but the venture ended in disaster when the steam-operated equipment blew up.

Cedar Brook (989-724-5241), one of the few farms in the state that raises brook trout, is open for anglers daily from noon until 6 p.m. from Memorial Day to Labor Day. After Labor Day, it is open weekends noon to 6 p.m. through Oct 15. The cost depends on the size of trout caught, but for $4 or $5 and a little fishing luck, you can depart with a hefty rainbow.

From the trout farm Lakeshore Drive continues north and in less than a half mile passes the marked side road to **Sturgeon Point Lifesaving Station** (989-727-4703; alconahistoricalsociety.com) and the preserved lighthouse, built in 1869. The last lightkeeper left in 1941, but the US Coast Guard continues to maintain the light. In 1982 the Alcona County Historical Society began renovating the attached lightkeeper's house and soon opened it to the public. The structure is a classic Michigan lighthouse, but the unique feature is that you can climb to the top of the tower (85 steps) and not only be greeted by a panorama of Lake Huron but still view a working prism as well. Amazingly, all that is needed to throw a light miles out on the Great Lake is this huge work of cut glass and an electric light no larger than your smallest finger.

Negwegon State Park

The only development **Negwegon State Park** has ever experienced since the state picked up the tract in 1962 is the construction of a parking area and a 10-mile trail system. What has never been improved is Sand Hill Road. This sandy, deeply rutted county road provides the only access to Negwegon and, in effect, has made it the most remote state park in the Lower Peninsula. Four-wheel-drive vehicles are recommended, and during extended dry spells, spinning tires in shifting mounds of sugary sand is not an uncommon occurrence.

After an agonizing 2.5-mile drive along the Alcona County road, most first-time visitors are stunned to arrive at a huge park sign and a wide, graveled entrance drive in the middle of nowhere. From the parking area at the end, they head into the woods and suddenly emerge at a crescent-moon bay framed by towering red pines on one side and the turquoise waters of Lake Huron on the other. In between is a sweeping shoreline of golden sand unmarred by beach blankets and beer coolers.

In short, paradise.

This is as far as most people get in the 1,775-acre park. If you can tear yourself away from the beach, Negwegon's trail system offers some interesting hikes. Departing south from the parking lot is the Potawatomi Trail, a 3.3-mile loop that hugs Lake Huron for more than a mile. To the north is the Algonquin Trail, which in 2 miles reaches the spectacular views at the tip of South Point.

To reach the park from US 23, head east on Black River Road and north on Sand Hill Road. Follow the two-track for 2.5 miles to the park entrance. It is best to stop first at **Harrisville State Park** (989-724-5126) on US 23 for a map and current road conditions before trying to reach Negwegon.

The lightkeeper's house is now a museum, with the 5 rooms downstairs furnished as a turn-of-the-20th-century residence for those who maintained the attached tower. The 4 rooms upstairs are also open, and each showcases a different aspect of the county's history: shipwrecks, fishermen, the original lightkeepers, and, perhaps the most interesting, the ice-collecting industry that boomed in the area during the winter so iceboxes could be kept cold in the summer.

The lighthouse museum is open from Memorial Day through Sept from 11:30 a.m. to 3:30 p.m. Mon through Thurs and from 11 a.m. to 4 p.m. Sat and Sun. The best time to drop in is Fri, Sat, and Sun from noon to 3 p.m.

when the lighthouse tower is open to visitors. There is no admission fee, but donations are accepted to maintain the lighthouse.

Alpena County

Lumbering turned **Alpena** from a handful of hardy settlers in 1850 into a booming town of 9,000 in 1884, and when the white pine ran out, the community sustained itself by becoming Cement City, utilizing its huge supply of limestone. From the cement factories emerged Besser Manufacturing Company, the world leader in concrete block-making equipment. Today Alpena is a manufacturing center that can boast the largest population (10,483) and the only enclosed shopping mall in northeast Michigan. The residents of this modern community also value their past and have begun restoring the historic downtown area as **Old Town Alpena.**

The original shopping area is clustered around N. Second Street and features small and specialized shops that could have been found here as early as the 1920s. An Old Town favorite is the **John A. Lau Saloon.** The restaurant dates to the 1880s when it was a rough-and-tumble waterhole for lumberjacks with a reputation that reached far into the woods. Part of the reason is that Lau always had three bartenders on staff, one who could speak German, one French, and the other Polish, so any logger, no matter where he came from, could order a beer-and-whiskey.

The restaurant still maintains that lumberman's decor with its thick plank floors, tin ceiling, crosscut saws on the walls, and historic photos of the original saloon. Dinners range from $12 to $25. The John A. Lau Saloon (989-354-6898; johnalausaloon.com) is at 414 N. Second Ave. Stories have long circulated that a ghost from the past haunts the John A. Lau Saloon. Fleeting images of a woman dressed in period clothing, strange knocking noises, odd unexplainable odors, and glasses that appear to move on their own accord all are the stuff of ghost tales surrounding the restaurant. Some say that the ghost is Agnes Lau, wife of the original saloon owner. Stop by and find out for yourself.

Alpena's **Jesse Besser Museum** is the only accredited museum in northern Michigan and boasts one of the finest collections of Great Lakes Indian artifacts in the country.

The museum also features a sky theater planetarium and outside a small historic village that is home to the *Katherine V*, a historic fish tug. Hours are

10 a.m. to 5 p.m. Tues through Sat. The museum (989-356-2202; bessermu-seum.org) is a block east of US 23 at 491 Johnson St. Admission is $5 for adults and $3 for children. Admission is free every Wed from 3 to 5 p.m.

Alpena's newest museum is devoted to its largest park, only this one is underwater. Off shore from the city, the ***Thunder Bay National Marine Sanctuary*** (989-356-8805; thunderbay.noaa.gov) extends over 448 square miles under Lake Huron and includes nearly 200 historic shipwrecks. The wrecks lie in water that ranges in depth from a few inches to 200 feet, making the sanctuary a popular destination for divers, snorkelers, and even kayakers who can look down and see pieces of wrecks in the clear, fresh water of Lake Huron.

Don't dive? Then the best—and driest—way to explore the shipwrecks is to visit the ***Great Lakes Maritime Heritage Center,*** the sanctuary's riverfront headquarters. The center's exhibits are a combination of a traditional maritime museum and a hands-on discovery center design for children. Inside the large hall is a life-size recreation of a historic Great Lakes schooner, historic displays and artifacts on shipwrecks, and interactive learning stations where kids can climb aboard a boat or follow "Discovery Tubes" to explore a wreck as if they're diving. And if you do want to see a real shipwreck, the staff will tell you where to get your toes wet.

The Great Lakes Maritime Heritage Center (989-356-8805; thunderbay .noaa.gov) is at 500 W. Fletcher St. and is open May through Labor Day 10 a.m. to 5 p.m. Mon through Sat and noon to 5 p.m. on Sun. The center is not open on Sun in the winter. There is no admission fee.

Presque Isle County

Jesse Besser, founder of the massive concrete block corporation, was also a humanitarian, and in Alpena the Besser Museum is named after him. But Besser also was responsible for leaving something in Presque Isle County— a small tract of land on Lake Huron whose towering white pines somehow escaped the swinging axes of lumbermen.

The industrial genius, realizing the rarity of the uncut pines and the beauty of the undeveloped Lake Huron shoreline, gave the area to the people of Michigan in 1966. Today it is the ***Besser Natural Area,*** managed by the Department of Natural Resources. The remote preserve, reached from

US 23 by taking County Road 405 to the south end of Grand Lake, offers a small niche of beauty and a little history in a quiet setting. Looping through the Besser Natural Area is a sandy 1-mile foot trail, which takes you past a small lagoon that once was part of Lake Huron. Look carefully at the bottom of the lagoon (you need polarizing sunglasses on sunny days) and you'll spot the hull of an old ship. The vessel served the community of Bell, which was located here in the 1880s and consisted of 100 residents, several homes, a sawmill, a saloon, a store, and a school.

The most noticeable remains of Bell are the rock pier along Lake Huron, a towering stone chimney, and the collapsed walls of a building whose steel safe and icebox counter indicate it might have been the saloon. Toward the end of the walk, you pass through some of the oldest and largest white pines remaining in a state once covered with the trees. There is no fee to enter the preserve, nor is there a visitor center or any other facility. Descriptive brochures that coincide with the footpath are available from a small box near the trailhead.

Visitors who exit US 23 for the east side of Grand Lake, which is the state's 19th-largest lake, with more than 5,000 acres of water, usually want to view lighthouses. They take in the beautifully renovated **Old Presque Isle Lighthouse** (989-595-6979) near the end of County Road 405 (Grand Lake Road). Built in 1840, this squat, stone lighthouse is open to the public and features an interesting museum crammed with artifacts and exhibits. The lighthouse is open daily from 9 a.m. to 6 p.m. from June 15 through Oct 15. There is a small admission charge.

Limestone Capital of the World

The world's largest open pit limestone quarry is Rogers City's **Port of Calcite** and located on the grounds is **Harbor View,** an observation area where visitors can watch huge freighters being loaded for ports throughout the Great Lakes. More than 500 US and Canadian freighters are loaded annually with each vessel carrying 12,000 to 30,000 tons of stone to be used in the production of steel, cement, chemicals, and construction materials. To reach Harbor View turn east on Quarry Road from Business US 23 and then right on Calcite Road and follow the signs. During the shipping season the port maintains a recorded message (989-734-2117) of what freighters are being loaded and when.

Take a Drive

The 56-mile stretch of US 23 between Mackinaw City and Rogers City is one of the most scenic drives in the Lower Peninsula, featuring a dozen parks and scenic turnouts overlooking Lake Huron.

Many of them are clustered around Rogers City. Five miles north of the town is *Forty Mile Point Lighthouse Park.* The small but delightful park is crowned by the towering lighthouse and includes a picnic area and beach. On the north side of Rogers City is *Seagull Point Park,* a mix of Lake Huron shoreline, low dunes, and woods that are best enjoyed in the fall by walking a 2-mile interpretive trail.

Just a mile north of it at 4500 E. Grand Lake Rd. is *New Presque Isle Lighthouse Park* (989-595-9917) with nature trails, picnic area, and a small museum of its own. Built in 1870, the New Presque Isle Lighthouse is one of the tallest on the Great Lakes, standing 109 feet tall. An unattached keeper's residence, constructed in 1905, is now a museum while in the original keeper's quarters in the lighthouse is a gift shop where for a small fee you can climb the 130 steps to the top of the tower. Needless to say the view is incredible. The lighthouse is open daily mid-May through mid-Oct from 9 a.m. until 6 p.m. The 1905 House Museum is open from Memorial Day through Labor Day from 11 a.m. to 5 p.m. Tues through Sat, and 1 to 5 p.m. Sun.

The *Fireside Inn* is yet another reason to come to this part of the country, especially for anyone whose idea of a vacation in northern Michigan is renting a quaint log cabin on the edge of a lake. The Fireside Inn began its long history as a resort when the original lodge was built in 1908, and the first few authentic log cabins soon began to appear around it. Little has changed about the lodge or the dining room inside with its rustic wooden beams, plank floor, and large windows looking over Grand Lake. They still ring a dinner bell to signal supper time and serve only

trivia

Posen, a village of 234 residents, is the agricultural heart of Presque Isle County with its farmers ranking third in the state as producers of packed and graded table potatoes. The best time to visit the community is during the *Posen Potato Festival* (989-766-8128; posenmi .org), held the first weekend after Labor Day.

one entree family-style; afterward guests still wander out to the rambling porch, an immense sitting area 215 feet long, to claim a favorite wicker chair or rocker.

You can rent one of the cabins with a wood interior and stone fireplace or just a room (shared bath) in the lodge itself. Rooms are $55 per person per day and cabins are $450 per week per person and either includes all meals. Or you can stop in just for dinner, a delightful experience in itself. Dinner prices range from $8 to $14, depending on what is being served that night, and you should call ahead if possible. The Fireside Inn (989-595-6369; firesideinngrandlake.com) is located off County Road 405 at the end of the spur at 18730 Fireside Hwy.

Presque Isle County is home to another unique inn, ***Nettie Bay Lodge.*** Located 14 miles west of Rogers City, the lodge is on the shores of Lake Nettie and surrounded by 2,000 private acres. Originally developed as a hunting and fishing camp, Nettie Bay Lodge has since become known as a wildlife-viewing destination, offering not only accommodations but also the use of photography and observation blinds that overlook marshes and other prime spots to sight wildlife.

Because of the area's diverse habitat, it is not unusual to sight 100 different birds in a single weekend. Loons nest on a small island right in front of the lodge, bald eagles and ospreys often feed in the shallow waters of the lake, flocks of wild turkeys can be spotted in the woods. Several times in May the Nettie Bay School of Birding is held at the lodge and includes 2 nights' lodging, some meals, and bird identification workshops and field trips with professional ornithologists.

Nettie Bay Lodge (989-734-4688; nettiebay.com) is west of Hawks on County Road 638 and offers 8 cottages and 2 rooms in the lodge. The birding school is $450 per person and includes lodging, meals, and instruction. The Cobblestone Restaurant at Nettie Bay Lodge also offers a sumptuous dinner followed by a musical performance. The weekend specials are by reservation only.

Montmorency County

One of the most popular attractions in Montmorency County isn't a museum or a scenic overlook but a 700-pound elk. Almost 1,500 elk thrive on state

Dinosaur Gardens

Though it sounds like a tacky roadside attraction, **Dinosaur Gardens** is actually an interesting, even eerie, place to visit. The 40-acre park was the creation of the late Paul Domke, a self-taught artist and sculptor. In the 1930s Domke built 27 life-size dinosaurs from concrete, wire, and deer hair within the tangled branches of a cedar swamp forest. A winding path leads through the dark woods where a dino lies waiting for you around every bend.

Eeek!

Dinosaur Gardens (877-823-2408; dinosaurgardensllc.com) is right on US 23, 10 miles south of Alpena. It's open daily from 9 a.m. to 6 p.m. from Memorial Day through Labor Day and 9 a.m. to 4 p.m. in May before Memorial Day and in Sept. Admission is $5 for adults and $4 for children.

forest land between Gaylord and Hillman, making it the largest herd east of the Mississippi River. A unique way to view the animals is an *Elk Viewing Sleigh Ride Dinner* arranged through the Best Western Thunder Bay Resort in Hillman. The popular wildlife-viewing adventure began in 1993 when Jack and Jan Matthias started offering sleigh rides to their 1940-vintage hunting cabin. But the high point for most guests was not the gourmet dinner at the cabin but seeing an elk along the way, including bulls whose antlers often exceeded a span of 4 feet.

The Matthiases eventually built a larger cabin to accommodate more people but still cook the 5-course meal—crown roast of pork, pear and apple crepes, and homemade soup, among other dishes—over a 1915 wood-burning stove. If you anticipate joining a sleigh ride, bundle up and grab one of the blankets that are provided. The ride through the snowy woods is a 45-minute trip each way.

The sleigh ride is offered each winter from Christmas through the third week of March. A 2-night weekend package including accommodations at the Thunder Bay Resort, breakfasts, and the sleigh ride is $246 per person, while the 1-night, midweek package is $186. When there is available space, you can also book just the dinner and sleigh at $89.50 per person. For more information or reservations, contact the *Best Western Thunder Bay Resort* (800-729-9375; thunderbayresort.com).

trivia

Located 11 miles inland from Rogers City along M 68 is *Ocqueoc Falls,* one of only two waterfalls in the Lower Peninsula. This cascade is a series of ledges that drops 6 feet in the Ocqueoc River. Ocqueoc is not the thundering waterfall that you experience throughout the Upper Peninsula, but it's still a beautiful spot, especially in the fall. The day-use area includes picnic tables and foot trails that follow the east bank of the river, while on the south side of M 68 is a rustic state forest campground.

Garland Resort near Lewiston has another cure for cabin fever. The best way to spend a winter afternoon at this sprawling resort of cozy cabins and romantic log lodges is by Nordic skiing and eating. At the same time. Every Saturday in January and February Garland (989-786-2211; garland usa.com) stages its famed Gourmet Glide when skiers follow the resort's well-groomed trails, stopping along the way at 5 buffet stations to feast on smoked trout, cheese fondues, spiced wine, and other treats. Which begs the question, are they skiing to eat or eating to ski? The cost is $69 for adults and $39 for children.

Oscoda County

The state bird of Michigan is the robin, but many argue that it should be the Kirtland's warbler. This small bird, the size of a sparrow, with a distinctive yellow breast, is an endangered species that breeds only in the jack pines of Michigan. It spends its winters in obscurity in the Bahamas and then migrates to areas between Mio and Grayling, arriving in mid-May and departing by early July. Only in these preserved nesting areas do birders and wildlife watchers have the opportunity to observe this rare bird, with fewer than 800 breeding pairs remaining.

The nesting areas are closed to the public, but you can join a *Kirtland's Warbler Tour,* which is sponsored by the US Forest Service. The tour, which lasts from 1.5 to 2 hours, includes a movie and a discussion by a Forest Service naturalist and then a short trip to the nesting area. The guided group hikes through the jack pines, usually covering 1 to 2 miles, until the warblers are spotted. Seeing a Kirtland's warbler is not guaranteed, but most tours do, especially in mid-May through June.

This tour is famous among birders, who come from all over the country for their only glimpse of the warbler, but it is also an interesting spot for anybody intrigued by Michigan's wildlife. The Forest Service office (989-826-3252), north of Mio on M 33, and the Michigan Audubon Society jointly conduct guided tours from May 15 through July 4, departing from the Ramada Inn in Grayling. Visit the front desk upon your arrival for the meeting location. The tours are offered on weekdays at 7 a.m. and on weekends and holidays at 7 and 11 a.m. Tours are free of charge.

Places to Stay in Michigan's Lake Huron Region

ALPENA

Days Inn
1496 M 32 West
(800) 582-9050
daysinn.com

AUGRES

Econolodge
510 W. US 23
(989) 876-4080
econolodge.com

BAY CITY

Americinn
3915 Three Mile Rd.
(989) 671-0071
americinn.com

Keswick Manor
1800 Center Ave.
(989) 893-6598
keswickmanor.com

FLINT

Red Roof Inn
G-3219 Miller Rd.
(810) 733-1660
redroof.com

Wingate by Wyndham
1359 Grand Pointe Court
(810) 694-9900
wingateflint.com

FRANKENMUTH

Bavarian Inn Lodge
1 Covered Bridge Lane
(888) 775-6343
bavarianinn.com

Frankenmuth Motel
1218 Weiss St.
(800) 821-5362
frankenmuthmotel.com

Zehnder's Splash Village Hotel
1365 S. Main St.
(800) 863-7999
zehnders.com

HARRISVILLE

Alcona Beach Resort
700 N. Lake Huron
Shore Dr.
(989) 724-5471

HAWKS

Nettie Bay Lodge
9011 W. County Hwy. 638
(989) 734-4688
nettiebay.com

HILLMAN

Thunder Bay Resort
27800 MI 32
(800) 729-9375
thunderbayresort.com

LEWISTON

Garland Resort
4700 N. Red Oak Rd.
(877) 442-7526
garlandusa.com

Pine Ridge Lodge
2730 Pine Haven Rd.
(989) 786-4789
pineridgelodgemi.com

MIDLAND

Sleep Inn
2100 W. Wackerly St.
(989) 837-1010
sleepinn.com

Valley Plaza Resort
5221 Bay City Rd.
(989) 496-2700
valleyplazaresort.com

OSCODA

Huron House Bed & Breakfast
3124 N. US 23
(989) 739-9255
huronhouse.com

OSSINEKE

Oakapiney Beach Cottages
9611 US 23 South
(734) 665-8876 or
(989) 471-2489
oakapiney.com

ROGERS CITY

Driftwood Motel
540 N. Third St.
(989) 734-4777

Manitou Shores Resort
7995 US 23
(989) 734-7233
manitoushores.com

SAGINAW

Fairfield Inn
5200 Fashion Square Blvd.
(800) 228-2800
fairfieldinnsaginawmihotel
.com

Hampton Inn
2222 Tittabawassee Rd.
(989) 797-2200
hamptoninn3.hilton.com

Montague Inn
1581 S. Washington Ave.
(989) 752-3939
montagueinn.com

TAWAS CITY

Paradise Beach Resort
1029 Lake St.
(800) 472-6518
tawasparadise.com

Tawas Bay Beach Resort
300 E. Bay St.
(800) 336-8601
tawasbaybeachresort.com

Places to Eat in Michigan's Lake Huron Region

ALPENA

Churchill Pointe Inn
5700 Bennett Rd.,
Hubbard Lake
(989) 727-2020
churchillpointeinn.com
Fine Dining

John A. Lau Saloon
414 N. Second Ave.
(989) 354-6898
johnalausaloon.com
American

The Olde Owl Tavern & Grille
121 W. Chisholm St.
(989) 356-6915
American

BAY CITY

Duece's Char House
432 Tuscola Rd.
(989) 893-5881
American

Krzysiak's House
1605 Michigan Ave.
(989) 894-5531
krzysiaks.com
Polish

SELECTED TOURISM BUREAUS

Alpena Area Convention and Visitors Bureau
235 W. Chisholm St.
Alpena 49707
(800) 425-7362
alpenacvb.com

Flint Genesee Regional Convention and Visitors Bureau
519 S. Saginaw St.
Flint 48502
(810) 600-6815
flint.travel
visitflint.org

Frankenmuth Convention and Visitors Bureau
635 S. Main St.
Frankenmuth 48734
(800) 386-8696
frankenmuth.org

Great Lakes Bay Regional Convention & Visitors Bureau
515 N. Washington Ave.
Sagniaw 48607
(800) 444-9979
visitgreatlakesbay.org

Rogers City Chamber of Commerce
292 S. Bradley Hwy.
Rogers City 49779
(800) 622-4148
rogerscity.com

Shiawassee County Convention and Visitors Bureau
215 N. Water St.
Owosso 48867
(989) 723- 1199
shiawassee.org

Tawas City Tourist Bureau
402 E. Lake St.
Tawas City 48764
(877) 868-2927
tawasbay.com

BIRCH RUN

Oscar & Joey's Roadhouse
12027 Dixie Hwy.
(989) 624-9349
oscarandjoeysroadhouse.com
Wild Game

EAST TAWAS

Northwoods Steak House
1222 US 23
(989) 362-5321
thenorthwoodssteakhouse.com
Steakhouse

FLINT

Bill Thomas' Halo Burger
800 S. Saginaw St.
(810) 238-4607
haloburger.com
Burgers

FRANKENMUTH

Bavarian Inn
713 S. Main St.
(800) 228-2742
bavarianinn.com
German

OTHER ATTRACTIONS

Chippewa Nature Center
Midland
(989) 631-0830
chippewanaturecenter.org

Crossroads Village and Huckleberry Railroad
Flint
(810) 736-7100

40 Mile Point Lighthouse
Rogers City
40milepointlighthouse.org

Great Lakes Lore Maritime Museum
Rogers City
(989) 734-0706
gllmm.com

Junction Valley Railroad
Bridgeport
(789) 777-3480
jvrailroad.com

Marshall M. Fredericks Sculpture Museum
Bay City
(989) 964-7125
marshallfredericks.org

Saginaw Children's Zoo
(989) 759-1408
saginawzoo.com

Saginaw Historical Museum
(989) 752-2861
castlemuseum.org

Sullivan's Black Forest Brew Haus
281 Heinlein Strasse
(800) 890-6877
blackforestbrewhaus.net
Brewpub

Harvest Coffeehouse & Beanery
626 Main St.
(989) 652-2203
harvestcoffeehouse.com
Cafe & Bakery

Zehnder's
730 S. Main St.
(800) 863-7999
zehnders.com
German

MIDLAND

Pi's
1815 S. Saginaw Rd.
(989) 832-5848
pischineserestaurant.com
Chinese

The Table
111 W. Main St.
(989) 633-6099
thetable.com
Fine Dining

OSCODA

Bavarian Bakery & Restaurant
5222 N. US 23
(989) 739-8077
German

Wiltse's Brew Pub
5606 F-41
(989) 739-2231
wiltsesbrewpub.com
Brewpub

SAGINAW

Crumb's Gourmet Cookie Cafe
4882 Gratiot Rd.
(989) 498-4010
crumbscaters.com
Cafe & Bakery

LAKE MICHIGAN

The Lake Michigan shoreline may be the Lower Peninsula's western edge, but many will argue that its heart lies in Chicago. The shoreline is now connected to the city by an interstate highway, but that has only cemented what was already a long and enduring relationship between the Windy City and this watery edge of Michigan.

It began with the Great Chicago Fire of 1871, which left the city smoldering in ashes. Chicago was rebuilt with Michigan white pine, and the mill towns along the Great Lake, communities like Muskegon and Saugatuck, worked around the clock to supply the lumber. Maybe it was during these excursions to the sawmills that Chicagoans discovered that this region of Michigan possessed more than towering trees and two-by-fours.

They discovered the sand, the surf, and the incredibly beautiful sunsets of the Lake Michigan shoreline. By the 1880s, the tourist boom was on, and it was being fed by vacationers from cities outside Michigan, places like St. Louis, and South Bend, Indiana, but most of all from Chicago. They arrived by steamships, trains, and eventually automobiles. They caused luxurious resorts and lakeside

LAKE MICHIGAN

cottages to mushroom, beginning in New Buffalo on the edge of the Indiana-Michigan border and continuing right up the coast: St. Joseph, South Haven, Saugatuck, Grand Haven, and Muskegon.

They call it the Michigan Riviera, and even Richard J. Daley, Chicago's famed political boss and mayor, had a summer home on the strip. With the completion of I-94, the two regions were linked by a four-lane belt of concrete. Many Chicagoans, eager to escape the city heat, were less than two hours from the cool breezes of their favorite resort.

The Lake Michigan shoreline is still the heart of Michigan tourism. This incredibly beautiful region is characterized by great dunes and watery sunsets, but it's also known for its bustling resorts, streets full of quaint shops, and attractive beachfront hotels. The region lies on the western edge of Michigan, but Chicago's influence is unmistakably clear.

AUTHOR'S TOP TEN PICKS

Gillette Sand Dune Visitor Center
Hoffmaster State Park
(231) 798-3573

Great Lakes Naval Memorial and Museum
Muskegon
(231) 755-1230
silversidesmuseum.org

Hackley and Hume Historic Site
Muskegon
(231) 722-0278
muskegonmuseum.org

Loda Lake Wildflower Sanctuary
White Cloud
(231) 745-4631

Ludington State Park
Ludington
(231) 843-2423

Picking apples at Tree-Mendus Fruit
Eau Claire
(877) 863-3276
treemendusfruit.com

Saugatuck Chain Ferry and Mount Baldhead Park
Saugatuck
(269) 857-4243

Shrine of the Pines
Baldwin
(231) 745-7892

Silver Lake State Park
(231) 873-2817
macwoodsdunerides.com

Windmill Island
Holland
(616) 355-1030
windmillisland.org

Just go to the beach and look at the license plates of the cars, listen to the baseball games the radios are tuned to, or see what city's newspaper someone is snoozing under. You're in Chicago's playland.

Berrien County

You barely cross the state border from Indiana before the first lakeshore communities appear on the horizon with their hotels and motels clustered near the water. Many are new, each with features little different from the one next door. But if you search a little, you can find an old inn from another era unique in its appearance and half-hidden in a quiet neighborhood near the lake. If you search harder, you might even find the *Inn at Union Pier.*

Union Pier is a cluster of well-shaded streets and 19th-century summer homes about 10 miles north of the border. Locate Berrien Street and you'll pass the inn, 3 nautical buildings painted light blue with white railings. The inn began in 1918 as a single building called the Karonsky Resort, but business was so good that by 1929 2 more structures had been added. An easy journey from Chicago (today it is only 90 minutes by car), the inn thrived in the golden age of the Lake Michigan resorts but by the 1960s was abandoned and closed up. In 1983, Bill and Madeleine Reinke purchased the place, gutted it, and after two years of renovation, opened for business.

From the outside the inn's most striking feature is the wraparound porch on one of the smaller lodges and the matching balcony above it, the ideal place to unwind after a day on the beach. Walkway decks connect the buildings; one has a large hot tub, and tables for breakfast outdoors are on another. Most of the rooms are furnished in light pine and include a Swedish ceramic woodstove. The heart of the main lodge is a spacious common area with a grand piano, overstuffed chairs and sofas, and lots to read. Guests begin each day with a full breakfast of local fruit and fresh baked goods on the deck and then

trivia

Former Chicago Mayor Richard M. Daley followed his father's footsteps by not only entering politics but also maintaining a second home in Michigan's Harbor Country, the communities along Lake Michigan from Indiana to Bridgman. Other celebrities with homes in the area include talk show hostess Oprah Winfrey, actor George Wendt of TV show *Cheers* fame, and the late film critic Roger Ebert.

head across the street to the beach, check out one of the inn's bicycles, or take to nearby roads for a winery tour or antiques excursion.

The Inn at Union Pier (269-469-4700; innatunionpier.com) has 16 rooms priced for double occupancy from $165 to $250 per night, including breakfast.

Three Oaks, in the southwest corner of Berrien County, is home to the *Three Oaks Spokes Bicycle Club.* Founded in 1974, the club is best known for the *Apple Cider Century* (888-877-2068; applecidercentury .com), when every September more than 7,000 cyclists depart from the tiny town on 1-day rides of 25, 50, 62, 75, or 100 miles.

But the club is also responsible for an interesting bicycle exhibit on the second floor of the *Three Oaks Library* at 3 N. Elm St. (269-756-5621; threeoaks.michlibrary.org). The room is full of historic two-wheelers, ranging

TOP ANNUAL EVENTS

MAY

Trillium Festival
Muskegon
(800) 250-9283
visitmuskegon.org

Tulip Time Festival
Holland
(800) 822-2770
tuliptime.com

JUNE

National Asparagus Festival
Shelby and Hart
(231) 259-0170
nationalasparagusfestival.org

JULY

Harbor Days/Venetian Nights
Saugatuck
(616) 886-1162
saugatuckvenetianfestival.org

Manistee National Forest Festival
Manistee
(800) 288-2286

AUGUST

National Blueberry Festival
South Haven
(800) 764-2836
blueberryfestival.com

SEPTEMBER

Apple Cider Century
Three Oaks
(888) 877-2068
applecidercentury.com

OCTOBER

Goose Festival
Fennville, October

from the Companion, a side-by-side two seater, to an 1860 velocipede, one of the earliest bicycles ever made, featuring two wheels, handlebars, and a seat—but no rubber tires, inflated inner tubes, or anything resembling a spring or a wire spoke. Thus its nickname: the Boneshaker.

At the *Three Oaks Spokes Clubhouse* in the historic *Dewey Cannon Trading Company Building* you'll find cycling information for the southwest corner of the state, a pedaler's paradise called Michiana. That includes the *Backroads Bikeway,* a selection of 14 tours throughout this Michigan/Indiana region that the club has posted with color-coded bike route signs. The tours range from 5 to 60 miles, and wind past sand dunes, wineries, cider mills, and one of the last stands of virgin hardwoods left in southern Michigan.

Along with maps of the Backroads Bikeway routes and a shop of cycling supplies, the club has changing rooms and bike rentals for $15 a day or $25 for the weekend. Three Oaks Spokes Bicycle Club (269-756-4255) is at 3 Dewey Cannon Ave. and open 10 a.m. to 5 p.m. Wed and Fri, 10 a.m. to 7 p.m. Thurs, and 10 a.m. to 3 p.m. Sat.

The *Lake Michigan dunes,* the most spectacular natural feature of the region, begin in Indiana and hug the shoreline almost to the Straits of Mackinac. The largest preserve of dunes in Berrien County is at *Warren Dunes State Park,* located on the lake 12 miles north of the state border. The park has more than 2 miles of fine sandy beaches and dunes that rise 240 feet above Lake Michigan. The dunes are a popular place in the summer for sunbathers and swimmers during the day and campers at night. What many people don't realize is that Warren Dunes is the only state park that permits hang gliding, and it is considered by most gliders to be one of the best places in the Midwest, if not the country, for soaring.

Gliders are drawn to the park because of *Tower Hill,* which looms over the beach parking lot. They trudge up the hill carrying their gliders and then soar into the winds from the top, flying over the sandy park or even above Lake Michigan. When the sport enjoyed its heyday in the mid-1970s, there would be almost 100 gliders on Tower Hill on a windy weekend, with as many as 20 in the air at one time. The park rangers were so burdened with accidents caused by unqualified fliers that they instituted a certification system and stricter regulations for gliders.

Strange as it Sounds

Tree-Mendus Fruit is like many U-pick fruit farms in western Michigan. The Eau Claire farm has 250 acres of apple orchards to pick, hayrides, a petting area with goats, chickens, and rabbits for children, a country store and gift shop featuring baked goods, jugs of cider, and apple and cherry products, and a picnic area.

But in some ways Tree-Mendus Fruit is the only farm of its kind. Take its International Cherry Pit Spitting Championship held annually on the first Sat in July. In 2003 the farm celebrated the event's 30th anniversary with the champion spitting a cherry pit 93 feet, 6.5 inches, a record effort at the farm.

Tree-Mendus Fruit (877-863-3276; treemendus-fruit.com) is 2 miles north of Eau Claire and east of M 140 on E. Eureka Road. The farm is open from July through Oct. Hours are 10 a.m. to 6 p.m. daily except Tues through Labor Day, and Fri through Mon in the fall.

What makes the park so attractive for these soaring adventurers, especially those just learning the sport, are the smooth winds that come off the lake and the soft and relatively forgiving sand below. Although not nearly the rage it was in the 1970s, arrive on a weekend in the fall or spring with a wind out of the north-northwest and it's still possible to watch a glider or two take off from the top of Tower Hill. Occasionally glider instructors still set up school in the park, taking students through a 1-day lesson or a tandem glide. To find such an instructor, call Warren Dunes State Park (269-426-4013) or check the state-by-state list of schools on the website of the United States Hang Gliding Association (ushpa.aero).

Lake Michigan does more than provide water for the beaches or a view from the top of sand dunes. It also tempers the winter storms that roll in from the Great Plains and moderates the sweltering summer heat felt elsewhere in the Midwest. These effects, combined with the light soil of the region, have turned the lakeshore strip into a cornucopia of orchards, berry farms, and especially vineyards. Michigan is the third leading wine-producing state in the country after California and New York. Paw Paw in Van Buren County is the unofficial center for the state's wine makers, with the largest vineyards, St. Julian Wine Company and Warner Vineyards, located right off I-94.

Smaller wineries are also found throughout the region, including a frequent winner in national competition, *Tabor Hill Winery,* in the center of Berrien County. The winery began when two Chicago salesmen who sold steel but loved wine brought a selection of hybrid grapevines back from France in 1968. They chose their vineyard site in the rolling hills of the county, hoping the conditions there were similar enough to those in France to bring success. They were. The transplanted vines thrived, and the winery produced its first bottle in 1970. Seven years later a bottle of its 1974 Baco won a gold medal in the American Wine Competition, and since then both the vineyard and Leonard Olson, steel-salesman-turned-winemaker, have won numerous awards. The winery remains small, producing 40,000 gallons (or about 15,000 cases) of wine annually in almost two dozen types of whites, reds, and blends.

The best way to view Tabor Hill is on a walking tour that begins where workers bottle the wine and then heads out into the rows of trellised vines for a history of the grapes. You also descend into the wine cellar for a look at the huge vats and hand-carved oak casks that age the wine, and then finish the tour in the tasting room for some tips on how to "judge" wine. The 25-minute tour ends with everybody age 21 or older sampling some of Tabor Hill's finest wines (kids can sample grape juice).

The winery also includes an excellent restaurant with tables that overlook the rolling vineyard and a huge deck outside. A favorite activity of many, especially during fall, is to pack a picnic lunch and enjoy it on the open deck with a bottle of Tabor Hill wine.

Bear Cave

Bear Cave near Buchanan is one of the few caverns in Michigan. Formed in rare "tura rock," the cave is 15 feet deep, 6 feet wide, and 15 feet high and is estimated to be 25,000 years old. The cave was part of the Underground Railroad for slaves in the mid-1800s and then in 1875 bank robbers used it to hide their loot. The heist inspired the 1903 movie, *The Great Train Robbery,* in which the cave served as a movie location.

Bear Cave (269-695-3050) is 6 miles north of Buchanan on Red Bud Trail. Tours of the cave are available during the summer and include following a winding stairway through the cavern.

Tabor Hill (800-283-3363; taborhill.com) is at 185 Mount Tabor Rd. and can be reached from I-94 by taking exit 16 and heading north on Red Arrow Highway to Bridgman. From Bridgman head east along Shawnee Road and keep an eye out for the signs. This vineyard is definitely off by itself. The free tours are offered every half hour from noon to 4:30 p.m. daily May through Nov.

In between the sand dunes, the orchards, and the wineries of Berrien County is a lot of history. Niles, the community of four flags, was the first settlement in the Lower Peninsula and claimed one of the first museums in the country when a private one opened here in 1842. Eventually it became the *Fort St. Joseph Museum,* and today it houses more than 10,000 historical items on 2 floors. Much of the museum's collection relates to its namesake fort, for which the French built the stockade in 1691. The British took it over in 1761, and the Spanish captured it 20 years later. In 1783, the Americans arrived and raised the fourth and final flag over Fort St. Joseph.

The museum's most noted displays, however, are devoted to the Sioux Indians of the Great Plains, not to the residents of Fort St. Joseph. Many of the Indian artifacts were obtained by Captain Horace Baxter Quimby, whose daughter moved to Niles. While the US Army captain was based in the Dakota Territory in 1881 and 1882, he became friendly with Sitting Bull, the most famous Sioux chief. Among the gifts Quimby received from Sitting Bull were 13 pictographs of the chief's greatest battles. The set of pictures is one of only three known collections of the Sioux chief.

The museum (269-683-4702) is right behind the Niles City Hall (ci.niles .mi.us) at 508 E. Main St. Niles can be reached from US 12, 23 miles east of I-94 or 33 miles west of US 131. Hours are 10 a.m. to 4 p.m. Wed to Fri and 10 a.m. to 3 p.m. Sat. There is no admission fee.

More history can be seen at Berrien Springs' *The History Center at Courthouse Square.* The courthouse itself was built in 1839 and at various times was a militia drill hall, a college, and even a church. In 1967, the courthouse was repurchased by the county and restored as the 19th-century courtroom where law was interpreted and justice dispensed in Michigan's early years of statehood. The classic Greek Revival–style structure is the centerpiece of the Berrien County Courthouse Square, a complex of 5 buildings that is listed on the National Register of Historic Places. It gives visitors a glimpse of the machinery of old-fashioned government.

You can climb the wooden stairs to the second-floor courtroom where former Michigan Supreme Court Justice Epaphroditus Ransom presided over the first session in April 1839. Little in the building has changed since then. The wooden floors still creak as you approach the bench, and floor-to-ceiling windows still illuminate the courtroom furnishings of pewlike benches, wood-burning stoves, and the curved railing that separated the participants from the gallery.

The historic complex (269-471-1202) is located in Berrien Springs at 313 N. Cass St. Berrien Springs is 11 miles southeast of exit 27 off I-94. Hours for the buildings are 10 a.m. to 5 p.m. Mon through Sat in the summer and Mon through Fri the rest of the year. Admission is free.

Van Buren County

South Haven has a long and colorful history spiced with Great Lakes vessels and shipbuilding, and much of it is explained at the *Michigan Maritime Museum,* which is dedicated to the boats that were built and used on the Great Lakes. Founded in 1976, the museum includes a 600-foot outdoor boardwalk around a historical fish tug and a vessel used in the US Life-Saving Service. Inside the museum hall the exhibits range from collections of small vessel motors and tools used by local shipbuilders to personal belongings of mariners and exhibits on the role of the Great Lakes in the War of 1812.

Michigan Maritime Museum (800-747-3810; michiganmaritimemuseum .org) is at 260 Dyckman Ave. where it crosses the Black River and is reached from I-196 by taking exit 20 and heading west on Phoenix Street. Turn north on Broadway Street and then west on Dyckman Street. From Memorial Day to Labor Day the hours are 10 a.m. to 5 p.m. Mon through Sat and noon to 5 p.m. Sun. The rest of the year hours are 10 a.m. to 5 p.m. Fri, Sat, and Sun. Admission is $6 for adults and $4.50 for children.

For excitement on the high seas, take a cruise on *Friends Good Will,* a tall ship sailing out of the Michigan Maritime Museum. The square topsail sloop is a replica of a ship of that name that fought for both the US and Great Britain during the War of 1812. The ship takes regularly scheduled sails on Lake Michigan from mid-May through mid-Sept, with crew dressed in full 1812-era regalia. During the summer months special "Pirate Chaser

Adventure Sails" are scheduled for the younger set Wed though Sat. *Lindy Lou* is an electric river launch that cruises up and down the Black River, starting at and returning to the Michigan Maritime Museum in South Haven. The launch is a recreation vessel designed to be a replica of river launches found in South Haven in the early 1900s. The launch cruises daily from May through Oct. Coming soon will be the *Bernida*, a prize-winning 1921 R Class yacht taking 4 passengers for sails on Lake Michigan. Cruises run $30 to $40.

The good life on the lakes can also be enjoyed at dinnertime aboard the **Idler Riverboat,** a restaurant floating in the Black River downtown in Old Harbor Village. The *Idler* was built in Clinton, Iowa, in 1897 for Lafayette Lamb, a lumber baron who used the 120-foot houseboat for his own personal enjoyment on the Mississippi. He never installed an engine in the *Idler* because he didn't want to be disturbed by the vibrations, so the vessel was always pushed up and down the river by a small tug.

The *Idler* appeared at the 1904 World's Fair in St. Louis, but in 1910 it burned to the waterline. It was immediately rebuilt and eventually captured the fancy of actor Vincent Price's father. He owned it for 58 years, and in a letter now framed and hanging in the restaurant, Price said that what his father liked most about the riverboat was playing the piano on board. Eventually the boat was purchased, and it was brought to South Haven in 1979. Today it has been beautifully restored, and topside is the Creole Tavern, an open-air bar with sweeping views of the town and the Black River from every table. In the restaurant, located below, you can dine on white linen in either the original dining quarters or one of 4 staterooms. Each accommodates a party of 6 for a private gastronomic evening. The menu lists more than 20 entrees priced from $14 to $26, and every day 6 new entrees are featured. Many local people know the restaurant best for its Cajun dishes— blackened fish and steak, barbecued shrimp, and Louisiana steak salad—and its sinfully rich cheesecakes. Also popular is the Bratburger—a full bratwurst on top of a burger.

Idler Riverboat (269-637-8435; millenniumrestaurants.com) is open daily from 11 a.m. to 10 p.m. Mon through Thurs and 11 a.m. to 11 p.m. Fri through Sun. Reservations are accepted, and dress is casual on the riverboat.

Sportfishing fans throughout Michigan head for the streams, inland lakes, and Great Lakes to fill their creels with a variety of catch. If they are passing through Van Buren County on M 43, they should also head for the

Caruso's Candy Kitchen

Since the Roaring Twenties, vacationing families have been stepping up to the Italian marble soda fountain bar at *Caruso's Candy Kitchen* in Dowagiac to sip a creamy soda or indulge in an ice-cream concoction served in a tall glass sundae dish. They're still doing it today because little has changed at this venerable ice-cream parlor.

Founded in 1822 by Antonio Caruso, who had just sailed to the United States from Italy with his wife, Caruso's still features pedestal stools, a wavy mirror behind the counter, lime green Hamilton Beach malt mixers, and high wooden booths. This is where you come for a real milk shake, made with hand-dipped ice cream in a metal malt glass. The specialty of the shop is the Green River: lime phosphate syrup on the bottom of a sundae dish, two scoops of vanilla ice cream, and topped off with crushed cherries, pineapple, mixed nuts, and real whipped cream. It is based on the green, white, and red flag of Italy and was Antonio Caruso's way of saluting his native country.

Caruso's (269-782-6001; carusoscandykitchen.com) is in downtown Dowagiac at 130 S. Front St. and is open from 9 a.m. to 5 p.m. Mon through Sat.

Wolf Lake State Fish Hatchery, one of the main reasons fishing is so good in Michigan. The hatchery dates to 1928 and by 1935 was the largest in the world. Construction of the present facility began in 1980, and three years and $7.2 million later, the technological upgrading had made Wolf Lake the finest complex in the country for producing both warm-water and cold-water species. No other hatchery in Michigan raises as many species as Wolf Lake, which hatches steelhead, brown trout, Chinook salmon, and grayling along with the warm-water species of tiger musky, northern pike, walleye, bass, and bluegill.

Hatchery tours should begin at the interpretive center, which will fascinate anybody who dabbles in sportfishing. Hanging on the wall in the lobby is the state record sturgeon—one very big fish—plus displays of trout fishing on the state's renowned Au Sable River. Off to one side is the "Michigan Room," a walk-through exhibit area that begins with an interesting series of habitat dioramas, cross sections of every type of water you might drop a line into, from trout streams to the Great Lakes. Each diorama shows the species that will be found, the habitat they like, and the lure of a frustrated angler trying to land the lunkers that lie below. There are also exhibits on fish anatomy, slide presentations of Michigan's commercial fisheries, and an area devoted to sportfishing gear, including a delightful display of more than 100 historic lures, plugs, and other tackle.

After viewing the exhibits and a short slide presentation in the auditorium, visitors are encouraged to wander through the hatchery itself to view millions of fish in the ponds. If you want to see something bigger, ask for some fish feed at the interpretive center and walk out on the small pier at the show pond. The small lake was developed so that people, especially children, could actually see some large fish. Among the species in it is a pair of sturgeons, each one more than 6 feet long and weighing more than 60 pounds. Imagine that at the end of your line!

The center (269-668-2876; michigandnr.com) is open Mon through Sun from 10 a.m. to 6 p.m. during the summer with guided half-hour tours at 10 and 11 a.m. and at 1, 2, and 3 p.m. The center has shorter hours in Mar, Apr, May, Sept, and Oct. There is no admission fee to visit Wolf Lake, which is reached from I-94 by heading north on US 131 for 4 miles and then west on M 43 for 6 miles.

Michigan has no short supply of vineyards and wine-tasting rooms to visit, but few have the old-world character of **Warner Vineyards** in Paw Paw. The building itself is a Michigan Historical Site, constructed in 1898 as the town's first waterworks station. The vineyard purchased it in 1967 and proceeded to renovate the structure using lumber from old wine casks to transform it into a wine haus and bistro.

trivia

Built in 1857, the *Park House* is the oldest residence in Saugatuck, and among the guests who have spent a night there was Susan B. Anthony. Today the Park House (800-321-4535; parkhouseinn.com) is a bed-and-breakfast inn.

Today the brick and stone building is reached by crossing a footbridge over the east branch of the Paw Paw River, which gurgles its way through the shaded grounds and around an outdoor deck. The whole setting is one of idyllic enjoyment. A self-guided tour of Warner's champagne caves will answer the question of how they get the bubbles into the bottle, or skip the tour and simply stop for a little wine tasting.

Warner Vineyards (800-756-5357; warnerwines.com) is reached from I-94 by taking exit 60 and heading north on M 40 into Paw Paw. The winery is at 706 S. Kalamazoo St. and open from 10 a.m. to 5 p.m. Mon through Sat and noon to 5 p.m. Sun.

Just down the road in Paw Paw at 716 S. Kalamazoo St. is the *St. Julian Winery,* the state's oldest and largest vineyard. Founded in 1921, St. Julian (800-732-6002; stjulian.com) produces 40 types of wines and also offers tours and tasting as well. Open Memorial Day to Labor Day (give or take) Mon to Fri from 11 a.m. to 8 p.m., Sat and Sun from 9 a.m. to 9 p.m.

Allegan County

On the map *Saugatuck* looks like just the next beachfront community along the lake, but in reality it is a trendy resort whose streets are lined with fine restaurants, quaint shops, and lots of tourists. Perhaps the most striking sight in Saugatuck are the docks along the Kalamazoo River, where moored at the edge of the shopping district is an armada of cabin cruisers and sailboats 30, 40, or 50 feet in length or even longer. You can pick up the boardwalk that winds past the boats anywhere along Water Street, and if you follow it north, eventually you'll come to the most unusual vessel afloat, the *Saugatuck Chain Ferry* (269-857-1701). It's the only chain-powered ferry in the state and has been carrying passengers across the Kalamazoo River since 1838. An operator hand-cranks a 380-foot chain attached at each shore, pulling the small white ferry through the water.

It's only $1 for the 5-minute ride, and it is your escape from the bustling downtown shopping district to one of the most beautiful beaches on the lake. Once on the other side, you walk north for a few hundred yards until you reach *Mount Baldhead Park,* with tables, shelter, and a dock on the river. There is also a stairway that takes you (after a little huffing and puffing) to the top of the 200-foot dune, where you are greeted with a glorious panorama of Saugatuck, Kalamazoo Lake to the southeast, and Lake Michigan to the west. On the other side you have a choice. You can descend to *Oval Beach* along the Northwoods Trail, an easy walk that includes a view of the lake and beach along the way. Or you can dash madly down the steep and sandy Beach Trail, right off the towering dune, across the beach, and into the lake for a cool dip.

Saugatuck's most entertaining tour by far is *Harbor Duck Adventures.* It's almost impossible to miss this big, blue half-boat and half-truck wheeling through town. What was an amphibious vessel in World War II has been turned into a 20-passenger wet taxi that offers a forty-five-minute narrated tour of Saugatuck and Douglas and even crosses the Kalamazoo River between them. Even better, you are free to leave the vessel to shop trendy Saugatuck and then board a later tour.

Harbor Duck Adventures (269-857-3825; harborduck.com) departs Coughlin Park at Colver Street in Saugatuck every hour from 10 a.m. to 7 p.m. May through Sept. Fare for adults is $17 and $9 for children 6 to 12, $5 for children 3 to 5.

Moving inland, another interesting attraction is the old *Allegan County Jail* in Allegan. Seriously. The imposing redbrick building was built in 1906 and features Greek Revival architecture with a peaked roof and columns along the porch. It has bars on the windows, a hexagonal turret in the corner, and a three-story grandeur that is lacking in its newer counterpart across the street.

But most unusual is the small red sign on Walnut Street that says *Allegan County Old Jail Museum.* Go to jail and get a history lesson in penitentiary punishment. Within the museum are a variety of exhibits, including a country store loaded with 19th-century merchandise, a display devoted to Allegan's General Benjamin Pritchard, whose men captured Confederate President Jefferson Davis during the Civil War, and a historical laundry room.

But coat hangers and wringers are not what draw more than 1,000 visitors to the museum every year. It's a macabre fascination with slammers and pokeys. To that end, a guide leads you through the sheriff's living quarters and the large kitchen, where his wife would prepare meals for up to thirty prisoners a night and then pass plates through a small door in

trivia

Beneath the sand near the mouth of the Kalamazoo River on Lake Michigan lies the site of *Singapore,* one of Michigan's most famous ghost towns. The town was founded in the 1830s by New York land speculators who hoped it would rival Chicago or Milwaukee as a lake port. Singapore bustled as a lumbering town for almost forty years, but once the trees were gone by the 1870s, the residents fled.

the wall. On the second floor are rows of 6-by-8-foot cells, complete with the graffiti that disheartened convicts scratched on the walls in the 1930s. You can even walk through the maximum-security cells, now filled with a historical toy collection, view the old padded cell, and examine the holding pen for "ladies."

The Old Jail Museum (269-673-8292; alleganoldjail.org) is open 10 a.m. to 4 p.m. Fri and Sat and there is no admission. To reach the museum, take M 222 (exit 55) off US 131 and head west into Allegan. The old jail is at 113 Walnut St., between Hubbard and Trowbridge.

Ottawa County

Every spring Holland bursts into a rainbow of colors thanks to the millions of tulips that residents plant seemingly everywhere. The event climaxes during the *Tulip Time Festival* (800-822-2770; tuliptime.com) in mid-May, when the flowers are in full bloom and the Dutch-founded city hosts more than a half-million visitors, who book hotel rooms months in advance.

But historical Holland can be an interesting trip the rest of the year as well. Founded in 1847 by Dutch religious dissenters, Holland celebrated its sesquicentennial in 1997 and today is the undisputed center of Dutch culture in Michigan. For a dose of old Holland, visit Nelis's *Dutch Village.* This fifteen-acre theme park is a re-created 19th-century Dutch village complete with canals, tulip gardens, and historical displays along with some kitschy attractions like a wooden-shoe slide to keep the kids happy. Among the many buildings are a wooden-shoe factory and Queen's Inn, Holland's only restaurant serving Dutch food.

At the wooden shoe factory, shoes are carved by hand and with antique automated machines. Try on a pair of klompen (wooden shoes), feed the farm animals, ride the restored antique carousel, and take a big swing on the Zweefmolen (Dutch Swing Ride). There is no extra charge for rides. Adults can step onto the Heksenwaag (a 200-year-old witch's scale) to find out who is guilty of witchcraft, hand crank an Amsterdam street organ, and sample Dutch specialty foods. Educational movies, enjoyed by both adults and children, are shown throughout the day. A Klederdracht (costume) Museum features authentic costumes in typical settings and a doll exhibit showcases 150 provincial costumes. New attractions include pedal-pumper cars, Dutch cheese making, Dutch Delftware making, Dutch dancing lessons, and walking the goat. Dutch Village (800-285-7177; dutchvillage.com) is along US 31, 2 miles northeast of downtown Holland. From Apr through mid-Oct the grounds are open from 10 a.m. to 5:30 p.m. daily with longer hours during Tulip Time. Admission is $10 for adults and $7 for children.

Windmill Island is a city park that features **De Zwaan,** the only working Dutch windmill allowed to be shipped out of the Netherlands. The 5-story-high windmill is still operating as it grinds whole wheat flour that is sold in shops nearby. Also at Windmill Island are the Posthouse Museum, Little Netherlands Museum, an 1895 carousel, and 36 acres of manicured gardens, dikes, canals, and picnic areas. The park (616-355-1030 or 888-535-5792; windmillisland.org) is just northeast of downtown Holland at Seventh and Lincoln Streets and open mid-Apr through mid-Oct 9:30 a.m. to 5 p.m. daily. Admission is $7.50 for adults and $4.50 for children ages 5 to 15.

Holland also has two wooden-shoe factories where you can buy the oaken loafers or simply see a demonstration of how they are made. The best is the **Deklomp Wooden Shoe & Delft Factory,** which also includes a display on the many kinds of wooden shoes worn in Europe. The Wooden Shoe Factory (616-399-1900; veldheer.com) is off US 31 just south of Sixteenth Street at 12755 Quincy Ave. Hours are 9 a.m. to 5 p.m. daily from Apr through Oct. At this double Dutch delight, you can talk with the artists as they mold, hand-paint, and glaze the only authentic blue and white delftware made in the US, or watch the wooden shoe carving on machines that were imported from the Netherlands. All handmade items, and other Dutch delicacies, are available for purchase.

Grand Haven has developed its waterfront along the Grand River and includes a riverwalk that extends several miles from downtown to the picturesque **Grand Haven Lighthouse** (grandhaven.org), out in Lake Michigan. But by far the most noted aspect of the river is the city's **Musical Fountain,** the world's largest, which performs nightly during the summer with electronically controlled and synchronized music. Performances begin around dusk and most people enjoy the free concerts by assembling in the Waterfront Stadium. Nightly performances begin Memorial Day weekend and run until Labor Day. From Labor Day through Sept, performances are only on Fri and Sat.

Muskegon County

In the late 1800s this county was the heart of lumbering on Michigan's western side, and the city of **Muskegon** grew during the prosperous era to be known as the Lumber Queen of the World. A drive down W. Webster Avenue shows how much money was made and where much of it went: The Victorian mansions are fabulous. The most elaborate houses were built by the two men who prospered most of all from Michigan white pine, Charles H. Hackley and his partner, Thomas Hume. They built their homes next to each other, and it reportedly took 200 artisans and craftsmen two years to complete the houses. Behind the homes the men shared the same carriage house. The **Hackley House** and **Hume House** are listed on the National Register of Historic Places and have been called two of the nation's most outstanding examples of Victorian architecture.

Although restoration continues, the homes are open for tours. The Hackley House is especially impressive, a virtual museum of carved woodwork that strikes you from the moment you walk into the home and are greeted by unusual figures along the walls. Almost every aspect of the house is overwhelming, from its original furnishings and stained-glass windows to the hand-stenciled walls and the 11 fireplaces, each made unique with imported ceramic tiles. If you see only one restored home in Michigan, it should be the Hackley House, where it's hard to imagine living in such style.

trivia

The world's largest weather vane is located in Montague. Erected in 1884 by the Whiteall Metal Studios across the street, the vane is 48 feet tall and weighs 3,500 pounds. It has a 26-foot-long arrow and directional letters that are 3 feet, 6 inches tall, and is topped off by a 14-foot-long schooner. The vane is right off Business US 31 in a park overlooking the town harbor.

The **Hackley and Hume Historic Site** (231-722-7578; muskegonmuseum.org) is at 484 W. Webster Ave. Tours are offered May through Oct, Wed through Sun from noon to 4 p.m. Admission is $3 for adults.

Another interesting museum in Muskegon is partly underwater. The USS *Silversides* is a US Navy submarine that was commissioned just eight days after the Japanese attacked Pearl Harbor on December 7, 1941. It went on to serve in the Pacific Fleet

Cruising to Milwaukee

Bored with Michigan or just hungry for a good bratwurst? An interesting side trip from Muskegon is Milwaukee. Wisconsin's beer-and-brat capital is only a 2.5-hour ride away thanks to *Lake Express LLC* (866-914-1010; lake-express.com). The company's high-speed catamaran connects the two cities with 3 round-trips across Lake Michigan daily from July through Aug and 2 trips daily in May, June, Sept, and Oct. During the summer you can arrive at Milwaukee before noon and not leave until 7 p.m. That's a lot of brats and fried cheese curds.

The round-trip fare for passengers is $135 for adults, $40 for children, and $165 if you choose to take your vehicle.

during World War II and ranked third among all US submarines for enemy ships sunk. Today *Silversides* is docked at the Muskegon Channel Wall in Père Marquette Park at 1346 Bluff St. and is the main attraction of the **Great Lakes Naval Memorial and Museum.**

The museum itself, at 1346 Bluff St., opened its doors in 2009 and features military exhibits, a theater, and a gift shop. From there guides lead tours on the USCGC *McLane*, a Prohibition-era "buck-and-a-quarter boat" (125 feet long) that earned the honor of sinking an enemy vessel during WWII, and then USS *Silversides*. The 312-foot-long submarine is often the first one most visitors have ever boarded and they find the cramped torpedo rooms, crew quarters, and the galley fascinating.

Great Lakes Naval Memorial and Museum (231-755-1230; silversides-museum.org) and the USS *Silversides* are open daily May through Oct from 10 a.m. to 5:30 p.m. and weekdays from 10 a.m. to 4 p.m. the rest of the year. Admission is $15 for adults and $10.50 for children.

The towering dunes along the eastern side of Lake Michigan are the world's largest accumulation of dunes bordering a body of fresh water and are renowned throughout the country. One of the best places for learning about dunes is the **Gillette Sand Dune Visitor Center** within P. J. Hoffmaster State Park. This beautiful facility was built in 1976 as a bicentennial project and then totally renovated in 2002. It's located at the base of Mt. Baldy, a towering sand dune, and its west wall is a 2-story viewing window where visitors can stare up at the migrating mountain of sand. As Michigan's

Michigan's Best: Dune Climbs

The first time my children saw the Dune Climb in Sleeping Bear Dunes National Lakeshore, it might as well have been Mt. Everest. And in a way it was. Climbing it was a knee-bender. Reaching the top was exhilarating. Bounding and leaping down the steep sandy slope is as close as they have ever come to rappelling.

In Michigan, a towering sand dune is the first mountain every kid (and their parents) needs to conquer. There is certainly no shortage of sand on the west side of the state but here are our top five dune climbs in no particular order:

Pikes Peak: In the 1970s Warren Dunes State Park (269-426-4013) was one of the most popular places to hang glide in Michigan. That's how steep and high its dunes are. Today thousands climb Pikes Peak in the day-use area to enjoy the views of Berrien County and the wide sandy beaches that greet them at the end of their romp.

Mount Baldhead: From downtown Saugatuck, you can hop on the city's Chain Ferry for a quick ride across Kalamazoo River and then tackle the 282 steps to the top of this 220-foot-high dune. Three routes lead down the other side; Northwoods Trail and South Ridge Trail are gentle descents through the woods. Skip them for Beach Trail, a wild run down through the sand that will have you at Saugatuck's beautiful Oval Beach (269-857-1701) in minutes.

Tunnel Park: This 22-acre Ottawa County park is home to a 140-foot dune with a tunnel through the middle of it so visitors can easily reach the beach on the west side. The east side of the sandy mountain is roped off as a dune climb and features a long staircase to make the climb even easier. From US 131 depart at the Lakewood Boulevard exit and head west to Lakeshore Drive where Tunnel Park (616-738-4810) is just a quarter mile to the south.

Silver Lake State Park: Lying between Silver Lake and Lake Michigan is a strip of some of the largest and purest dunes in the state, giant mountains of windblown sand, lacking trees, scrub, even dune grass. From the Dune Pedestrian Parking Area, it's a 10-minute hike to the dunes that tower right above the beaches on Silver Lake's west side. Run and dive! From US 31, depart at Shelby Road and head west for 6 miles to County Road B15 and follow the signs to Silver Lake State Park (231-873-3083).

Dune Climb: This is the original, a steep sandy slope that rises 130 feet above a picnic area in Sleeping Bear Dunes National Lakeshore (231-326-5134) near Empire. It's a major effort for little legs but the view of Glen Lake from the top is stunning and the run back down wild.

official sand dune interpretive center, Gillette is a natural history museum filled with state-of-the-art displays devoted to the state's unique sand dunes.

Its main exhibit hall is entitled "Michigan Coastal Sand Dunes . . . Like Nowhere Else on Earth" and features dioramas that depict dune habitats in all seasons, an animation station where visitors can see how sand dunes are formed, and an interactive computer station that outlines the great sand dune areas in the state. There is also an 82-seat auditorium where multimedia presentations on the dunes are shown, a gift shop, and classrooms that host a wide range of nature programs throughout the year.

Most visitors view the exhibits and then tackle **Dune Climb Stairway** that begins near the center. This 193-step structure climbs 190 feet to the top of one of the park's largest parabolic dunes where an observation deck gives way to a sweeping view of Lake Michigan and the surrounding sand dunes. There is a vehicle permit fee to enter the state park (231-798-3573), which is reached by heading south of Muskegon on US 31, exiting at Pontaluna Road, and heading west. The Gillette Visitor Center at 6585 Lake Harbor Dr. is open daily during summer from 10 a.m. to 5 p.m.; the rest of the year, hours are Tues through Fri noon to 4 p.m. and Sat 10 a.m. to 4 p.m. The center is closed mid-Nov through mid-Jan for annual maintenance.

Newaygo County

The most distinctive structure in the southern Newaygo County town of **Grant** is its wooden water tower. Built in 1891, it's the classic *Petticoat Junction* water tower, the last one standing in the state. Driving down Main Street, you half expect to see Uncle Joe and the rest of the cast from that zany old sitcom.

Drive through the town to see the water tower, but stop because of its train depot. Chuck Zobel has transformed the once bustling passenger station into the **Grant Depot Restaurant,** one of the county's best eateries—unless you're a railroad enthusiast, then it's a fascinating train museum that serves a very good Mile High Lemon (meringue) Pie.

After purchasing the empty depot in 1979, Zobel spent a year renovating it, and in the process of tearing down walls and replacing floors, he turned up a variety of artifacts from the era of the iron horse: tickets and train orders from 1903, bottles, telegrams, signs, even the remains of a copper sulfate battery that powered the telegraph before the age of electricity. Today you can sit at a table in what a century ago was the passenger waiting room, or in a bay window overlooking the tracks, where a station agent once worked a telegraph. What was the baggage room is now the kitchen, and the dining room walls are covered with memorabilia—from lanterns and oilcans to warning lights, tickets, and an engineer's manual on how to operate a locomotive.

trivia

One of the most unusual festivals in Michigan is the *Blessing of the Bikes*, which is held the third weekend in May in Baldwin. Hundreds of motorcyclists, many of them riding classic Harley-Davidsons, arrive in town for the weekend and gather on Sunday at the local airstrip to have their bikes blessed by a priest.

The Grant Depot Restaurant (231-834-7361) is open from 5:30 a.m. to 8 p.m. Mon through Thurs, 5:30 a.m. to 9 p.m. Fri and Sat, and 8 a.m. to 3 p.m. Sunday. From I-96 in Grand Rapids, head north on M 37 (exit 30). Grant is reached in 24 miles, and the depot is right off M 37 at 22 W. Water St.

Wildflower lovers ought to stay on M 37 in Newaygo County to reach the *Loda Lake Wildflower Sanctuary*. In 1938, Forest Service rangers invited the Federated Garden Clubs of Michigan to help them create a sanctuary for native plants, including endangered and protected species, to ensure their survival. Although part of the Manistee National Forest, the preserve is still managed by the Federated Garden Clubs, and over the years it has evolved into a unique haven for botanists, wildflower enthusiasts, and families who just want to know the difference between Michigan holly and Holly, Michigan.

The self-guiding trail is a mile loop of easy hiking where you encounter the first numbered post in less than 20 feet, and before you return to the picnic area, you'll pass 38 others. The interpretive posts mark the locations of trillium, blueberries, swamp rose, insect-eating sundew plants, and fragrant water lily, among other plants, and they correspond to a trail guide available near the parking area.

From White Cloud head north on M 37 and then left on Five Mile Road, where the directional sign to Loda Lake is posted on the corner. Head a mile west and turn right on Felch Road. The entrance to the sanctuary is a mile to the north. For a trail guide, call or stop at the **US Forest Service Ranger Station** (231-745-4631) at 650 N. Michigan Ave. in Baldwin.

Lake County

When you look at a stump, what do you see? A stump? Is a tree root just a tree root? Not to Ray Overholzer. This hunting guide-turned-craftsman would stroll along the Père Marquette River, find a stump left over from Michigan's logging era, and see a table or maybe a piece of a rocking chair. Then he would spend months fashioning it by hand until his unique vision became reality. This is woodworking as an art, and it's preserved today at the **Shrine of the Pines,** a small but—to those of us who struggled in shop class just to build that birdhouse—intriguing museum.

Overholzer constructed a rocking chair from roots that is so perfectly balanced it rocks 55 times with a single push. His gun rack holds 12 hunting rifles and rotates on hand-carved wooden balls like ball bearings—not a screw or a hinge in the elaborate cabinet. A stump became a bootlegger's table with a hidden compartment for the whiskey bottle and another for the shot glasses. Perhaps most amazing is the dining room table that began as a 700-pound stump of a giant white pine. By the time Overholzer was done working with the piece of discarded wood, it was a 300-pound table with roots carved into legs and storage bins hollowed out of the sides. In 1940 and 1941 Overholzer built a huge lodge on the banks of the Père Marquette and originally intended to operate it as a hunting lodge. But his furniture was too dear to him by then and, fearing it would get scratched, he changed his mind. The intended lodge became a museum of more than 200 pieces, the world's only collection of handcrafted white pine furniture.

The Shrine of the Pines (231-745-7892; shrineofthepines.com) is open from 10 a.m. to 6 p.m. Mon through Sat and 1:30 to 6 p.m. Sun from mid-May to mid-Oct. Admission is $5 for adults and $12.50 for families.

Oceana County

County Road B-15 turns off from US 31 north of Whitehall and swings west toward Lake Michigan before returning to the highway at Pentwater, the bustling resort community at the northwest corner of Oceana County. Along the way the county road passes *Silver Lake,* an impressive sight that slows most cars bearing sightseers to a crawl. The lake is bordered to the west by a huge dune that towers over it, and from the car window you see beach and sunbathers, crystal clear lake and sailboats, the mountain of sand and dune climbers. Much of what you see, including the strip of dunes between the inland lake and Lake Michigan, is part of *Silver Lake State Park.*

Silver Lake is different from other state parks along Lake Michigan because the dunes have been divided into three areas for three types of users. The section in the middle is the pedestrian area, where people scramble up the huge dunes and hike across them to Lake Michigan.

The region to the south is one of only two places in the state where dune rides are offered in large open-air jeeps that hold up to 12 passengers. *Mac Wood's Dune Rides* date back to the 1930s, and today thousands enjoy the popular rides every year from early May through early October. The scenic 40-minute ride takes passengers through the heart of the Silver Lake dune country from the top of the tallest dunes to the edge of Lake Michigan. It's a wild ride down sandy hills and through the surf of Lake Michigan, but never too scary for small children to handle. The tour is even more spectacular near sunset on a clear summer evening.

Mac Wood's Dune Rides (231-873-2817; macwoodsdunerides.com) is on Sixteenth Avenue at Scenic Drive just south of the state park campground. Hours are 9:30 a.m. to sunset daily from Memorial Day to Labor Day. The cost is $17 for ages 12 and up, $11 for children 3 to 11.

Tiny *Hart,* population 1,900, is known for two things: asparagus and rail trails. Hart hosts the *National Asparagus Festival* (231-259-0170; nationalasparagusfestival.org) in the second weekend of June because Oceana County grows more of the green stuff per capita than anywhere else in the world. The 4-day event includes parades, farm tours, fun runs, and the opportunity to feast on the asparagus that has been prepared every which way, from dip to cakes.

Not into vegetables? Then arrive with your bicycle. Hart is the northern end of the *Hart-Montague Trail.* The 22.5-mile paved path became one of the first rail trails in Michigan when an abandoned track of the Chesapeake and Ohio Railroad was converted into recreational use in 1987. A trailhead with maps and parking is located in Hart's John Gurney Park. The northern 8 miles of the trail, from Hart to Shelby, is by far the most scenic section.

Mason County

Continue on S. Lakeshore Drive, pass the huge Ludington Power Plant, and then after a few miles keep an eye on the east side of the road for **Bortell's Fisheries.** From the outside the fish market is not glamorous, but it has been in business since 1937 and gradually has evolved into western Michigan's finest shop for fish and seafood. It carries a variety of frozen seafood, makes delicious marinated herring in cream and wine, and smokes one of the best selections of fish in the state, including trout, chub, salmon, sturgeon, blind robin, and menominee. Want something fresher? When in season, its cases are filled with fresh perch, pike, walleye, trout, and even smelt in the spring, all half buried in ice.

Still not fresh enough? Then you can wander around back with a pole and catch a rainbow trout out of one of its stocked ponds. Bortell's will cook any fresh fish right there in the market and serve it with french fries and homemade potato salad or coleslaw. You can enjoy your meal outside at one of a half dozen picnic tables next to the market, or better yet, cross the street to Summit Park, where you have a view of Lake Michigan from your

Lake Michigan Car Ferry

In 1897 the *Père Marquette* departed Ludington, offering the first ferry transportation across Lake Michigan between Michigan and Wisconsin. A century later you can still hop on a ferry for a trip to Manitowoc, Wisconsin, thanks to the **SS Badger,** the only steam-powered auto passenger ship on the Great Lakes.

Launched in 1952, the 410-foot ferry was extensively refurbished in 1991 and now includes staterooms, a maritime museum, food and beverage service, theater and bingo hall, an outdoor deck, and live entertainment. The 60-mile crossing takes 4 hours but saves you the 450-mile drive around the lake between the two cities. The cruise, a throwback to when luxurious steamers sailed the Great Lakes in the 1920s, is so popular that the company offers a single-day ticket. The round-trip fare for an adult without a vehicle is $128 and $39 per child.

In the summer the ferry departs Ludington at 8 a.m. and 7:55 p.m. and Manitowoc at 1:15 p.m. and 12:30 a.m. For tickets or reservations call the SS *Badger* at (800) 841-4243 or go online at ssbadger.com.

table. The freshest fish, good food, and beautiful scenery at a little out-of-the-way county park—it doesn't get much better than that.

Bortell's Fisheries (231-843-3337) is 7 miles south of Ludington on S. Lakeshore Drive between Meisenhiemer and Deren Roads. From May through Sept the store is open daily from 11 a.m. to 8 p.m. Cash only.

The first frame house in Mason County was built by Aaron Burr Caswell in 1849. Six years later the 2-story home was still the only frame building in an area that was trying to organize itself into Michigan's newest county. So that year Caswell offered the front half of his home as the first courthouse and county seat of Mason. Today the preserved building is a state historic site and the centerpiece of *White Pine Historic Village,* a museum complex operated by the Mason County Historical Society.

The village at 1687 S. Lakeshore Dr. is composed of some 20 preserved buildings or replicas, all from the surrounding county and set up along streets on a bluff overlooking Lake Michigan. Each of the buildings, which range from an 1840s trapper's log cabin to a hardware store of the early 1900s, is completely renovated inside and can be viewed on a leisurely self-guided walk. Throughout the village people in traditional dress ply their trades, everything from a blacksmith to a turn-of-the-20th-century housewife cooking on a woodstove to a violin maker.

What makes White Pine Village an enjoyable experience is the active visitor participation in the exhibits. A documented trial that was held in the Caswell home in the 1860s is reenacted today with visitors filling in as the jury, and 9 out of 10 times handing down the same verdict as the first time. A log chapel on the rise overlooking the area still holds a Sunday service,

Death of Father Jacques Marquette

Located on Lakeshore Drive just north of White Pine Village is a memorial to *Father Jacques Marquette,* a 45-foot-tall metal cross set in stone. The 17th-century missionary explorer is famous for founding St. Ignace and Sault Ste. Marie and for joining Louis Jolliet on a 3,000-mile paddle in discovering the Mississippi River. Realizing he was losing his health, Marquette tried to return to his beloved St. Ignace mission in 1675 but never made it. Instead he died on the banks of Lake Michigan in Buttersville at the site of the cross. He was buried here, but his remains were later exhumed and taken to St. Ignace for final burial.

Skyline Trail

Anyone who loves boardwalk paths with benches will savor the Skyline Trail, a short but spectacularly scenic hike in Ludington State Park. The path follows the crest of a wooded dune, and erosion of the original trail prompted the park staff to replace it with a boardwalk path in 1981. The two-year project included use of Air National Guard helicopters to airlift much of the lumber to the top of the dune.

The sweeping views of Lake Michigan and the park's open dune country are so good that numerous benches were built into the boardwalk. Sure, the trail is only a half mile long, but if you sat on every bench and admired the scene, it would take you most of the afternoon to hike it. The view from the bench at Post Number 11 is especially scenic as you gaze south at the miles of open dunes stretched out to the Lake Michigan shoreline, the Ludington Harbor Lighthouse, and, on a clear day, even the Silver Lakes dunes 25 miles away.

Beside the benches are 13 numbered posts along the boardwalk that correspond to information in a brochure available from map boxes at the foot of each staircase. They identify the three common evergreens in Michigan, explain dune country succession, and point out stumps and other remnants of the loggers who arrived in 1851 to cut down the white pine.

and afterward people are encouraged to help the village cooks and enjoy their fresh-baked treats.

White Pine Village (231-843-4808; historicwhitepinevillage.org) is open from late Apr until mid-Oct Tues through Sat from 10 a.m. to 5 p.m. In the summer the museum is also open 1 to 5 p.m. Sun. The museum complex is located off US 31, 3 miles south of Ludington, and is reached by exiting west onto Iris Road and then turning north at S. Lakeshore Drive for a quarter of a mile. Admission is $9 for adults, $6 for children, and $25 for families.

From Ludington the famous dunes of Lake Michigan continue to the north, and the area immediately adjacent to the city has been preserved as *Ludington State Park.* It's a popular place where visitors enjoy miles of beach, rolling dunes, and modern campgrounds, or a hike to historic Point Sable Lighthouse. Along with a 300-site campground, the state park (231-843-2423; michigandnr.com) also features the Great Lakes Interpretive Center, an unusual nature trail in Hamlin Lake for canoers, and a lighthouse that can only be reached on foot.

At the tip of the Big Sable Point is **Big Sable Point Lighthouse,** whose black-and-white tower is Ludington State Park's distinctive trademark. The classic structure was authorized by President James Buchanan in 1858 after the barge, *Neptune*, sank off the point and 37 people drowned. Actual construction began in 1866 and a year later its light was illuminated by Burr Caswell, Mason County's first resident and the first caretaker of the lighthouse.

The light was placed on the National Register of Historic Places in 1983 and today is an interesting maritime museum that is reached on foot by following the lighthouse service road or the beach, either one a 1.5-mile walk. The attached lightkeeper's residence contains furnished rooms, historic displays, and a gift shop. You can then climb a circular, iron stairway of 130 steps to the top of the tower and step outside. The view is worth every step as the park's sandy shoreline lies to the east and the blue horizon of Lake Michigan to the west.

Big Sable Point Lighthouse (231-845-7343; bigsablelighthouse.org) is open from 10 a.m. to 5 p.m. daily from May through Oct. Admission is $2 for adults and $1 for children. Outside there are picnic tables while nearby is the marked Lighthouse Trail that heads east to the heart of the park and the rest of the trail system.

Where Ludington State Park ends, the **Nordhouse Dunes** begin, a 1,900-acre preserve in Manistee National Forest that is not as well known or as frequently visited as the state park but is equally beautiful.

A Michigan governor called the Nordhouse Dunes "one of the most outstanding scenic resources" in the state, and in 1987 they were given a federal wilderness designation. What makes these dunes unique is that the area is entirely undeveloped. Travel through the dunes is only on foot either along 10 miles of easy-to-follow trails or by simply making your way across the open hills of sand. The area is the only place in Michigan where you can hike in and camp among the dunes. Because of its inaccessibility to motorized traffic, the dunes area also offers those willing to hike in the opportunity of having a beach to themselves along its 4 miles of sandy lakeshore.

Access into Nordhouse Dunes is through the Lake Michigan Recreation Area, a semiprimitive campground on the northern end of the preserve that is maintained by the national forest's **Manistee Ranger District** (231-723-2211). Trails into the dunes begin from the recreation area, which also contains 100 camping sites, a beach, and observation towers overlooking the lake. To reach the recreational area, take US 31 to Lake Michigan Road (also known as Forest Road 5629) located 10 miles south of Manistee. Follow Lake Michigan Road 8 miles west to the area. There is a $5 vehicle permit fee for exploring the dunes or for day use of the recreational area. There is a $16 nightly fee for camping.

Manistee County

Manistee is another lakeshore town that boomed during the lumbering era; at one time in the late 1800s, it boasted 32 sawmills and 17 millionaire lumber barons among its residents. Almost the entire town was destroyed in the Great Fire of 1871 on the same day Chicago experienced its famous blaze. One of the first buildings erected after the fiery mishap was the **Lyman Building,** which was a place of business throughout its existence until the Manistee County Historical Society turned it into the only "store-front museum" in the state.

The Lyman Building Museum is not just another county museum displaying local artifacts. The many fixtures, walk-in vault, and wraparound balcony have been preserved, and part of the first floor has been restored as an early drugstore with brass apothecary scales, pill makers, an impressive selection of antique medicines and balms, and fading posters on the walls selling Pe-Ru-Na, which "cures catarrh." The other half of the first floor is set up as a general store, while in the back is an old newspaper office with original Linotype machines. Upstairs are 10 more rooms, including a dentist's office, a bank, and the living room of an early 1900s home. The hallway between the rooms is filled with Victor talking machines and Victrolas. The Lyman Building Museum (231-723-5531; manisteemuseum.org), at 425 River St. in downtown Manistee, is open from 10 a.m. to 5 p.m. Mon through Sat from June through Sept; 10 a.m. to 5 p.m. Thurs through Sat, Jan through Mar; and 10 a.m. to 5 p.m. Tues through Sat, Apr through May and Oct through Dec. Admission is $3 for adults and students.

Manistee is a city full of museums and one of them isn't even on dry land. Permanently moored on Manistee Lake at the Moonlite Motel and Marina is the **SS City of Milwaukee,** the last traditional Great Lakes railroad car ferry still afloat. The 360-foot long steamship was built in 1931 for the Grand Trunk Western Railroad and could hold an entire freight train of 32 boxcars on its freight deck and 300 passengers on the cabin deck above. Its triple expansion engines were monsters at 1,400 horsepower each, and their combined power could propel the ship at 14 mph or break through 3 feet of solid ice. The ship served as "Rails Across the Water" until 1981 when the state of Michigan shut down its cross-lake ferry system.

Destined to be scrapped, the SS *City of Milwaukee* was saved by residents of her homeport, Frankfort, and in 2000 was declared a National Historic Landmark and towed to a new home in Manistee. Today this floating maritime museum offers guided tours that take you from the freight deck to the engine room to the wheelhouse to the Pullman staterooms and everywhere in between. In October the railroad ferry becomes a "Ghost Ship" haunted house to the delight of wide-eyed children. Visitors are invited to experience lodging aboard a 1920s Great Lakes steamship. Passenger, crew, and other cabins are available for overnight stays. Walk the decks and enjoy the stars from a deck chair or watch a movie in the observation room.

The SS *City of Milwaukee* (231-723-3587; carferry.com) is open for tours from 11 a.m. to 6 p.m. Thurs through Mon from June through Aug and on Fri, Sat, and Sun mid-Apr through mid-Sept. Admission is $8 for adults, $5 for children, and $25 for families. Overnights are $25 per single person, $15 per extra person in a cabin.

trivia

A historical marker in Orchard Beach State Park 2 miles north of Manistee commemorates the Great Fire of 1871. On October 8, the day the famous Chicago fire began, fires also broke out in Michigan after an exceptionally long, hot summer. Most of Holland and Manistee was ruined within hours, with the flames sweeping east across the state and eventually reaching Port Huron.

Places to Stay in the Lake Michigan Area

DOUGLAS

Sherwood Forest Bed & Breakfast
938 Center St.
(800) 838-1246
sherwoodforestbandb.com

GRAND HAVEN

Boyden House Bed & Breakfast
301 S. Fifth St.
(616) 846-3538
boydenhouse.com

Harbor House Inn
114 S. Harbor Dr.
(800) 841-0610
harborhousegh.com

LUDINGTON

Ludington Pier House
805 W. Ludington Ave.
(231) 845-7346
ludingtonpierhouse.com

Viking Arms Inn
930 E. Ludington Ave.
(231) 843-3441 or
(800) 748-0173
vikingarmsinn.com

MANISTEE

Lakeshore Motel
101 S. Lakeshore Dr.
(231) 723-2667
lakeshoremotelmanistee.com

Ramsdell Inn
399 River St.
(231) 398-7901
ramsdellinn.net

Riverside Motel
520 Water St.
(231) 723-3554

NEW BUFFALO

Harbor Grand Hotel
111 W. Water St.
(888) 605-6800
harborgrand.com

ONEKAMA

Portage Point Inn
8513 Portage Point Dr.
(231) 889-4222
portagepointinn.com

OTHER ATTRACTIONS

Curious Kids Museum
St. Joseph
(269) 983-2543
curiouskidsmuseum.org

Fernwood Botanic Gardens
Buchanan
(269) 695-6491
fernwoodbotanical.org

Manistee Fire Hall
Manistee

Ramsdell Theatre
Manistee
(231) 723-9948
ramsdelltheatre.org

Southwestern Michigan College Museum
Dowagiac
(800) 456-8675
museum.swmich.edu

Trillium Ravine
Niles

PENTWATER

Hexagon House
760 Sixth St.
(231) 869-4102
hexagonhouse.com

SAUGATUCK

Maplewood Hotel
428 Butler St.
(800) 650-9790
maplewoodhotel.com

Rosemont Inn
83 Lakeshore Dr.
(888) 767-3666
rosemontinn.com

Twin Gables Country Inn
900 Lake St.
(269) 857-4346 or
(800) 231-2185
twingablesinn.com

SOUTH HAVEN

Inn at the Park
233 Dyckman Ave.
(269) 639-1776
innpark.com

Old Harbor Inn
515 Williams St.
(800) 433-9210
oldharborinn.com

Sunset Inn
72 N. Shore Dr.
(800) 720-2468
sunsetinn.us

ST. JOSEPH

Boulevard Hotel
521 Lake Blvd.
(800) 875-6600
theboulevardinn.com

South Cliff Inn
1900 Lakeshore Dr.
(269) 983-4881
southcliffinn.com

UNION PIER

Inn at Union Pier
9708 Berrien St.
(269) 469-4700
innatunionpier.com

Lakeside Inn
15251 Lakeshore Rd.
(269) 469-0600

WHITE CLOUD

The Shack
2263 W. Fourteenth St.
(231) 924-6683
theshackbedandbreakfast
.com

Places to Eat in the Lake Michigan Area

BUCHANAN

Tabor Hill Winery
185 Mount Tabor Hill Rd.
(800) 283-3363
taborhill.com
Fine Dining

GRANT

Grant Depot Restaurant
22 W. Main St.
(231) 834-7361
American

HOLLAND

Alpen Rose
4 E. Eighth St.
(616) 393-2111
alpenroserestaurant.com
Austrian

Boatwerks Waterfront Restaurant
216 Van Raalte Ave.
(616) 396-0600
boatwerksrestaurant.com
American

84 East Food & Spirits
84 E. 8th St.
(616) 396-8484
Italian

LUDINGTON

Jamesport Brewing Company
410 S. James St.
(231) 845-2522
jamesportbrewing
company.com
Brewpub

Old Hamlin Restaurant
122 W. Ludington Ave.
(231) 843-4251
oldhamlin.com
American

P. M. Steamers
502 W. Loomis
(231) 843-9555
pmsteamers.com
American

SELECTED CHAMBERS OF COMMERCE & TOURISM BUREAUS

Grand Haven Area Convention and Visitors Bureau
225 Franklin Ave.
Grand Haven 49417
(800) 303-4092
visitgrandhaven.com

Holland Area Convention and Visitors Bureau
76 E. Eighth St.
Holland 49423
(800) 506-1299
holland.org

Ludington Convention and Visitors Bureau
5300 W. US 10
Ludington 49431
(877) 420-6618
pureludington.com

Manistee Convention and Visitors Bureau
310 First St.
Manistee 49660
(877) 626-4783
visitmanistee.com

Muskegon Convention and Visitors Bureau
610 Western Ave.
Muskegon 49440
(800) 250-9283
visitmuskegon.org

Saugatuck/Douglas Visitors Bureau
2902 Blue Star Hwy.
Douglas 49406
(269) 857-1701
saugatuck.com

South Haven Convention and Visitors Bureau
546 Phoenix Rd.
South Haven 49090
(800) 764-2836
southhaven.org

Southwestern Michigan Tourist Council
2300 Pipestone Rd.
Benton Harbor 49022
(269) 925-6301
swmichigan.org

MACATAWA

Piper Restaurant
2225 S. Shore Dr.
(616) 335-5866
piperrestaurant.com
American

MONTAGUE

Dog 'n Suds
4454 Dowling St.
(231) 894-4991
dog-n-suds.com
American

NEW BUFFALO

Casey's Bar & Grill
136 N. Whittaker
(269) 469-5800
caseysnewbuffalo.com
American

Ozzies Eatery
603 E. Buffalo St.
(269) 469-9437
American

ONEKAMA

Fish Tale Cafe
5159 Main St.
(231) 889-4099
American

PENTWATER

Boathouse Bar & Grille
5164 W. Monroe Rd.
(231) 869-4588
boathousebarandgrille
.com
American

SAUGATUCK & DOUGLAS

Everyday People Cafe
11 Center St.
(269) 857.4240
everydaypeoplecafe.com
Fine Dining

Mermaid Grill
360 Water St.
(269) 857-8208
mermaidofsaugatuck.com
Seafood

Saugatuck Brewing Company
2948 Blue Star Hwy.
(269) 857-7222
saugatuckbrewing.com
Brewpub

SOUTH HAVEN

The Idler
515 Williams St.
(269) 637-8435
millenniumrestaurants.com
Cajun

Tello Italian Bistro
524 Phoenix Rd.
(269) 639-9898
tellobistro.com
Italian

STEVENSVILLE

Tosi's
4337 Ridge Rd.
(269) 429-3689
tosis.com
Italian

ST. JOSEPH

Bistro on the Boulevard
521 Lake Blvd.
(269) 983-6600
theboulevardinn.com
Fine Dining

Clementine's Too
1235 Broad St.
(269) 983-0990
ohmydarling.com
American

THREE OAKS

Froehlich's
26 N. Elm St.
(269) 756-6002
shopfroehlichs.com
Bakery & Cafe

UNION PIER

Red Arrow Roadhouse
15710 Red Arrow Hwy.
(269) 469-3939
redarrowroadhouse.com
American

NORTHWEST MICHIGAN

In many ways Northwest Michigan is a continuation of the region stretching along Lake Michigan. It's accented by vast tracts of dunes, miles of beaches, and a handful of well-developed resort towns whose specialty shops bustle in the summer and winter. But it is also distinctly different.

This is "the land of many little bays," with scenic Grand Traverse Bay dominating the center of the region, Little Traverse Bay farther up the shoreline, and remote Sturgeon Bay at its northern tip. For many tourists this is Mackinaw City, a tour of Fort Michilimackinac, and a ferry ride to Mackinac Island, the summer resort island known throughout the country for its horse-and-carriage transportation and the Grand Hotel.

Most of all, this is Michigan's Cherry Country. Moderate weather from the Great Lakes and light soils help this region produce 80 to 85 percent of the state's total cherry crop. Drive along US 31 from Traverse City to Charlevoix in spring, and you'll pass rolling hills of trees in full bloom and air scented by cherry blossoms.

Arrive in July and you can enjoy the bountiful harvest these fruit farms produce. Along this 50-mile stretch of road,

you'll pass dozens of farms and will undoubtedly see harvesting crews "shaking" one tree after another, with the cherries ending up in a large metal tank of water.

You'll also see numerous roadside fruit stands that will be hard to pass up, and you shouldn't even try. The most common sweet cherries sold are Bing and Schmidt; tourists often call them black cherries, though if they are, the fruit is overripe. Look for cherries that are firm and dark maroon, and be prepared when you bite into your first one. The juice will explode from the cherry, dribble down your chin, and send your taste buds into a state of ecstasy. There are few things as wonderful in this state as a northern Michigan cherry in July.

Benzie County

One of the smallest counties in the state, Benzie is also one of the most scenic. It features rolling forested hills, spring-fed trout streams, towering sandy bluffs, and endless beaches along Lake Michigan and Crystal Lake, a body of water whose clarity lives up to its name. In the natural beauty of this north woods setting, Gwen Frostic emerged as one of Michigan's most noted poets and publishers from her background as an artist and a conservationist. Her love of nature has always been with her, but she began writing and carving blocks for prints in the mid-1940s in the blue-collar community of Wyandotte, south of Detroit. In the early 1960s she moved to a wooded spot 2 miles west of Benzonia and set up *Gwen Frostic Prints* on a personal wildlife sanctuary of 285 acres.

Her large gallery is housed in a building of native stone, glass, and old wood, which seeks to "bring the outdoors in" while blending into the natural surroundings. She accomplished that surprisingly well. Inside you'll walk below rough-cut beams past huge stone fireplaces and view the tumbling water of natural fountains. You'll be surrounded by Frostic's woodblock prints, tables covered with books of her poetry, and bird carvings by some of the country's leading wildlife carvers. There is a small library overlooking a pond where waterfowl usually are feeding, and another room displays all the honors she has received, including a Michigan governor's proclamation of an official "Gwen Frostic Day."

AUTHOR'S TOP TEN PICKS

Avalanche Peak
Boyne City
(231) 582-6222

Beaver Island
Charlevoix
(888) 446-4095
beaverisland.org

Dennos Museum Center
Traverse City
(231) 995-1055
dennosmuseum.org

Grass River Natural Area
Bellaire
(231) 533-8576
grassriver.org

Gwen Frostic Prints
Frankfort
(231) 882-5505
gwenfrostic.com

Historic Mill Creek Discovery Park
Mackinaw City
(231) 436-7301
mackinacparks.com

Michigan Forest Visitor Center
Hartwick Pines State Park
(989) 348-7068
michigan.gov/dnr

Pierce Stocking Scenic Drive
Empire
(231) 326-5134

South Manitou Island
Leland
(231) 256-9061
nps.gov

**Tunnel of Trees Shore Drive
and Legs Inn**
Cross Village
(231) 526-2281

Most impressive, perhaps, is the publishing aspect of the gallery. From a balcony above, visitors can view 12 original Heidelberg presses clanking away as workers print a wide selection of cards, notepaper, wall prints, and books, all using block designs carved by Frostic, featuring natural subjects and sold in the gallery.

Gwen Frostic Prints (231-882-5505; gwenfrostic.com) is at 5140 River Rd., 2 miles west of US 31 and 6 miles east of M 22 in Frankfort. The gallery is open from 9 a.m. to 4:30 p.m. daily from May through Sept and Mon and Fri the rest of the year. The presses are in operation only Mon through Fri.

More art in an unusual outdoor setting can be seen at the ***Michigan Legacy Art Park*** (231-378-4963; michlegacyartpark.org). This "gallery," a 30-acre forest at Crystal Mountain Resort on M 115 near Thompsonville, can be viewed any time of the year, even on cross-country skis in the winter, but is a perfect fall destination.

Scattered along a wooded ridge and reached by short footpaths are 35 major works of art, ranging from wind machines and poetry rocks to a winding piece that incorporates 3,500 cubic feet of oak logs. The park is open year-round from dawn to dusk, and in early October the outdoor sculptures are framed by colorful foliage that is almost as appealing as the art itself. Admission is a suggested donation of $3 per person or $10 per family.

Back in the 1930s a small group of Frankfort residents discovered the thrill of soaring in gliders. They would take off from the high bluffs overlooking Lake Michigan and fly through the air, sometimes for hours, before landing on the beach. What emerged was the ***Northwest Soaring Club of Frankfort,*** which at one time hosted a national soaring championship in this small town.

trivia

In 1873 a canal was built to Lake Michigan that drained the water out of inland Crystal Lake. The level of Crystal Lake dropped 25 feet, creating the beautiful beaches that make it such a popular resort area today. The canal, on the other hand, eventually became a swamp.

The art of soaring has changed over the years, but the club is still around, offering lessons and, for visitors passing through on vacation, introductory rides. Passengers join a certified pilot in a 2-seat glider 25 to 35 feet long, with a wingspan of about 50 feet. The glider is towed to a height of 2,000 to 3,000 feet by a small plane and then released. What follows is a spectacular ride along the Lake Michigan shoreline with extensive views of the lake, sand dunes, and beautiful Crystal Lake. The length of the ride depends on the wind and thermal conditions, but it ranges from 30 minutes to sometimes several hours.

Introductory rides are offered from May through Oct and cost $35 per person for a 3,000-foot tow, $45 for a 4,000-foot tow, and $85 for a 5,300-foot tow. The higher the tow, the longer the flight. Participants also must pay a daily membership fee of $50. Interested persons should contact the Northwest Soaring Club (231-352-9160; northwestsoaringclub.org). Club rides take off from Frankfort Airport, located on Airport Road south of M 115.

Of all the dunes along Lake Michigan, the best known are those in ***Sleeping Bear Dunes National Lakeshore,*** administered by the National

Hit the Trail in Michigan

When somebody in Michigan tells you to "hit the trail" they mean it . . . literally. That's because the state is blessed with thousands of trails and footpaths. The Michigan State Park system and four National Forests are laced with nature walks, footpaths, and mountain bike areas, while crisscrossing the state are more than 2,000 miles of rail trails. Isle Royale National Park has 160 miles of hiking trails; Michigan State Forests have 65 pathways that total 750 miles. The North Country Trail crosses the Upper Peninsula and then the Lower Peninsula for a hike of 1,150 miles!

Where to find a path? Here are a few websites that will lead you to the trail of your choice:

michigantrails.org: Go to the Michigan Trails & Greenways Alliance and click on "Trail Finder" to locate a rail trail.

mmba.org/trail-guide: The Michigan Mountain Biking Association has information on more than 100 mountain bike trails across the state.

northcountrytrail.org: On the North Country Trail Association website you'll find maps and descriptions for much of the NCT in Michigan and other states.

michigantrailmaps.com: Maps, photos, and descriptions for hiking and backpacking trails around the state with the ability to locate them by county.

traversetrails.org: Traverse City is home to Michigan's premier trail network, all managed by TART Trails and used by cyclists, inline skaters, Nordic skiers, hikers, and mountain bikers.

Park Service. Thousands of people visit the area every year, and many head straight to the **Dune Climb,** a 150-foot-steep hill of sand located right off M 109 in Leelanau County. This is the park's most famous feature, a kneebending climb up the towering dune and a wild run down through the soft sand. In addition, there are other aspects of the park, many having nothing to do with dunes and often overlooked by visitors who rush through the area in an afternoon.

The national lakeshore begins in Benzie County and includes one of the most scenic beaches on Lake Michigan. **Platte River Point** is a long, sandy spit divided from the mainland by the crystal clear Platte River. It's pure sand, this narrow strip, with endless Lake Michigan on one side, the knee-deep salmon and trout river on the other, and panoramas of towering dunes off in the distance. To reach it, sunbathers turn west from M 22 onto the marked Lake Michigan Road and follow it to the end. Then it's a quick wade through the rippling waters of the Platte River with dad holding a young one or the picnic lunch high on his shoulder. There is no bridge.

People at Platte River Point swim, build sand castles, and beachcomb as on any other beach, but the favorite activity here is floating. They bring out an old inner tube or an air mattress, hike a few hundred yards up the point, and then let the Platte River give them a free ride right out to Lake Michigan if they wish. It's debatable who enjoys it more, the kids or the parents. If you don't have an inner tube, you can rent one from *Riverside Canoe Trips* (231-325-5622; canoemichigan.com) located on M 22 right before you turn off for the beach. Tubes for 1 to 4 people can be rented, and there are drop-off and pickup services for those who want to spend an afternoon "tubing" the Platte River from the Platte Lake to the Great Lake. Rental rates depend on the length of your float and the size of your tube.

Best Cherry Pie in Northern Michigan

A sure way to start an argument in northern Michigan is to ask who bakes the best cherry pie in this land of cherries. You're bound to get a wide range of opinions, and one of them will surely be the Cherry Hut.

Located in Beulah, right on US 31, the **Cherry Hut** has been around since 1922 and has been run by the Case family since 1959. Locals call the smiling cherry on the restaurant sign "Cherry Jerry" and know it marks a good place to go for turkey dinners or giant cinnamon rolls.

But it's a thick slice of cherry pie, made with locally grown tart cherries and wrapped in a golden flaky crust, that is the Cherry Hut's claim to fame and why it has received recognition from such national media powerhouses as the *New York Times, People* magazine, *Bon Appétit* magazine, and National Public Radio. The fruit in the pies is so fresh that on the menu is this warning: "Cherries may contain an occasional pit."

The Cherry Hut (231-882-4431; cherryhutstore.com) is open from Memorial Day weekend through Oct from 11 a.m. to 8 p.m., serving lunch and dinner. A slice of cherry pie is $2.95, and a whole pie is $7.75.

Might as well buy a whole pie—they're that good.

TOP ANNUAL EVENTS

MAY

National Morel Mushroom Hunting Festival
Boyne City
(231) 582-6222
morelfest.com

JULY

Alpenfest
Gaylord
(800) 345-8621

Au Sable River Canoe Marathon and River Festival
Grayling
(989) 348-4425
ausablecanoemarathon.org

Blissfest
Cross Village
(231) 348-7047
blissfest.org

National Cherry Festival
Traverse City
(231) 947-4230
cherryfestival.org

AUGUST

Buckley Old Engine Show
Buckley
buckleyoldengineshow.org

Traverse City Film Festival
(231) 392-1134
traversecityfilmfest.org

Harbor Days
Elk Rapids
(231) 342-1058
elkrapidsharbordays.org

Suttons Bay Art Fair
Suttons Bay
(231) 271-9895
suttonsbayartfestival.org

Waterfront Art Fair
Charlevoix
(231) 547-2675
charlevoixwaterfrontartfair.org

SEPTEMBER

Celtic Festival
Beaver Island
(231) 448-2505
beaverisland.org

Harbor Springs Cycling Classic
Harbor Springs
(800) 530-9955
birchwoodinn.com

OCTOBER

Apple Festival
Charlevoix
(234) 547-2101

You can relive the 1950s and catch a flick in Benzie County at the *Cherry Bowl Drive-In,* Northern Michigan's last drive-in movie theater. The drive-in has been showing movies since 1953 and still honors that swinging era by serving malts and chili fries in its diner while workers dress as if they were in the cast of *Happy Days*. Admission includes 2 movies, and kids 12 years old and younger get in free. Families haven't paid so little to see a movie since, well, the 1950s.

Cherry Bowl Drive-In (231-325-3413; cherrybowldrivein.com) is on US 31 just a mile west of Honor at 9812 Honor Hwy. Admission for adults is $8.50. The drive-in promises that it will never show any movie stronger than PG-13 or any movie that glorifies teen drinking or drug use.

Leelanau County

For a view of spectacular dune terrain, take a ride along the **Pierce Stocking Scenic Drive** at Sleeping Bear Dunes National Lakeshore. Often called "the slowest, shortest, but most scenic stretch of pavement in the state," the drive is only a 7.4-mile loop but passes three stunning overlooks of the national lakeshore's perched dunes. Pierce Stocking, the self-taught naturalist who built the road in the early 1960s and operated it until his death in 1976, charged each car $2. The next year the National Park Service took over the road and changed its name to honor the man who'd built it.

The speed limit is only 15 miles per hour, but even that seems fast at times. Along with the scenic viewing points of the dunes and the sweeping shoreline, there are also 12 interpretive stops that correspond with information in a brochure provided at the fee station. From the Dune Overlook you can also walk the Cottonwood Trail, a short nature trail that leads you to within view of the Dune Climb. Feel energetic? There is also a bicycle lane along the road, but keep in mind that it's a very hilly bike ride. Above all, pack a lunch and plan to picnic at the Lake Michigan Overlook.

The entrance to Pierce Stocking Scenic Drive is on M 109, 3 miles north of the **Sleeping Bear Dunes National Lakeshore Visitor Center** (231-326-5134; nps.gov/slbe) in Empire. A weekly or annual vehicle pass is required to enter the drive.

The dunes are one of the main attractions of the area today. At the turn of the 20th century, however, the noted feature was the **Manitou Passage,** between the Manitou Islands and the mainland. During the heyday of Great Lakes shipping from the 1860s to 1920, when a hundred vessels might pass through on a single day, this was a shoal-lined shortcut they all took. The narrow Manitou Passage's shallow, reeflike shoals, and often violent weather, produced more than their share of shipwrecks, and eventually several lighthouses and lifesaving stations were built on the mainland and the islands.

One of them has been preserved by the National Park Service as *Sleeping Bear Point Coast Guard Station Maritime Museum.* The facility began its service in 1901 as a US Life-Saving Station and was actually situated on Sleeping Bear Point. When a migrating sand dune threatened to bury it in 1930, the US Coast Guard (having replaced the US Life-Saving Service) moved the buildings 1.5 miles toward Glen Haven. The station ended its duty in 1942 and now is a well-restored museum that tells the story of the US Life-Saving Service, which monitored the coastline all around the country.

Anywhere from 6 to 10 men would live at the remote station, and their former living quarters, a huge 2-story building, is now the main exhibit area. It allows visitors a glimpse of the regimented work they performed and the isolated life they lived. Nearby the boathouse contains the lifesaving boats, complete with tracks down to the beach for a quick launch, and other equipment, including the beachcart. When ships ran aground within 400 yards of shore, the lifesavers would pull out the beachcart and use the

Michigan's Famous Dune Climb

The Dune Climb in Sleeping Bear Dunes National Lakeshore is the most popular dune to climb in Michigan and possibly the country. Park officials estimate that more than 300,000 people climb it annually . . . or try to. This is no easy climb.

It's 130 feet to the top of the first hill at the Dune Climb and another 130 feet to the top of the second hill, or a total ascent of 260 feet. Jockey's Ridge on the Outer Banks of North Carolina, the largest dune on the Atlantic coast, is just a little over 100 feet. Then there is the fact that you're trudging through soft sand that gives way under each step. You may be taking a 12-inch step up the dune but the sand gives way underneath and your foot slides down 8 inches. Thus the net gain is only 4 inches, so in reality you will climb the dune three times before reaching the top.

The Dune Climb is a little easier to climb in the spring when the sand just below the surface is still damp, but it gets harder as thousands of visitors churn up the sand to dry in the summer sun. The easiest time to climb is a cool, cloudy day just after a rainfall. No matter when you climb or how hard it is, the effort is well spent as the view of Glen Lake to the east is stunning, one of the best in Sleeping Bear Dunes National Lakeshore.

small cannon on it to shoot a guideline to the distressed vessel. That rope was used to string more lines across the water, and a breeches buoy was sent to the ship on a pulley. Then, one by one, sailors would step into the breeches buoy and ride the line to the shore and safety. The museum is open daily from 11 a.m. to 5 p.m. from Memorial Day through Labor Day, and noon to 5 p.m. Sat and Sun Sept through mid-Oct. A vehicle permit is required to enter. Check with the park headquarters (231-326-5134) for other information. During summer at 3 p.m. each day, there is a re-enactment of a breeches buoy rescue drill using Raggedy Ann and Andy as shipwreck victims. Children are encouraged to participate in the drill.

From the Dune Climb, M 109 climbs to a panoramic view of Lake Michigan and the Manitou Islands then sharply descends to Grand Haven on the shores of Lake Michigan.

What used to be lumber baron D. H. Day's company town in the mid-1800s is now the *Glen Haven Historic District* with several of the buildings restored as museums.

You can view a collection of historic wooden boats and motors at the *Cannery Boathouse,* watch a blacksmith turn iron into horseshoes at the *Blacksmith Shop,* and step inside the *Glen Haven General Store* as it appeared in the 1920s.

A vehicle permit is required to visit Glen Haven. The General Store (231-334-3710) is open noon to 5 p.m. daily from July to Labor Day and the same hours on Fri, Sat, and Sun in May and June. The Blacksmith Shop and the Cannery Boathouse have slightly shorter hours, depending on volunteers.

Just east of Glen Haven is *Glen Arbor,* a small village on M 22 that bustles in the summer with shops, restaurants, and galleries. One of the most unusual stores is *Cherry Republic,* the self-proclaimed world's largest cherry retailer whose goal is "to put a cherry in every home."

Needless to say, everything here is cherry. In the Cherry Republic cafe you can choose from 12 different flavors of cherry ice cream, sip a glass of cherry lemonade, or feast on a cherry hotdog, cherry hamburger, or cherry chili. Next door in its Winery, people taste sparkling cherry wine or cherry ginger ale while its Great Hall of the Republic is a store stocked with everything from dried cherries and jars of cherry salsa to salad bowls carved out of cherry wood.

Leelanau Cheese

From humble beginnings as a converted gas station in Omena come Michigan's most honored cheesemakers, Anne and John Hoyt of Leelanau Cheese. The couple began producing handcrafted wedges of raclette cheese and containers of fromage blanc in the former gas station in 1995 after learning the cheese-making trade in Switzerland. Raclette is a semihard Swiss melting cheese made from whole cow's milk, with each 8-pound wheel aging 90 days before it is sold.

Eventually the couple was honored as the state's top cheesemakers four out of five years at the Michigan State Fair as well as winning many national honors at cheese competitions throughout the country. In 2000 they moved their operation to *Blackstar Farms,* an elegant inn and vineyard at 10844 E. Revold Rd. near Sutton's Bay. At the farms you can go horseback riding, sip locally produced wines, or watch the Hoyts make their cheese and taste samples. You can even spend the night, as the inn has 8 guest rooms that are $295 to $395 a night during the high season from June through Oct. For reservations contact Blackstar Farms at (231) 271-4970 or blackstarfarms.com.

Cherry Republic (800-206-6949; cherryrepublic.com) is at 6026 S. Lake St. and open from 9 a.m. to 9 p.m. daily during the summer with shorter hours in the winter.

The village of Leland's trademark is a row of weathered dockside shacks along the Leland River that at one time housed commercial fishermen and today is a historic district known as *Fishtown.* All the commercial fishermen except Carlson Fisheries have disappeared from the strip, but their buildings have been preserved and now house specialty shops and stores. With its unique setting and atmosphere, Fishtown is the proper place to begin a nautical adventure to *South Manitou Island,* a portion of the Sleeping Bear Dunes National Lakeshore located 17 miles from Leland in Lake Michigan.

Island visitors board a ferry at the end of Fishtown and begin with a 90-minute cruise to South Manitou that passes a lighthouse and the scenic shoreline of Sleeping Bear Dunes. The island, with its hardwood forests and natural harbor, attracted settlers, a lighthouse, and a lifesaving station as early as 1840, and it has an interesting history. The ferry has a 4-hour layover at the national park dock, more than enough time to view the small museum at the visitor center, climb the 116 steps to the top of the lighthouse, and enjoy a lunch on a nearby beach.

For the more energetic, there are trails and old farm roads across the island, and it's possible to hike the 6-mile round-trip to the **Francisco Morazan** and return to the mainland the same day. The *Morazan* was a Liberian freighter that ran aground in November 1960 at the southwest corner of the island, and a large portion of the battered vessel is still visible above the waterline today. For the best adventure on South Manitou, camp for a night or two at Weather Station Campground, a national park facility that is free. The campground is a 1.5-mile hike in from the dock, and you can explore the tract of sand dunes on the west side of the island. The dunes, perched on bluffs high above Lake Michigan, are probably the most remote and least visited ones in the state.

All visitors must bring their own food to South Manitou, and campers have to be self-sufficient with tent, sleeping bags, and other equipment. Contact **Manitou Island Transit** (231-256-9061; manitoutransit.com) about the ferry that sails to the island daily from June through Aug. The round-trip fare is $35 for adults and $20 for children 12 and under.

The growing conditions in southwest Michigan that made Paw Paw the wine-producing center of the state are also found in **Leelanau** and **Old Missionary,** two peninsulas filled with fruit farms and a half dozen vineyards of surprising quality. All the vineyards have a tasting room, and an interesting day can be had visiting each of them. The first bonded wine cellar in the area—and many think the most beautiful one in the state—is **Boskydel Vineyard,** a small winery on the shores of Lake Leelanau. There is no restaurant at Boskydel or even any picnic tables outside, but it is built on the side of a hill, and from the parking lot you have a view of the sloping vineyard leading down to the huge lake, framed by the rolling hills of the Leelanau Peninsula. All this prompted one wine critic to proclaim Boskydel the most beautiful site for a winery in the country.

It was within the family tradition that Bernie Rinke should plant a vineyard. He grew up on an Ohio farm, and his father bootlegged wine during Prohibition. Rinke began planting his vineyard in 1964 and now cultivates 25 acres of grapes, producing 6,000 gallons (2,500 cases) annually of several dry and semidry red and white table wines. The tasting room is open daily year-round from 1 to 5 p.m., and if you want a tour of the winery, Rinke will lead you through a 10-minute look at his facility.

A Fall Driving Tour

If you visit Leelanau in the fall, use it as your springboard for a driving tour of Northwest Michigan. This popular color tour is a 190-mile drive that focuses on two delightful peninsulas: Leelanau and Mission. Both are crowned by a light-house in a park (Leelanau State Park and Old Mission Point) and feature more than two dozen vineyards where you can stop, taste, and purchase some of Michigan's finest wines. The other highlight of the tour is Sleeping Bear Dunes National Lakeshore. Fall colors peak between late September and mid-October. For a wine trail map check the **Leelanau Peninsula Vintners Association** website at lpwines.com.

Actually, Rinke would rather stay in the small tasting room, plop a large wine glass in front of you (no plastic cups here), and talk—about his grapes, about wine tasting, about his days as Northwestern Michigan College's first librarian in nearby Traverse City. (Ask him where the name of the winery comes from.) Something new at Boskydel is a chestnut orchard where the experimental vineyard used to be. And these chestnuts are not intended for wine. The Chinese chestnuts growing here are low in fat and highly nutritious. They also make a lovely appetizer with your favorite Boskydel wine and they are available for purchase at the winery. Visitors to the winery can sample the chestnuts in winter, roasted on an open fire. Cost: $5 per pound (limited supplies).

A beautiful vineyard, a most delightful wine maker, and not a bad wine either, Boskydel (231-256-7272; boskydel.com) is 3.5 miles southeast of the town of Lake Leelanau at County Road 641 and Otto Road.

At the tip of the Leelanau Peninsula is the 1,350-acre *Leelanau State Park.* From this park you can enjoy spectacular views along miles of lakeshore, from platforms on top of dunes, and even from the tower of a lighthouse. In addition to a campground, picnic area, and hiking trails, the park also includes the historic Grand Traverse Lighthouse.

Built in 1916, the *Grand Traverse Lighthouse* is the most recent light in a series of lighthouses that have guided ships around the peninsula since 1852. Today it is an interesting maritime museum where visitors can

Traverse City Film Festival

It's not the Sundance Film Festival, not yet, but it's getting there. When Academy Award–winning filmmaker Michael Moore, whose antiwar film *Fahrenheit 9/11* is the highest-grossing documentary of all time, founded the *Traverse City Film Festival* in 2005 many questioned his intentions. As it turns out, all he wanted to do was show great films near his home in Northern Michigan.

The Traverse City Film Festival was a huge hit from the start. It has become one of the biggest film festivals in the Midwest, registering 80,000 admissions to nearly 100 screenings and pumping millions of dollars into the Traverse City tourism economy. Staged in the first week of August, the festival presents the best of independent, foreign, and documentary cinema in several indoor movie houses, including the city's State Theatre, the City Opera House, and the Old Town Playhouse. Even more popular are the classic movies shown free of charge on a giant, inflatable outdoor screen overlooking Grand Traverse Bay at dusk.

For more information on the Traverse City Film Festival or to book tickets, call (231) 392-1134 or go online at traversecityfilmfestival.org.

tour the first floor, which has been restored as a lightkeeper's home of the 1920s, and then climb the tower for a grand view of Lake Michigan. The foghorn building next door has also been restored and is now a gift shop with a maritime theme.

Leelanau State Park is located 8 miles north of Northport on County Road 629. The Grand Traverse Lighthouse (231-386-7195; grandtraverselighthouse.com) is open 10 a.m. to 5 p.m. daily Memorial Day through Labor Day, noon to 4 p.m. daily May, Sept, and Oct, and noon to 4 p.m. on Sat and Sun in Nov. A state park vehicle permit is required to enter the park, and admission to the lighthouse is $4 for adults and $2 for children.

Grand Traverse County

The most noted feature of the county is **Grand Traverse Bay,** a beautiful body of water with Traverse City at the south end and old Mission Peninsula splitting it up the middle. Its protected waters have become a haven for sailboats, catamarans, and sailboarders, but by far the most impressive vessel afloat during the summer is the **Manitou,** a replica of a two-masted, gaff-rigged, topsail 1800s coasting cargo ship. The 114-foot, 100-ton ship was built in 1983 to look and sail like a traditional schooner, and it's that love for old wooden boats that draws most of its passengers on deck. From May through Sept the *Manitou* offers 3 sailings daily, with 2-hour cruises at noon and 3 p.m. and a 2.5-hour evening sail with picnic meal—the most popular trip, of course—at 6:30 p.m. Passengers who dream about a life on the high seas go a step further and book a cabin on the *Manitou*, which at night becomes Michigan's only floating bed-and-breakfast. The quarters are tiny, with bunks built into the curves and angles of the hull. The head (bathroom) is shared, and the showers are back on land. In the evening guests wander topside to take in Traverse City lights shimmering on the bay or snuggle up in their bunks to be put to sleep by the gentle swells and the creaking of the wooden hull.

The *Manitou* is operated by the **Traverse Tall Ship Company** (800-678-0383; tallshipsailing.com). Its office and dock are at 13390 S.W. Bay Shore Dr. Daily cruises range from $39 to $47 for adults, and overnight accommodations, which include a hearty breakfast with the crew in the galley, range from $130 for singles to $230 for doubles.

A Singer Named Jewel

In the mid-1990s, regulars at Ray's Coffeehouse in Traverse City remember, they would hear a young singer with a distinctly sweet and high voice. By 1997 they knew her well, though she had been gone for years. Her name—the only name she goes by—was Jewel. Jewel was a student at the *Interlochen Fine Arts Camp* that summer and playing for tips in local coffeehouses. In time she would become one of the hottest singers on the pop music scene.

You can catch other possible future stars at the internationally acclaimed music camp that overlooks Green Lake near the town of Interlochen. The camp hosts more than 750 performances each year by faculty members, students, and big-name entertainers, with many of them taking place in its open-air pavilion overlooking Green Lake. For ticket information call (800) 681-5920.

You can also enjoy the water from above through *Grand Traverse Balloon,* which offers hot-air balloon rides across Grand Traverse Bay, often beginning at the Château Grand Traverse vineyards on Old Mission Peninsula. This may well be the most spectacular view from any hot-air balloon in Michigan, as below you lies the narrow peninsula, the rippling waters of the bay, Traverse City, and the endless rows of the cherry orchards to the northeast. The entire flight takes 3 hours, with an hour in the air, and flights are always at sunrise or sunset because there's less wind turbulence. They are priced at $349 per person for sunrise flights and $399 per person for sunset flights. Jeff Geiger, the Traverse City balloonist who runs Grand Traverse Balloon (231-947-7433; grandtraverseballoons.com), recommends reservations but says he can usually fulfill last-minute urges to float above the bay.

For another unusual view of the bay, head to the highest ridge on the Mission Peninsula just before sunset. At this high point Robert Begin has built the state's newest vineyard, *Château Chantal,* and included a brick terrace that overlooks both the West Arm and East Arm of Grand Traverse Bay. With vineyards and cherry orchards at your feet, you settle back with a glass of Chardonnay or a semidry Riesling and some sharp cheeses or freshly cut fruit and watch the sky melt into a collage of oranges and reds over the bays of northern Michigan.

Begin and his wife have built the unique winery on a former ridgetop cherry farm and named it after their daughter. You can stop by for a tour or a sip in the vineyard's wine-tasting and sales area, a great room that features hardwood floors, a polished granite bar top, and a grand piano in front of a 20-foot-wide bay window overlooking Grand Traverse Bay. Or you can simply stop for the night and unwind. That's because this winery is also a bed-and-breakfast, featuring 6 rooms and suites with sitting areas and private baths.

Château Chantal (800-969-4009; chateauchantal.com) is located just off M 37 on Mission Peninsula, 12 miles north of Traverse City. Tours are offered daily during summer at 1, 2, and 3 p.m. The tasting room is open year-round from Memorial Day through Labor Day, Mon through Sat from 11 a.m. to 8 p.m., Sun 11 a.m. to 6 p.m.; from Sept through Oct, Mon through Sat from 11 a.m. to 7 p.m., Sun from 11 a.m. to 6 p.m.; Nov through early June, Mon through Sun from 11 a.m. to 5 p.m. Rooms range from $190 to $265 per night.

One of Michigan's newest art museums is no stuffy gallery with ancient masterpieces in gilded frames. Located on the campus of Northwestern Michigan College, the *Dennos Museum Center* at 1410 College Dr. opened in 1991 after more than a decade in the planning.

The jewel of the museum is its permanent Inuit Art Gallery, a collection that began in 1960 and was housed in the college library. Today there are 550 pieces of sculptured soapstone and colorful prints depicting the harsh life and fascinating culture of these Arctic people. Carvings and prints depict hunters pulling a walrus out of the ice with a rope, kayaking through the open seas, bedding down in an igloo, and waiting patiently at a breathing hole in the frozen Arctic Ocean for a seal to surface.

But families and kids usually head for the Discovery Gallery, which combines art, science, and technology into an intriguing set of hands-on displays. One of the exhibits is the Recollections Piece. With the use of video cameras and computer-generated images, visitors can watch themselves "come alive in color" as they move in front of a room-size screen. The museum staff calls it "painting with your body."

From downtown Traverse City head north on US 31 to the Northwestern Michigan College campus. The Dennos Museum Center (231-995-1055; dennosmuseum.org) is on the small campus. The center is open Mon, Tues, Wed, Fri, and Sat from 10 a.m. to 5 p.m., Thurs from 10 a.m. to 8 p.m., and Sun from 1 to 5 p.m. Admission is $6 for adults and $4 for children.

More fun for kids is located on the west side of Traverse City at the **Great Lakes Children's Museum,** whose hands-on and interactive exhibits are focused on water and the Great Lakes. At the museum's Lighthouse Keeper's Quarters, children can dress up and experience life in a lighthouse while the Water Table lets them create standing waves and eddies and channel flowing water a hundred different ways without getting too wet. Never been on a freighter before? There's one at the museum especially sized for kids to explore. When the sun is out you want to be on the beach in Traverse City, but if it's raining this is a great place to spend an afternoon with the family.

The Great Lakes Children's Museum (231-932-4526; greatlakeskids.org) is at 13240 S.W. Bayshore Dr. (M 22) and is open 10 a.m. to 5 p.m. Tues through Sat and 1 to 5 p.m. on Sun. During the summer the museum is also open on Mon from 10 a.m. to 5 p.m. Admission is $6 per person.

If you're traveling just north of Traverse City on US 31 and pass a place called the **Music House,** turn off the car stereo. Strip the headphones and MP3 players from your kids' ears and toss that huge boom box in the trunk. Then turn around and see how music used to be enjoyed. Housed in an old granary built in 1905, the Music House is a showcase for automatic musical instruments from the 1880s to the 1920s. Visitors are entertained rather than educated, as the hour-long tour is a musical journey with toe-tapping demonstrations ranging from small music boxes to one of the largest ballroom dance organs ever made.

Tours begin in the phonograph gallery, where a huge model of Nipper, the famous RCA Victor dog, greets you. There are rows of "talking machines" beginning from 1900 with their wax cylinders instead of records and colorful morning glory horns instead of speakers. In the main portion of the barn are larger musical machines set up in the environments in which they were enjoyed. The most impressive sight for many visitors is upstairs in the loft, which is home to the 30-foot facade of the Amaryllis dance organ. Built in 1922 for a palace ballroom in Belgium, the instrument plays a folded perforated cardboard book using hundreds of wooden and metal pipes along with percussion instruments.

The Music House (231-938-9300; musichouse.org) is located on a 180-acre cherry farm off US 31, 1.5 miles north of the highway's junction with M 72 or 8 miles north of Traverse City at 7377 US 31 North. It is open daily from "cherry blossoms through fall colors," or, to be more exact, May 1 through Oct 31, 10 a.m. to 4 p.m. Mon through Sat and noon to 4 p.m. Sun. From mid-Nov through Dec, it is open Sat and Sun 10 a.m. to 4 p.m. Admission is $11 for adults and $4 for children

Antrim County

Speeding along US 131 in the middle of Antrim County, you pass one of the most spectacular inland viewing points in the Lower Peninsula, though you would never know it from this road. The side road to **Deadman's Hill** is 7 miles north of Mancelona, but there is little fanfare about the scenic overlook: Only a small brown sign points the way. Follow Deadman's Hill Road for 1.5 miles until it dead-ends at a pair of Department of Natural Resources pit toilets and a wood-chip path. Some 15 yards up the path is a spectacular panorama from a high point of more than 1,200 feet. You take in a 180-degree view of the Jordan River valley stretching 15 miles to rugged hills that fill the horizon. During October the view from this spot is priceless, as the entire valley with the river winding through it is on fire with autumn reds and oranges.

Deadman's Hill earned its name from the logging era at the turn of the 20th century. The steep hills made the Jordan River valley a treacherous place to log, and numerous accidents occurred. But people grieved the most in 1910 when "Big Sam" Graczyk, 21 years old and soon to be married, was killed while driving a team of horses and a big wheel of logs. The name for the ridge stuck. You can admire the view and have a picnic while sitting on the edge, and the more adventurous can hike the Jordan River Pathway, which begins at this point. Part of the trail is a 3-mile loop down to the river and back, or it can be turned into an 18-mile overnight walk to a hike-in campground for backpackers.

Where there is a boardwalk or similar planking along a trail, there is usually a swamp, marsh, or bog surrounding it. At the **Grass River Natural Area,** there are an awful lot of boardwalks. Some trails are nothing but boardwalks, because a good slice of this 1,165-acre Antrim County park is sedge meadow, marsh, and cedar swamp.

Grass River itself is only 2.5 miles long and just chest deep. It's a crystal clear waterway that connects Lake Bellaire to Clam Lake as part of Antrim

County's "Chain of Lakes." But the extensive floating sedge mats and other wetlands that surround the river are so intriguing that they prompted a fund-raising effort to buy the land and dedicate it as a natural area in 1976.

They've been building boardwalks ever since. Along with an interpretive center, which features several rooms of displays and a small bookstore, Grass River has a 5-mile trail system that is marked with interpretive posts and winds through a variety of habitats.

The Woodland/Wildfire Trail is the longest at 2.2 miles; the quarter-mile Tamarack Trail is designed to be accessible for people with disabilities. But to many the Sedge Meadow Trail is the most enjoyable. It's one long boardwalk—almost every step of it is on wood—that passes through a variety of wetlands where plants have been identified and numbered posts correspond with information in a trail guide. Eventually the trail emerges at the edge of Grass Lake where observation platforms and towers have been built on the boardwalk along with a series of benches.

From US 131 in Mancelona, head west on M 88 toward Bellaire and within 2 miles continue on Alden Highway (County Road 618). The entrance road to Grass River Natural Area (231-533-8576; grassriver.org) is off CR 618 before you reach Alden. Exciting news happened in October 2011 when the long-awaited (original plans were developed 42 years ago) Grass River Center was opened. The building sits exactly where it was planned, in a fern field off the cabin trail. The building offers teaching facilities, restrooms, and covered areas for water quality studies, eating, meeting or just plain resting.

The trails are open from dawn to dusk. The interpretive center is open daily from 10 a.m. to 4 p.m. June through Aug. Winter hours are 10 a.m. to 4 p.m. Sat and Sun.

Charlevoix County

South of Charlevoix off US 31 is yet another state park along Lake Michigan. *Fisherman's Island State Park* possesses many of the same features as the other parks: 3 miles of sandy shoreline, excellent swimming areas, scenic views of the Great Lake. But Fisherman's Island also has a couple of unique features. Not nearly as popular or crowded as some other locales, the park offers 10 rustic campsites right on Lake Michigan. Each one is tucked away in the trees with a table and a spot to pitch a tent only a few feet from the lapping waters of the lake. These are some of the most beautiful campsites in the Lower Peninsula, and naturally they are the first to be chosen in the campground. But you can reserve those particular sites, or any other in the park, up to 6 months in advance through the *Michigan Campground Central Reservation System* (800-447-2757; midnrreservations.com). The other noted feature of the state park is the *Petoskey stones.* The state stone is actually petrified coral, a leftover fragment of the many coral reefs that existed in the warm-water seas from Charlevoix to Alpena some 300 million years ago. Today the stones are collected by rock hounds, and many of them end up polished and used in jewelry, paperweights, and other decorative items. Dry stones are silvery with no apparent markings to the untrained eye, but when the rocks are wet, it's easy to see the ringlike pattern that covers them. Rock hounds searching for the stones are usually seen closely inspecting the waterline or washing off handfuls of rocks in the lake.

The 2.5-mile park road begins at the ranger station and ends at the sandy beaches of the state park but along the way passes an extended

Splashing & Sliding at Avalanche Bay

In 2005 Michigan's largest ski resort, *Boyne Mountain,* opened the state's largest indoor water park, *Avalanche Bay.* While some traditionalists in the ski industry wondered about combining water slides with ski slopes, the indoor park was envisioned as a solution to Michigan's finicky winters and a way to attract more families in the summer to what is basically a golf resort.

Now while dad is out hitting the links, the kids are making a splash in 88,000 square feet of spraying gushers, falling water, splash pools, and wild rides. To the theme of a Swiss village hit by an avalanche, the park offers more than a dozen rides and attractions all surrounding Splasherhorn Mountain, a 3-story structure that at the sound of a horn dumps 800 gallons of water on the unsuspecting below. Kids can also float down a lazy river in an inner tube, ride the wild Vertigo tube slide, even surf a simulated rip curl.

Parents can join in the watery fun or soak away weary ski muscles in a pair of giant Jacuzzis known as Glacier Hot Springs.

Boyne Mountain is on US 131 just south of Boyne Falls. For information on skiing, lodging, or golf vacation packages call the resort (800-862-6963) or go online at boyne.com.

rocky shoreline. Many gem enthusiasts say this is one of the best places in northern Michigan to find Petoskey stones. Stop at the ranger station for a park map and information on the famous stones. There is a vehicle fee to enter Fisherman's Island State Park (231-547-6641) and an additional charge to camp overnight.

The Great Lakes, which have blessed Michigan with miles of magnificent shoreline, also have given it many islands that have become unique destinations for visitors. The most popular is *Mackinac Island,* a nonmotorized resort (no cars or buses) that tourists flock to each summer, taking ferries out of Mackinaw City on the Lower Peninsula or St. Ignace across the Mackinac Bridge on the Upper Peninsula. There are also many islands without the crowds, commercialization, and fudge shops of Mackinac that make for an interesting side trip. One of the largest is *Beaver Island,* reached by a ferry from Charlevoix.

Known as Emerald Isle for its strong Irish heritage, Beaver Island lies 32 miles northwest of Charlevoix and is 55 square miles of forests, inland lakes, and farms. Its recorded history dates to 1832, when Bishop Frederic Baraga, the "Snowshoe Priest," brought Christianity to a small Indian settlement here. The island's most bizarre period began in 1847 after James Jesse Strang arrived. Strang and his band of Mormon followers had just broken away from the leadership of Brigham Young and established St. James, the island's only village. Eventually Strang would crown himself "king of Beaver Island" and rule the island and its religious sect with an iron fist before being shot in 1856 by a disgruntled subject. Irish immigrants followed in the 1870s to fish the waters of northern Lake Michigan, and today many of the 551 people who live year-round in or near St. James have roots back in Ireland.

Beaver Island has an assortment of lodge and hotel accommodations and restaurants for overnight visitors, but on Saturdays in July and August, it also makes an ideal day trip. You can depart from Charlevoix at 8:30 a.m. on the ferry and reach the island by 10:30 a.m. for a 6-hour visit before catching the last ferry back to the mainland at 5:30 p.m. In St. James there are several museums, including the *Old Mormon Print Shop* (231-448-2254), which was built by King Strang in 1850, and the Marine and Harbor Museum, a 1906 net shed dedicated to the time when the area bustled with fishermen.

ttle Traverse Bay on Lake Michi-n. Thus they avoided a paddle

The museums are open from June through Aug. Hours are 11 a.m. to 5 p.m. Mon through Sat and noon to 3 p.m. Sun. There is a small admission charge.

Another interesting attraction in St. James is the **Toy Museum and Store** (231-448-2480). Once known as "the last nickel toy store in the US," the Toy Museum is still affordable to anybody on a weekly allowance: Chinese fans 3 for a dollar, a disappearing dagger for 75 cents, and green army men at a nickel apiece. Suspended from the high-peaked ceiling is the "museum," an interesting collection of antique toys that range from foot-pedal Roadsters and "rocket cars" from the 1930s to clay marbles and dolls that predate the 1900s. The shop at 37970 Michigan Ave. is open daily from 1 to 4 p.m. in June and from 11 a.m. to 4 p.m. in July and Aug.

You can also rent a mountain bike or a Jeep and tour the island, which has more than 100 miles of roads, most of them dirt and gravel. On a pleasant summer day, this is a most delightful adventure and a great way to see the old farmhouses, inland lakes, remote shoreline, and lighthouse located outside St. James. Pack a picnic lunch and plan on driving 3 to 4 hours to circle Beaver Island.

The **Beaver Island Boat Co.** (888-446-4095; bibco.com) operates the ferry and charges $48 for a round-trip adult ticket and $26 for children during non-peak times and $54 for adults and $30 for children during peak times. You can rent a vehicle for $55 a day from **Gordon's Auto Clinic** (231-448-2438) or a mountain bike from **Lakesports Rentals** (231-448-2166). For a complete list of island businesses, lodging, and sites, contact the **Beaver Island Chamber of Commerce** (231-448-2505; beaverisland.org).

trivia

By following Michigan's Chain of Lakes (Mullett, Burt, and Crooked Lakes), Native Americans and fur traders had only one short portage in traveling from Lake Huron to Little Traverse Bay on Lake Michigan. Thus they avoided a paddle through the Straits of Mackinac and facing its strong winds and wicked currents.

A number of writers have ties to Northwest Michigan but none as famous as **Ernest Hemingway,** who spent the summers of his youth at his family's cottage on Walloon Lake. Hemingway buffs often tour the area to see artifacts and places that made their way into his writing. Most begin in Petoskey's Little Traverse Historical Museum (see Emmet County) and then head down US 141 past Walloon Lake. Some go to *Hemingway Point* on the south shore of Lake Charlevoix, to which the young author once fled (it was owned by his uncle) when being pursued by a game warden.

Of course, almost all eventually stop at the *Horton Bay General Store,* located across the lake on Boyne City Road. Built in 1876 with a high false front, the store's most prominent feature is its large front porch with benches and stairs at either end. Hemingway idled away some youthful summers on that porch and fished nearby Horton Creek for rainbow and brook trout. He also celebrated his first marriage in Horton Bay's Congregational Church, and eventually the general store appeared in the opening of his short story "Up in Michigan." The Horton Bay General Store has had a string of owners, but remarkably little has changed about its appearance. It is still the classic general store; only the bright red benches outside receive a new coat of paint every now and then.

You enter through a flimsy screen door with a bell above it, and inside you find the worn wooden floors and shelves stacked with canned goods and other merchandise. There is an old wooden tub filled with ice and cold drinks, a small freezer that holds 4 or 5 flavors of ice cream, and the lunch counter where the morning coffee drinkers gather. Then as your eyes wander toward the ceiling, you realize this is more a preserved shrine to Hemingway than a store for the local residents. On one wall hang guns, old traps, mounted deer heads, and a panel of photographs of the author during his days in Northwest Michigan. Horton Bay General Store at 05115 Boyne City Rd. (231-582-7827; hortonbaygeneralstore.com) is open from 8 a.m. to 4 p.m. Mon through Thurs, 8 a.m. to 9 p.m. Fri and Sat, and 8 a.m. to 3 p.m. Sun. The store closes in the winter.

From Horton Bay you can continue around Lake Charlevoix in a scenic drive that will take you past Young State Park, through the historic downtown area of Boyne City, and near Hemingway Point, where Ferry Road abruptly ends at the South Arm of the lake. If you want to continue, you have to take passage on the *Ironton Ferry,* one of Michigan's most delightful boat rides, even though it's only 5 minutes long.

Ferry service on the South Arm dates back to 1876, when the first barge was pulled back and forth by horses. It was apparently a moneymaker right from the start, as the 1884 rates are still listed on the side of the ferry office. The present ferry was installed in 1926 and is guided by cables 35 feet down on the lake bottom, making it, say officials, one of two cable-operated automobile ferries in the country.

That's only one of the Ironton Ferry's many little oddities, the reason it was once featured in *Ripley's Believe It or Not*. Consider its size (so small it holds only 4 cars), the length of its trip (a mere 575 feet of water), and the fact that it doesn't have a rudder. Perhaps most unusual is that the Ironton Ferry doesn't make regularly scheduled crossings. It's operated on demand because the South Arm is so narrow that passengers can be seen waiting on the other side.

The ferry operates from mid-Apr to Thanksgiving Eve, 6:30 a.m. to 10:30 p.m. daily. A trip across is $3.25 per vehicle or 50 cents per walker.

On the shores where Hemingway's family had their cottage are a number of historic buildings, including the **Walloon Lake Inn.** The century-old inn has a number of rooms upstairs, a fine lakeside restaurant downstairs, where you can arrive by car or boat, and, during the winter, the **Fonds du Cuisine Cooking School.** For 4 days small groups of students spend their mornings in the restaurant's kitchen working with owner/chef David Beier and their afternoons in the dining room eating lunch. From Tues through Fri they are up to their elbows in sauces and batters at a school where textbooks are replaced by mixing bowls and wire whisks.

Classes are held between the countertop and the range, as the students receive their own ducks to truss and rainbow trout to fillet. Class ends with the midday meal, a lavish affair that may last 2 hours and usually involves

trivia

At one time Michigan was a favorite nesting ground for the passenger pigeon. Vast quantities of beechnuts attracted them, and each spring immense flocks arrived, literally darkening the skies for hours at a time as they flew over.

At Crooked Lake in Emmet County, a nesting in 1878 covered 90 square miles, drawing the attention of thousands of hunters who quickly converged on the area. Millions of birds were killed, packed in barrels, and shipped to Petoskey. Such wanton slaughter led to the extinction of the passenger pigeon by 1914.

a little wine tasting and comparing of each other's creations. Walloon Lake Inn at 4178 West St. (800-956-4665; walloonlakeinn.com), in the heart of Walloon Lake Village, is 8 miles south of Petoskey and is reached from US 31 by heading west a quarter of a mile on M 75. The school is offered two dozen times from Sept through June and costs $310 per person for the 2-day class and $565 for the 4-day class. Either class includes lodging, breakfast, and daily luncheon.

Emmet County

Housed in Petoskey's Chicago and West Michigan railroad depot, which was built in 1892, the *Little Traverse Historical Museum* is the first logical stop on any Hemingway tour. The display case is small but contains photographs, other memorabilia, and some rare first-edition books that Hemingway autographed for his friend Edwin Pailthrorp, whom he visited in Petoskey in 1947. There is also a display case devoted to another famous writer, Bruce Catton, who was born in the Emmet County town and grew up in nearby Benzonia. Later Catton would pen *A Stillness at Appomattox*, for which he won a Pulitzer Prize in 1953. The original manuscript of that book and other personal artifacts are in the museum.

The museum (231-347-2620; petoskeymuseum.org) is at 100 Dock Street on Petoskey's picturesque waterfront and is open Memorial Day to Sept from 10 a.m. to 4 p.m. Mon through Fri and 1 to 4 p.m. Sat and Sun. Admission is $3 for adults, free for children under 10. From the well-developed resort town of Harbor Springs, M 119 heads north and hugs the coastline for 31 miles until it ends at Cross Village. The drive is often cited as a scenic one, but not for the views of Lake Michigan you might expect when tracing it on a map. This is the *Tunnel of Trees Shore Drive,* a narrow road that climbs, drops, and curves its way through the thick forests along the rugged coast. At times the branches from trees at each side of the road merge overhead to form a complete tunnel, shading travelers even when the sun is beaming down at midday. You finally emerge from the thick forest at Cross Village, a small hamlet and home of *Legs Inn.*

The inn is the creation of one man, Stanley Smolak, a Polish immigrant who fell in love with this part of Michigan and moved here from Chicago in 1921. Smolak quickly made friends with the local Ottawa Indians, who inducted him into their tribe as Chief White Cloud. Then in 1930, with a Polish past, a love for northern Michigan, and his new Indian heritage, Smolak began building the inn. He combined the driftwood and stones he found along the shoreline to construct an unusual building on a bluff overlooking Lake Michigan. From the outside the architecture of the Legs Inn is bizarre at best, but the interior is even more fascinating, for Smolak loved to carve the driftwood. He would take a piece, see something in it, and then whittle away. The inn has several rooms, all filled with Smolak's driftwood sculpture.

Naturally, the menu reflects Smolak's homeland and includes entrees of pierogi, gotabki, and bigos, a hearty Polish stew. The restaurant even serves a beer imported from Poland. The Legs Inn (231-526-2281; legsinn.com) is located in the heart of Cross Village at 6425 N. Lake Shore Dr. (you'll know it when you see it) and is open mid-May to mid-Oct from noon to 8 p.m. and even later in July and Aug. Dinner entrees on the menu range from $15 to $20. Rooms are priced from $59 to $119.

Cheboygan County

The residents are certainly friendly in **Cheboygan.** Arrive in this Lake Huron town of 4,826 during the summer or early fall and the first place people want you to go is the jail. Stay as long as you like, they say. Plan to spend a few minutes in each cell, because that's where you'll find the pride and heritage that is Cheboygan—in the **Cheboygan History Center** located in the old county jail. At this museum you not only get to view the history of the area in an interesting series of displays and exhibits, you also have the opportunity to wander through a 19th-century jail. It's debatable which is more fascinating.

Built in 1890, the facility served as the area jail until 1970, when the county board of commissioners gave the building to the historical society. You enter the attached brick home where the county sheriff and his family lived, and the first room you walk into is a huge kitchen, where his wife cooked not only for him and his family but for all the prisoners as well. From the home you pass through a metal door, entering the jail. Little has changed about the facility except that the historical society has filled each cell with a display, ranging from the town's first hardware stores to its maritime history to an exhibit on logging. Call it "history behind bars."

The museum is at Huron and Court Streets at 427 Court St. From US 23 within town, head south on M 27 and then west on Court Street for 3 blocks. The jail museum (231-627-9597; cheboyganhistorycenter.org) is open from June through Sept from 1 to 4 p.m. Tues through Sat. Adult admission is $5; children have free admission.

Built in 1995, Spies Heritage Hall houses primary exhibits which chronicle the history of Cheboygan County. Exhibits include the Native American presence in the Straits Area, the military service of local residents in wars from the Civil War to wars in Iraq and Afghanistan, the maritime industry, and the lumber industry.

trivia

You can only drive north on I-75 so many times before the billboard about a "man-eating clam" entices you off the highway at exit 326 and into the parking lot of Sea Shell City.

Inside the huge gift shop, between the rows of rubber tomahawks and other tacky souvenirs for tourists, is a 505-pound giant clam (*Tridacna gigas*) from the Philippines. This is reputed to be the largest mollusk in the world and "has the capacity to snuff out a man's life with one sharp snap of its shells." Reality is that the clam is a vegetarian that feasts on algae.

A Native American log cabin built in the mid-1800s was moved to the center. It was one of three remaining cabins when the Cheboygan County sheriff dispatched deputies in 1900 to foreclose on property because of unpaid taxes. The cabins were part of a Native American village on Burt Lake in the late 1800s. Most of the cabins were burned. The cabin had been used as an ice house and then a storage shed. When it was moved to the history center, the cabin was taken apart log by log. Each log was numbered to permit exact reconstruction of the cabin. Notice the notched corner construction of the cabin, which assured a close fit and stability. Originally, the chinking—the filler between the logs—was moss, clay, or mud. The roof is covered with wood shingles. The original floor was hard packed dirt, which could be swept or even scrubbed if it was packed hard enough. The cabin had a loft for storage and sleeping. The ladder to the loft could be pulled up at night for security. The door is made of wood split lengthwise. It is locked by unknotting the rope pull and pulling it through to the inside at night. By removing the rope, the door could not be opened from the outside.

Another intriguing historical spot in Cheboygan County is just a few miles north on US 23. *Historic Mill Creek Discovery Park* is an excellent destination for families, especially for those with children who think history is "borrrring!" The Mackinac Historic State Park was opened in 1984 after the site was "rediscovered" in 1972 by a local archaeologist. It dates to the 1780s, when a Scottish trader named Robert Campbell obtained a 640-acre tract of land around the only stream in the area with enough power to operate a mill, making the creek one of the oldest industrial centers in the Midwest. There was a great demand for lumber at the time, since the British were moving their military post from Fort Michilimackinac at the tip of the Lower Peninsula to Mackinac Island. The island's high limestone bluffs made it easier to defend against the Americans, who were thought to be on their way.

Today the 625-acre park is a combination of re-created history and high adventure. You learn the history of Mill Creek from exploring the interactive exhibits in its museum and watching interpreters cut logs at a reconstructed sawmill or by hand in a saw pit. Then you can hit the park's 3.5 miles of forest trail for a little adventure that includes the Forest Canopy Bridge, Nature Trail Climbing Wall, the 50-foot-high Treetop Discovery Tower, and Eagle's Flight Zip Line that sends you flying through the canopy over Mill Creek like an eagle. History has never been so fun.

The park is reached from I-75 by taking exit 338 and heading south on US 23 for 4 miles. Mill Creek (231-436-4226) is open from May through mid-Oct from 9 a.m. to 4 p.m. daily and until 5 p.m. from mid-June through Aug. Admission is $8 per adult and $4.75 per child and the Adventure Tour, which includes the zip line, climbing wall, canopy bridge, and tower, is an additional $7 per person.

Otsego County

The eastern elk, once a common sight to Indians in the Lower Peninsula, disappeared from Michigan around 1877. After several unsuccessful attempts to reintroduce the animal in the early 1900s, seven Rocky Mountain elk were released in Cheboygan County in 1918, and today biologists believe Michigan's herd of 1,400 elk descended from those animals. The herd ranges over 600 square miles in Cheboygan, Montmorency, Otsego, and Presque

Isle Counties, but its heaviest concentration is in the wilderness areas of the
Pigeon River Country State Forest.

The 95,000-acre state forest features rustic campgrounds, miles of hiking
trails, and fishing opportunities, but come fall most visitors have their hearts
set on seeing the elk. As big as the adults are (ranging from 700 to 900
pounds), they're tough to spot during the summer, for they break up into
small groups or are solitary and lie low in the thick forest. But in September
the bulls begin the "bugling season," when they move into open areas and
form harems of 15 to 20 cows by calling out to them with a high-pitched
whistlelike sound. Watchers will see from 30 to 100 elk gathered in an open
field and then hear the most amazing sound—the huge bull making his
high-pitched mating call.

To witness one of Michigan's great wildlife scenes, head to the Pigeon
River forestry field office (989-983-4101), 13 miles east of Vanderbilt, just
off Sturgeon River Road. The office is open from 8 a.m. to 4:30 p.m. Mon
through Fri, and workers can provide maps and suggest open areas to view
the elk. The rule of thumb is that 2 weeks on either side of Sept 20 is the
best time to catch the bugling, or rutting, season. Plan to be at an open
area just before dawn or dusk, and sit quietly to await the movement of the
herd. One traditional spot to see elk is off Ossmun Road near Clark Bridge
Road northeast of the forestry office. Here you will find a large open field,
a small parking lot off the road, and a few elk viewers waiting patiently
during September.

If you can't find an elk in Pigeon River Country State Forest, head south
to *Gaylord's Elk View Park.* The city herd began in 1995 when three elk
needed a home after a local nature center closed. Today the herd numbers
around 70 and lives on a 108-acre enclosure. A few of the bulls tip the scales
well over 800 pounds and stand 6 feet tall, donning massive horns during
the fall and winter and dropping them in the spring.

The most popular viewing area of Elk View Park (800-345-8621) is
adjacent to the Elk's Lodge (how appropriate!) and reached by departing
I-75 at exit 279 and heading north on S. Otsego Avenue and then east on
Grandview Boulevard.

Crawford County

The best-known attraction in this county is **Hartwick Pines State Park** and its **Michigan Forest Visitor Center,** the new interpretive center dedicated to Michigan's lumber era at the turn of the 20th century. On the outside the building, decks, and wooden walkways blend naturally into a grove of pines. Inside there are sitting areas with glass walls looking out over the ancient trees, the reason the state park was created.

The hands-on displays, dedicated to Michigan's vast forests, are excellent. There is a mounted wolf that looks so real a sign was needed saying PLEASE DON'T PET THE WOLF. Instead you touch a piece of fur and immediately a pack of wolves begins to howl all around you. The Living Giant is a white pine that talks to you, explaining what heartwood is or how its needles

The Holy Waters

The most revered trout stream east of the Mississippi River is an 8-mile stretch of the Au Sable River east of Grayling that is known among fly fishers as the Holy Waters. It was on the banks of the Holy Waters that Trout Unlimited was founded in the 1950s.

Ironically, trout are not native to the river but were introduced. The original fish of the Au Sable was grayling, the trout-like fish with the distinctively high dorsal fin. These were first classified by biologists in 1864, and within a decade, after railroads had penetrated northern Michigan, anglers from all over the country were arriving in Grayling to fish for grayling.

The fishing was so easy that anglers could often catch three or four grayling at a time by tying multiple hooks to their line. Such heavy fishing pressure and the deforestation caused by the lumber industry made the Michigan grayling rare by the turn of the 20th century and extinct by 1930.

For more on the history of fly fishing or to see a grayling stop at the **Crawford County Historical Museum** (989-348-4461; grayling-area.com/museum) at 97 Michigan Ave. in Grayling. The historical complex surrounds the Grayling Depot and in the depot itself is an intriguing first-floor exhibit of trout fishing in the Au Sable. Along with century-old bamboo rods and flies are displays on early Au Sable boat builders, guides, and a mounted grayling that measures 18 inches in length. During the trout season the museum is open Wed through Sat from 10 a.m. to 4 p.m.

produce food. But the most captivating display is "Reading the Rings." The computerized program displays a cross section of a white pine. Touch one of its rings and the screen flashes to what happened that year, including 1994 when the tree was blown down in a windstorm and cut up for firewood.

From the interpretive center you can walk the *Virgin Pines Trail* that loops through a 49-acre stand of 300-year-old virgin white pine. Along the way you will pass through a reconstructed loggers' camp with various lumber machines on display, including "Big Wheels" that were used to haul giant logs out of the woods.

The state park (989-348-7068) is north of Grayling and can be reached by exiting I-75 at M 93 and following the park signs. The Michigan Forest Visitor Center is open from 10 a.m. to 6 p.m. daily from Memorial Day to Labor Day and 9 a.m. to 4 p.m. the rest of the year. A vehicle permit is required to enter the park.

In 1959, in a cabin called the Barbless Hook on the banks of the Au Sable River, 16 anglers met one evening and formed *Trout Unlimited.* Today TU is the most recognized organization dedicated to the protection of cold water fisheries and it's no surprise to anybody who tosses a fly in search of a trout in Michigan that it was founded in Crawford County.

The county is steeped in the history of trout fishing and nowhere is that better seen than tiny *Lovells,* a village split by the North Branch of the Au Sable and home of the *Michigan Historic Trout Fishing Museum.* Set up in 2002 by the Lovells Township Historical Society, the cabin is the only museum in the state dedicated to the history of trout fishing, particularly fly fishing. Its display cases are filled with rods, reels, the fly collection of noted fly tier Bob Smock, and a lot of historical photos and articles from Lovells' golden era of fly fishing at the turn of the century.

Located on Twin Bridge Road, the museum is open Sat and Sun from 9 a.m. until 4 p.m. during the summer but the best time to visit is the last Saturday in April when Lovells stages its annual Trout Opener Festival with speakers, fly tying demonstrations, and casting competitions.

More trout fishing history is only a short walk away. What began as the Douglas Hotel in 1916 is today the *Fuller's North Branch Outing Club,* a lodge overlooking the North Branch of the Au Sable that is still dedicated to fly anglers. At its height, the North Branch Outing Club boosted

Whitefish on a Plank

The most valuable fish caught in the Great Lakes isn't walleye, lake trout, or even perch, it's whitefish (*Coregonus clupeaformis*) and during the summer Michigan restaurants from the Thumb to the Upper Peninsula serve it every way imaginable; from baked in a pastry puff to grilled on a cedar plank. This is especially true in the northwest corner of the Lower Peninsula.

Whitefish is a deep-bodied fish characterized by a small head with a blunt snout overhanging the lower jaw. The average commercially caught whitefish is 17 to 22 inches in length and weighs 2 to 4 pounds but in 1918 a 41-pounder was landed in Lake Superior, still the heaviest on record. The fish itself isn't actually white; rather, the skin is greenish-brown on the back, with silver sides and a silvery-white belly.

But its delicate flesh is white and possesses such an exceptional flavor that whitefish has been extolled ever since the first commercial nets were dropped into the Great Lakes. In 1918 the renowned *Fannie Farmer's Boston Cooking School Cookbook* called whitefish "the finest fish found in the Great Lakes."

There is still active commercial fishing for whitefish in Northern Michigan and it's possible to purchase filets that were swimming just the day before. The best-known commercial shop is **Carlson's** (231-256-9801; 205 W. River St.) in Leland's Fishtown that sells both fresh and smoked whitefish throughout the summer.

Even better is to let somebody else prepare it for you. Whitefish grilled on cedar planks is the most popular way to serve it, but restaurants also encrust it in ground pecans or macadamia nuts, blacken it Cajun style, or sauté the filets in a white wine, garlic, and caper sauce, to name but a few of the ways whitefish is served. A few of the restaurants where you can find good fish include **Whitecaps** (231-348-7092; whitecapsrestaurant.com) in Petoskey, **The Cove** (231-256-9834; thecoveleland.com) in Leland, and **Old Mission Tavern** (231-223-7280; oldmissiontavern.com) on Mission Peninsula. Even **Legs Inn** (231-526-2281; legsinn.com) in Cross Village, renowned for its Polish entrees, serves whitefish 3 different ways.

Another northern Michigan treat is smoked whitefish spread where the fish is blended with cream cheese, herbs and spices, and sometimes even a touch of brandy and then enjoyed on a slice of crusty bread. Some of the best whitefish spread is made and sold at **Burritt's Market** (231-946-3300; burrittsmarket.com; 509 W. Front St.) in Traverse City.

such members as Henry and Edsel Ford, Harvey Firestone, and the Dodge brothers. In 1996 the Fuller family bought the historic but vacant lodge and opened it as a 12-room inn after two years of extensive renovation. Fuller's North Branch Outing Club (989-348-7951; fullersnboc.com) is at 6122 E. County Rd. 612 and is a classic angler's inn. The lodge overlooks 400 feet of the North Branch and features a complete fly shop on the first floor, a comfortable lounge and dining area, and a room to hang and dry out your waders. Outside there are often as many Au Sable River boats in the parking lot as cars.

Wexford County

Hunting and fishing have a long tradition in Michigan. How long? In 1994 the state celebrated the 100th year in which deer licenses had been issued. There is no better place to see the history of hunters and anglers in Michigan than at the *Carl T. Johnson Hunting and Fishing Center,* a state interpretive site in Cadillac. Located adjacent to Mitchell State Park along M 115, the center features a variety of exhibits and hands-on displays, including a marsh diorama, a wall-size aquarium stocked with native fish, and a full-size stuffed elk, a species reintroduced to the state thanks to the efforts of sportsmen's groups. Push a button and you can hear the call of the elk along with the calls of many other Michigan species in the exhibit hall. From the center a trail leads north into the Heritage Nature Study Area, which includes observation platforms and marshes where you have a reasonably good chance of spotting many of Michigan's wild species.

The Carl T. Johnson Hunting and Fishing Center (231-779-1321) is open daily from 10 a.m. to 6 p.m. from Memorial Day through Dec 1 and the rest of the year from noon to 5 p.m. Fri and 10 a.m. to 5 p.m. Sat and Sun. A $10 recreation passport is required for vehicle entry into the park.

Places to Stay in Northwest Michigan

BAY VIEW

Stafford's Bay View Inn
US 31
(800) 258-1886
staffords.com/bayview

Terrace Inn
1549 Glendale St.
(800) 530-9898
theterraceinn.com

BEAVER ISLAND

Beaver Island Lodge
St. James
38210 Beaver Lodge Dr.
(231) 448-2396
beaverislandlodge.com

The Emerald Isle Hotel
St. James
37985 Kings Hwy.
(231) 448-2376
emeraldislehotel.com

BELLAIRE

Grand Victorian Bed & Breakfast
402 N. Bridge St.
(877) 438-6111
grandvictorian.com

CHARLEVOIX

Inn at Grey Gables
306 Belvedere
(231) 547-2251
innatgreygables.com

Pointes North Inn
101 Michigan Ave.
(866) 547-0055
pointesnorthcharlevoix
.com

Weathervane Terrace Hotel
111 Pine River Lane
(800) 552-0025
weathervane-chx.com

ELK RAPIDS

White Birch Lodge
571 Meguzee Point Rd.
(231) 264-8271
whitebirchlodge.org

ELLSWORTH

House on the Hill Bed & Breakfast
9661 Lake St.
(231) 588-6304
thehouseonthehill.com

FRANKFORT

Chimney Corners Resort
1602 Crystal Dr.
(231) 352-7522
chimneycornersresort.com

GAYLORD

Heart Lake Resort Cottages
9603 Old 27 South
(888) 595-5081
heartlakeresort.com

Marsh Ridge Resort
4815 Old US 27
(800) 743-7529
marshridgelodging.com

GLEN ARBOR

Lakeshore Inn
5793 S. Ray St.
(231) 334-3773
lakeshoreinnmotel.com

HARBOR SPRINGS

Birchwood Inn
7291 S. Lakeshore Dr.
(800) 530-9955
birchwoodinn.com

Colonial Inn
210 Artesian Ave.
(231) 526-2111
harborsprings.com

LELAND

Falling Waters Lodge
200 W. Cedar St.
(231) 256-9832
fallingwaterslodge.com

Whaleback Inn
1757 N. Manitou Trail
(M 22)
(800) 942-5322
whalebackinn.com

OMENA

Sunset Lodge Bed and Breakfast
12819 E. Tatch Rd.
(231) 386-9080
omenasunsetlodge.com

SELECTED CHAMBERS OF COMMERCE AND TOURISM BUREAUS

Beaver Island Chamber of Commerce
26215 Main St.
Beaver Island 49782
(231) 448-2505
beaverisland.org

Benzie County Visitors Bureau
P.O. Box 204
Benzonia 49616
(800) 882-5801
visitbenzie.com

Boyne County Convention and Visitors Bureau
401 E. Mitchell St.
Petoskey 49770
(800) 845-2828
petoskeyarea.com

Charlevoix Area Convention and Visitors Bureau
100 Main St.
Charlevoix 49720
visitcharlevoix.com
(800) 367-8557
charlevoixlodging.com

Gaylord Area Convention and Tourism Bureau
101 W. Main St
Gaylord 49735
(800) 345-8621
gaylordmichigan.net

Mackinaw Area Tourist Bureau
10800 US 23
Mackinaw City 49701
(800) 666-0160
mackinawcity.com

Sleeping Bear Dunes Visitors Bureau
6748 S. Dunes Hwy.
Glen Arbor 49630
(888) 334-8499
sleepingbeardunes.com

Traverse City Convention and Visitors Bureau
101 W. Grandview Pkwy
Traverse City 49684
(800) 940-1120
traversecity.com

PETOSKEY

Apple Tree Inn
915 Spring St.
(800) 348-2901
appletreeinn.com

Comfort Inn
1314 US 31
(231) 347-3220

Stafford's Perry Hotel
100 Lewis St.
(800) 737-1899
staffords.com/perryhotel

TRAVERSE CITY

Beach Haus Resort
1489 US 31 North
(231) 947-3560
beachhausresort.com

Cherry Tree Inn
2345 US 31
(800) 439-3093
cherrytreeinn.com

Grand Beach Resort Hotel
1683 US 31 North
(800) 968-1992
tcbeaches.com

Grand Traverse Resort
100 Grand Traverse
Village Blvd. (Acme)
(800) 236-1577
grandtraverseresort.com

Park Place Hotel
300 E. State St.
(231) 946-5000
park-place-hotel.com

Traverse Victorian Inn
461 Munson Ave.
(800) 506-5525
traversevictorian.com

Places to Eat in Northwest Michigan

BEAVER ISLAND

Dalwhinnoe Bakery
St. James
38240 Michigan Ave.
(231) 448-2736
mcdonoughsmarket.com
Deli

Stoney Acre Grill
St. James
26420 Carlisle Rd.
(231) 448-2560
stoneyacregrill.com
Bistro

BEULAH

Cherry Hut
216 N. Michigan Ave.
(231) 882-4431
cherryhutstore.com
American

BOYNE CITY

Red Mesa Grill
117 Water St.
(231) 582-0049
magnumhospitality.com
Tex-Mex

CHARLEVOIX

Grey Gables Inn
308 Belvedere Ave.
(231) 547-9261
greygablesinn.com
Fine Dining

Whitney's
307 Bridge St.
(231) 547-0818
whitneysofcharlevoix.com
Seafood

ELLSWORTH

Rowe Inn
6303 E. Jordan Rd.
(231) 588-7351
roweinn.com
Fine Dining

ELK RAPIDS

Pearls
617 Ames St.
(231) 264-0530
magnumhospitality.com
Cajun

Riverwalk Grill
106 Ames St.
(231) 264-9121
tcgrills.com
Outdoor Dining

Siren Hall
151 River St.
(231) 264-6062
sirenhall.com
Fine Dining

FRANKFORT

Chimney Corners Resort
1602 Crystal Dr.
(231) 352-7522
chimneycornersresort.com
American

GAYLORD

Diana's Delights
138 W. Main St.
(989) 732-6564
American

GRAYLING

Spike's Keg o' Nails
301 N. James St.
(989) 348-7113
spikes-grayling.com
Tavern

HARBOR SPRINGS

New York Restaurant
101 State St.
(231) 526-1904
thenewyork.com
American

OTHER ATTRACTIONS

Benzie Area Historical Museum
Benzonia
(231) 882-5539
benziemuseum.org

Colonial Michilimackinac
Mackinaw City
(231) 436-8705
mackinacparks.com

Empire Area Museum
Empire
(231) 326-5568

Gaslight Shopping District
Petoskey

Leelanau Historical Museum
Leland
(231) 256-7475
leelanauhistory.org

Lighthouse Park
Old Mission Peninsula

Sunset Park
Petoskey
(231) 347-2500

LAKE LEELANAU

Kejara's Bridge
202 W. Main St.
(231) 256-7720
kejarasbridge.com
Organic

LELAND

Bluebird
102 E. River
(231) 256-9081
leelanau.com/bluebird
Seafood

The Cove
111 River St.
(231) 256-9834
thecoveleland.com
Outdoor Dining

MISSION PENINSULA

The Jolly Pumpkin Cafe
13512 Peninsula Dr.
(231) 223-4333
jollypumpkin.com
American

Mission Table
13512 Peninsula Dr.
(231) 223-4222
missiontable.net
Fine Dining

Old Mission Tavern
17015 Center Rd.
(231) 223-7280
oldmissiontavern.com
American

PETOSKEY

City Park Grill
432 E. Lake St.
(231) 347-0101
cityparkgrill.com
Eclectic

Jesperson's
312 Howard St.
(231) 347-3601
American

Palette Bistro
321 Bay St.
(231) 348-3321
palettebistropetoskey.com
Fine Dining

Roast & Toast
309 Lake St.
(231) 347-7767
roastandtoast.com
American

Whitecaps
215 E. Lake St.
(231) 348-7092
whitecapsrestaurant.com
Fine Dining

TRAVERSE CITY

Blue Tractor
423 S. Union St.
(231) 922-9515
bluetractorcookshop.com
American

Don's Drive-In
2030 US 31 North
(231) 938-1860
Burgers

Ham Bonz
1108 E. Eighth St.
(231) 929-9288
Barbecue

North Peak Brewing Company
400 W. Front St.
(231) 941-7325
northpeak.net
Brewpub

Poppycock's
128 E. Front St.
(231) 941-7632
poppycockstc.com
Vegetarian

Red Ginger
237 E. Front St.
(231) 944-1733
eatatginger.com
Asian

EASTERN UPPER PENINSULA

The "Mighty Mac" sounds like a hamburger with the works, but to most Michiganders it's the Mackinac Bridge, the only link between the Lower and Upper Peninsulas and the third-longest bridge in the country. Building a bridge was first considered in 1884, but the 5-mile span wasn't built until 1957, finally uniting a state that for its first 120 years was divided by a stretch of water known as the Straits of Mackinac.

Most travelers view the **Mackinac Bridge** as a very scenic drive. A trip across the Mighty Mac is a 360-degree panorama of shorelines, Great Lakes, and islands scattered everywhere, while below, the straits bustle with ferries, freighters, and fishing boats. The bridge is also the link between two worlds. Unlike industrialized southern Michigan, the Upper Peninsula's economy was based on lumbering and mining. After the majestic white pines were cut and the mines closed, this section of Michigan fell upon hard times, which in some ways continue today. Residents of the north, however, are quick to point out that the first permanent settlement in the state was not Detroit but Sault

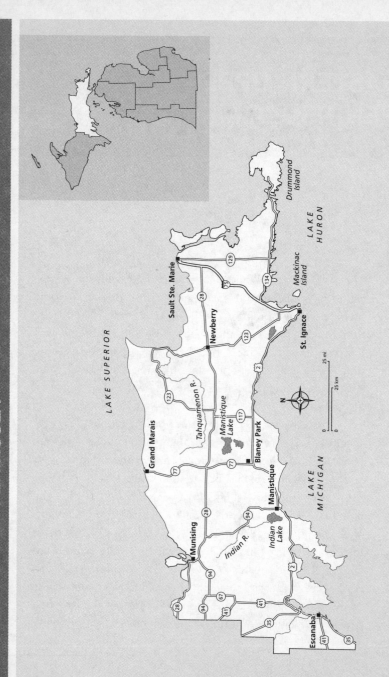

EASTERN UPPER PENINSULA

LAKE SUPERIOR

LAKE HURON

LAKE MICHIGAN

Drummond Island

Mackinac Island

Sault Ste. Marie

Newberry

St. Ignace

Grand Marais

Manistique Lake

Blaney Park

Manistique

Munising

Indian Lake

Indian R.

Tahquamenon R.

Escanaba

25 mi

25 km

N

Ste. Marie and that their endurance proves their long history is not about to end anytime soon. Survival is a way of life in the U.P.

What travelers will quickly discover upon crossing the bridge is a place of remote beauty and unique character, where interstate highways are almost nonexistent, and motel chains and fast-food restaurants are few and far between. Almost every road in the U.P. is "off the beaten path," offering natural beauty, family-run inns and cafes, and outdoor opportunities that will satisfy any lover of pristine forests, lakes, and streams.

Mackinac County

Sometimes in our rush to see one place, we overlook another. Such is often the case of a place like *St. Ignace.* This historical town, the second oldest settlement in Michigan, has a scenic harbor and a main street full of shops and restaurants. Only who takes the time to look around when we're all racing through to catch the next boat to Mackinac Island?

AUTHOR'S TOP TEN PICKS

Fayette State Park
Garden
(906) 644-2603

Fort Mackinac
Mackinac Island
(906) 847-3328

Grand Hotel
Mackinac Island
(800) 334-7263
grandhotel.com

Great Lakes Shipwreck Museum
Paradise
(906) 635-1742
shipwreckmuseum.com

Kitch-Iti-Kipi
Manistique
(906) 644-5134

Peninsula Point Lighthouse
Stonington
(906) 474-6442

Pictured Rock Boat Cruises
Munising
(906) 387-2379
picturedrocks.com

Seney National Wildlife Refuge
Germfask
(906) 586-9851

Soo Locks Park
Sault Ste. Marie
(800) 647-2858

Tahquamenon Falls
Paradise
(906) 492-3415

A Legitimate Tourist Trap

Before there was Mystery Spot and Sea Shell City with its "man-eating clam" or a miniature golf course in the shape of Michigan, there was *Castle Rock.*

In a region of the state lined with tourist traps and gift shops selling rubber toma-hawks and "I Am a Yooper" refrigerator magnets, Castle Rock is the original. It is also one of the most affordable attractions on either side of the Mackinac Bridge and, located right at exit 348 off I-75, a great leg stretcher after the long drive north.

What the heck, let's stop.

There is nothing phony about the rock itself. Castle Rock is a sea stack, one of a handful in and around St. Ignace, the result of limestone caves collapsing and waves eroding the remaining rock into pillars and arches more than 4,000 years ago. The most famous are Sugar Loaf and Arch Rock on Mackinac Island, while in downtown St. Ignace there's St. Anthony's Rock. At 183 feet, Castle Rock is not only the tallest one but also the only one you're allowed to climb.

The slick brochure promoting Castle Rock states that it was used by Indians as a lookout and that Pontiac, the great Ojibway chief, was thought to have stood on it. Of course it also says that the legendary giant Paul Bunyan and his blue ox, Babe, once sat at the base of it. Believe what you want.

What is known is that historical photos show people climbing the rock as early as 1911 and that in 1930 Clarence Eby purchased the rock and 80 acres surround-ing it. He built a souvenir stand at the base of it and a stairway to the top of it, and

Slow down. St. Ignace is an intriguing city, and you don't have to go any farther than the *Museum of Ojibwa Culture* to discover why. The city-operated museum gives a vivid picture of the Straits of Mackinac in the 1600s and 1700s when the Ojibway, Huron, and Odawa Indians mingled with the French in what is now downtown St. Ignace. The museum is housed in a former Catholic church, and through video presentations and exhibits it focuses on the Woodland Indian culture and how these indig-enous people survived the harsh winters of the Upper Peninsula. Outside there is a replica of a Huron longhouse that can be viewed.

The Museum of Ojibwa Culture (906-643-9161; museumofojibwaculture .net) is at 500 N. State St., next door to the St. Ignace Chamber of Commerce office. Hours are 9:30 a.m. to 8 p.m. Mon through Sat and noon to 5 p.m.

he charged people 10 cents to climb it, enticing them with signs that read: "Stop and climb. Still only a dime!"

That's one of the most amazing things about Castle Rock—its admission fee. It remained 10 cents until 1979, when it was raised to 25 cents. Finally, in 2001 the fee was increased to 50 cents. Still, it's cheaper to climb Castle Rock than to cross the Mackinac Bridge.

To reach the sea stack, you first have to pass through Castle Rock Curios Shop, and this is where you might lose the kids. The large gift shop is stocked with thousands of souvenirs people expect you to bring home from the Upper Peninsula: polished agates, Mackinac Bridge playing cards, Daniel Boone raccoon caps, fake arrowheads, and a bald man's hairbrush (it has no bristles).

From the shop you head outside where there is a giant statue of Paul Bunyan and Babe (life-size?) and the stairway to the top of Castle Rock, a climb of 170 steps.

The climb is worth it as the view is magnificent. Spread out below you is St. Ignace, while offshore is Mackinac Island and in between them a handful of ferries hustling tourists back and forth. You can see Lake Huron, Lake Michigan, even the towers of the Mackinac Bridge.

The view is so expansive that it's easy to envision Indians using Castle Rock as an observation post. But as for Paul Bunyan using it as a backrest . . . that's still a stretch for this flatlander.

Castle Rock (906-643-8268; castlerockmi.com) is open May through Oct from 9 a.m. to 9 p.m. daily.

Sun, from late June to Labor Day. In early June and from Sept to mid-Oct, the museum is open from 9 a.m. to 5 p.m. Admission is by donation.

Next door to the museum is ***Marquette Mission Park,*** while across State Street is one end of the ***Huron Boardwalk.*** Together the small park and the 2-mile-long boardwalk take you back more than 300 years into the life of this town.

Marquette Mission Park features Father Marquette's grave and several outdoor exhibits that retrace the significance of this little plot of land. From the park you then cross the street to Huron Boardwalk, which winds south along the St. Ignace waterfront. The boardwalk features its own series of historical displays, which cover everything from "Nineteenth-Century St. Ignace" to the "Legacy of White Pine" in text and photos. Between the displays are benches, each with a million-dollar view of Mackinac Island, the ferries making high-speed runs to the resort island and the rest of the bustling waterfront. To reach Marquette Mission Park and Huron Boardwalk from I-75 on the north side of the Mackinac Bridge, take exit 344A and follow Business Loop I-75 to State Street, which parallels the boardwalk.

trivia

Labor Day is the only time of the year that people are allowed to walk across the Mackinac Bridge. More than 70,000 people trek across the 5-mile-long bridge that day, including most governors of Michigan and, in 1992, President George H. W. Bush. Walkers begin on the north side of the bridge and jump on free shuttle buses to return to their cars afterward.

There are numerous forts to visit in Michigan, but without a doubt the most famous and probably the most beloved is *Fort Mackinac* on *Mackinac Island.* Built and first occupied by the British in 1779, the fort is part of *Mackinac Island State Park* and is the scene of cannon firings and other living-history demonstrations throughout the summer. The Officer's Stone Quarters, constructed of limestone in 1781, is the oldest building in Michigan. The scene of the white stockade looming above the island's downtown area is probably one of the most photographed in the state.

The fort is open daily from 9:30 a.m. to 7 p.m. from mid-June through Aug and 9 a.m. to 4:30 p.m. from mid-May to mid-June and after Labor Day through mid-Oct. Admission is $11 per adult, $6.50 per child, which also covers 6 other interesting museums in the downtown area of Mackinac Island including Mission Church, the oldest church in Michigan; Indian Dormitory, with displays and craft demonstrations on Native American cooking and weaving; and Beaumont Memorial.

Mackinac Island State Park actually covers 1,800 acres, or 83 percent of the island, and offers much more than just cannon demonstrations twice a day. There are 140 miles of roads and trails, open to use by hikers, cyclists, and equestrians, but not cars, which are not allowed on the island. The roads and trails loop through a surprisingly rugged and wooded terrain, past some of the most interesting natural formations in Michigan, including *Arch Rock,* the almost perfect 50-foot-wide limestone arch. The vast majority of

When Mackinac Is Mackinaw

Let's see; there's Mackinac Island and Mackinaw City and Fort Michilimackinac and the mackinaw, which some people still wear. No wonder many out-of-staters are tongue-tied when they visit this region of Michigan.

The word Mackinac—or Mackinaw—is a shorter form of Michinnimakinong, which was the Native Americans' description of the area; mish-inni-maki-nong or "great connecting place." That's a good description for the Straits of Mackinac, which connects Lake Michigan and Lake Huron. Thus on the north side you have Mackinac Island and Fort Mackinac, and on the south side there's Mackinaw City and Fort Michilimackinac. A mackinaw is also a regional cloth or coat made from thick woolen material.

To sound like a Yooper (somebody who lives in the Upper Peninsula), just make sure you always end any of those words in "awe" and never "ack." Mackinac should never rhyme with "bric-a-brac," but rather with "Saginaw." The only time you say "ack" is when you call the Mackinac Bridge by its nickname . . . the Big Mac.

visitors reach these attractions on a bicycle, which can either be brought to the island on the ferry or rented in the downtown area.

For more information contact Mackinac Island State Park (906-847-3328; mackinacparks.com). For information on the three ferry companies that provide transportation to the island, call *Arnold Transit* (800-542-8528), *Shepler's Mackinac Island Ferry* (800-828-6157), or *Star Line* (800-638-9892).

Scenic shoreline drives abound in Michigan, but it's hard to argue when someone says the most spectacular of all is the stretch of US 2 from St. Ignace to the hamlet of Naubinway. The views of Lake Michigan, beaches, dunes, and offshore island are rarely interrupted along this 42-mile segment. One of the places to spot for a

trivia

Mackinac Island was the site of one of the most celebrated moments in Michigan's history. After Americans took over Fort Mackinac diplomatically, the British recaptured it during the War of 1812 by secretly landing in the middle of the night and dragging a cannon up a bluff overlooking the fort. When the American garrison woke up the next morning and saw what was aimed at them, they gave up without firing a single shot.

Somewhere in Time Celebrated at Grand Hotel

On a whim, a young playwright from Chicago decides to take a trip and stay at the **Grand Hotel** (800-334-7263; grandhotel.com) on Mackinac Island. Although he is a success in his profession, Richard Collier feels lonely and unhappy. He has never found his special love.

Wandering around the historic hotel to pass the time, the writer steps into the Grand Hotel Hall of History. There he encounters the photo of an actress who appeared at the hotel in 1912. Drawn to the picture, the young man feels driven to will himself back in time to meet the beautiful actress, his destiny Elise McKenna. Somehow or other, he succeeds.

Of course, this is all a Hollywood movie. And it was made way back in 1980, for goodness sake. But, if you visit the Grand Hotel on a special October weekend, you would never know the story wasn't true or that the tale was filmed decades ago. Ladies in long dresses and frilly hats will be enjoying tea in the hotel lobby, walking the beautiful grounds with dainty parasols to protect them from the sun or watching the sunset from the world's longest front porch. Men in turn-of-the-century suits and gentlemanly hats will be sipping fine wine, discussing the merits of strong steeds pulling the passing carriages or taking a turn on one of the island's many bicycles.

It will truly be like turning back the clock to Somewhere in Time, the 1980 movie that critics bashed but moviegoers loved. "I've never seen anything like it," says

panoramic view on this drive is **Cut River Gorge Roadside Park** on US 2, 26 miles west of St. Ignace.

Actually there are 3 parks on both sides of this stunning gorge that are connected by the impressive Cut River Bridge, a steel-arch cantilever structure that was built in 1948 and stands 147 feet above the river. You can walk across the bridge for an impressive view of Lake Michigan or follow one of 3 foot trails that wind down to the Cut River and then out to a beautiful beach on the Great Lake. By combining two of the trails with a walk across the bridge itself, you'll enjoy an interesting loop of between 1 and 1.3 miles.

A much less traveled but equally scenic route is east of the Mackinac Bridge on M 134. The road follows the U.P. shoreline along northern Lake Huron, passing the intriguing Les Cheneaux Islands and ending at De Tour,

Bob Tagatz, historian at the Grand Hotel. "I've been here almost 20 years and there has not been a single day that someone has not asked me about the movie. The following of the movie borders on bizarre."

Starring Jane Seymour and Christopher Reeve, the classic movie featured the Grand Hotel as its backdrop. In fact, some folks swear the 1887 Victorian hotel is actually the scene stealer. Perched high over the Straits of Mackinac, the hotel seems to have gotten even more beautiful with the passing years.

The annual *Somewhere in Time* weekends officially started in 1991, but movie fans were staging their own impromptu tributes even before that. R.D. Musser, owner of the Grand Hotel, allowed the facility to be used by Universal Studios for free. All filming took place in the height of the season, with the hotel fully booked. The film company worked around the dining of paying guests, filming the dining room during the night.

Every setting required by the *Somewhere in Time* script was found on Mackinac Island. The movie was filmed entirely on the island, except for a few brief scenes shot in Chicago.

"It's just a beautiful movie," Tagatz says. "I am an historian so time travel is something I am very interested in. Then the theme of the movie that love transcends death is something I think everyone wants to believe in."

Hint: The two lovers are not destined to live happily ever after in 1912. But they eventually do find each other again—somewhere in time.

the departure point for remote Drummond Island, a haven of fishing resorts. The best stretch is the 24 miles from Cedarville in Mackinac County to De Tour in Chippewa County. This segment is one continuous view of the lake, the islands, and long stretches of sand where there are more than a dozen turnoffs and roadside parks, allowing everybody an uncrowded beach for a lazy afternoon in the sun.

Chippewa County

Sault Ste. Marie is synonymous with the Soo Locks, the world's largest and busiest locking system, the crucial link for freighters passing between Lake Superior and Lake Huron. The city of 14,253 is Michigan's oldest and has

Feasting on Mackinac Island

Dinner began downtown, near Huron Street, where daytime visitors, with a rubber tomahawk under one arm and a 1-pound box of fudge under the other, were scurrying toward the ferries to get off this historical island before dark. We went in the other direction.

We signaled for a horse-drawn taxi and then settled back in the cushioned carriage seats as it clip-clopped its way past the Grand Hotel, up a steep hill, and finally into the island's wooded interior. Some 15 minutes later we emerged from the trees at the impressive Stonecliffe Mansion, home of the **Woods Restaurant** (906-847-3331; grandhotel.com).

Built in 1905, it was once the site of several religious and educational institutions and today houses the Woods Restaurant. The interior is a cross between a hunting lodge and a Bavarian mountain retreat with clunky wooden chairs, a huge stone fireplace, and enough stuffed animals on the walls to make any hunter feel at home.

We feasted on veal Wiener schnitzel, Austrian steak soup, and wild mushroom stew, and then enjoyed a second bottle of wine, not worrying about drinking and driving because, as our waiter pointed out, "there are no cars on the island to drive." We topped off the evening with another carriage ride back to our hotel.

And you thought the only thing to eat on Mackinac Island was fudge.

There is more to dining at this summer retreat than its legendary candy shops. Dozens of restaurants, cafes, and pubs cater to thousands of tourists each summer, satisfying even those with the most finicky taste buds. But the key to a memorable dining experience is to stick around after the last ferry has pulled out, to book a room in a hotel or a bed-and-breakfast, and then indulge in that time-honored tradition of a late and leisurely dinner, enjoyed long after the daytime crowds have vanished.

Reserve a room by first calling the **Mackinac Island Chamber of Commerce**

been an important center since the French Canadian voyagers in the 1700s portaged their long canoes and bales of furs around St. Mary's Rapids.

Most of this colorful history of shipping can be appreciated by walking along Water Street, beginning at its east end, where the **SS Valley Camp** is docked next to the Chamber of Commerce Information Center. The 550-foot freighter was once owned and used by the Republic Steel Corporation

(800-454-5227; mackinacisland.org) for a list of accommodations. Then hop on the first ferry leaving the mainland and take a gastronomic romp around the island:

Horn's Gaslight Bar: In the 1920s Ed Horn was working for the Life-Saving Service at the Round Island Lighthouse when he and his wife opened up a pool hall and snack shop on Huron Street. After Prohibition, Horn acquired one of Michigan's first liquor licenses, and his pool hall became Horn's Gaslight Bar in 1933. It still is, and the interior includes the original tin roof, historical photos on the walls, a long polished bar, and, of course, a honky-tonk piano player. Try the tequila prawns, oversize shrimp sautéed in tequila, lime, and garlic. Horn's is located at 7200 Main St. (906-847-6154; hornsbar.com).

Grand Hotel Main Dining Room: Everybody knows there is a $10 fee during the day to stroll along the world's longest porch if you're not a guest. Few people realize you can have dinner at the hotel's main dining room without either booking a room or paying that fee. And everybody should, at least once. Dinner at the Grand Hotel (800-33-GRAND; grandhotel.com) is an experience, not a meal. You begin by strolling through the middle of the huge, 760-seat dining room along the carpeted runway affectionately known as "Peacock Alley." Go ahead, strut a little on the way to your table.

An army of 55 waiters will tend to your needs as you indulge in such entrees as broiled whitefish and trout scaloppine, sliced veal loin with sweetbreads, or herb-roasted prime rib of beef. Afterward you can enjoy a fine cigar and a snifter of brandy on the porch.

Fort Mackinac Tea Room: There's more to this fort than just the musket and cannon demonstrations. The Tea Room Restaurant (800-33-GRAND; grandhotel .com) in the Officer's Stone Quarters is a string of yellow-canopy tables overlooking the island's bustling harbor, the Mackinac Bridge, the two Great Lakes that meet there, and so on.

Thus at the fort they boast that you can enjoy sandwiches, soups, and salads in the oldest building on Mackinac Island (1781) with the best view in the state.

and frequently passed through the locks. Today it has been turned into one of the largest Great Lakes marine museums and is listed as a National Historic Site. From the pilothouse and the 1,800-horsepower steam engine to the captain's quarters and the galley, visitors are free to roam the ship for a close-up look at life aboard an ore carrier, where a crew of almost 30 worked, slept, and ate. Down below, in its massive cargo holds, are models and displays of Great Lakes vessels, aquariums of the freshwater fish that abound nearby, and a room devoted to wreckage of the *Edmund Fitzgerald*, the ore carrier that sank in raging Lake Superior in 1975, taking its captain and crew of 28 with it.

The SS *Valley Camp* (888-744-7867) is open daily from 10 a.m. to 5 p.m. and 11 a.m. to 5 p.m. Sun mid-May through June, 9 a.m. to 6 p.m. in July and Aug, and 10 a.m. to 4 p.m. and Sun from 11 a.m. to 5 p.m. from Sept through Oct 15. Admission is $12 for adults and $6 for children ages 6 to 16.

Another interesting stop in any tour of the city is the ***River of History Museum.*** Through the use of 8 exhibit galleries and a state-of-the-art audio system, the museum takes you on an 8,000-year journey along the shores of St. Mary's River. You begin with the sounds of ice melting and the rapids roaring as a glacier carves out the river valley. You move on to the sprawling Indian camp that was once here and then see the first French explorers paddling ashore in 1662.

The River of History Museum (906-632-1999; riverofhistory.org) is at 531 Ashmun St. It's open mid-May through mid-Oct from 11 a.m. to 5 p.m. Mon through Sat. Admission is $7 for adults and $3.50 for children.

To reach the locks to the north, return to and follow Water Street, which in 1982 was renovated into the ***Locks Park Walkway,*** providing an excellent overview of the city's 350-year past. The walkway is marked by blue symbols of freighters, and interpretive plaques explain the history of various areas and renovated buildings. Along the way you'll pass the Baraga House, the 1864 home of Bishop Frederic Baraga, a missionary and historian known as the "Snowshoe Saint" who was the first bishop of the U.P. Nearby is the Johnston House, which was constructed in 1794 for an Irish fur trader, making it the oldest surviving home in Michigan. The walkway also passes the site of Fort Brady, built by the Americans in 1823 and the spot where in 1820 General Lewis Cass lowered and removed the last British flag to fly over US soil.

Water Street ends at ***Soo Locks Park*** in the heart of downtown Sault Ste. Marie. The US Army Corps of Engineers maintains the park and visitor center, and next to the locks it has built a raised viewing platform that provides an excellent view of ships being raised and lowered to the various lake levels. Your chances of seeing this take place are quite good; some 12,000 vessels pass through the locks annually. During the summer an average of 30 freighters pass through each day.

The interesting visitor center was doubled in size in 1995 and tells the history of the locks, beginning with the construction of the first American lock in 1853. Exhibits include a short video and a working model of a lock. The *Soo Locks Information Center* (906-253-9101) is open mid-May through mid-Oct from 9 a.m. to 9 p.m. There is no admission fee.

You can experience the locks directly through *Soo Locks Boat Tours,* which offers a 2-hour cruise up and down St. Mary's River, first passing through an American lock and then returning through the Canadian one. Boats depart daily from mid-May through mid-Oct, beginning

trivia

More than 82 million tons of cargo pass through the Soo Locks annually, with more than half of it iron ore from mines in the Upper Peninsula and Minnesota. Coal being shipped north accounts for 15 million tons, and Minnesota wheat being shipped east, 9 million tons.

at 10 a.m. and ending with the last cruise at 4 p.m. Soo Locks Boat Tours (800-432-6301; soolocks.com) maintains 2 docks, both on Portage Avenue south of the SS *Valley Camp.* Tickets are $23 for adults and $11 for children ages 5 to 12 (4 and under free).

As well known to locals as the locks is *The Antlers,* an Irish bar and restaurant on Portage Avenue. The exterior of the simple stone building that houses the eatery is misleading. Inside, the decor is a museum of collectibles (or, some say, junk) including hundreds of mounted animals on the walls, a birch-bark canoe hanging from the ceiling, and a 15-foot boa constrictor overlooking the bar. No wall is left bare. Hockey great Gordie Howe (whose picture also adorns the walls) was a frequent patron of the restaurant, which is known for its steaks and "Paul Bunyan" hamburgers. The Antlers (906-253-1728) is open daily from 11 a.m. and dinner prices range from $9 to $19.

One of the more interesting drives in the U.P. follows Whitefish Bay, beginning at Brimley (reached from M 28) and ending at desolate Whitefish Point. At Brimley follow Lake Shore Drive to the west as it hugs the shoreline, with frequent views of beaches and Lake Superior. In 7.5 miles, you'll come to the *Point Iroquois Lightstation.* The classic lighthouse was built in 1870 and operated until 1963, when sophisticated radar made it obsolete. The Coast Guard turned it over to the US Forestry Service, which worked with local historical societies to open it to the public in 1984. It has since been added to the National Register of Historic Places and features a few displays and artifacts in 3 rooms of the lightkeeper's house. This lighthouse is mainly popular for its curved staircase of 70 steps that leads to the top of the tower and a view of the surrounding area. The panorama, needless to say, is impressive, as you can see almost the entire coastline of Whitefish Bay and miles out into Lake Superior, including any freighter that happens to be passing by. The lighthouse (906-437-5272) is open May 15 through Oct 15 from 9 a.m. to 5 p.m. daily. Winter hours from Oct 16 to May 14 are 10 a.m. to 3 p.m. Sat and Sun.

trivia

The only Michigan highway not used by cars or trucks is M 185, the 8-mile blacktopped road that circles Mackinac Island. Except for emergency vehicles—fire trucks and ambulances—travel on M 185 is restricted to pedestrians, bicyclists, and horses.

Lake Shore Drive, with its numerous turnoffs and scenic beaches, ends at M 123. The state road is well traveled as it first heads north along Whitefish Bay and then swings west at Paradise to head inland to Tahquamenon Falls. Though the popular falls, second in size only to Niagara Falls east of the Mississippi River, is the destination for most travelers, there is a good reason to continue heading north on Whitefish Point Road. At the very end, at the very tip of the remote peninsula that juts out into Lake Superior, is the ***Great Lakes Shipwreck Museum.*** Whitefish Point is a combination of sandy beach, small dunes, and thunderous Lake Superior waves crashing along the shoreline. It also marks the eastern end of an 80-mile stretch that sailors knew as the Graveyard of the Great Lakes. Raging northwest storms, built up over 200 miles of open water, have caused 300 recorded shipwrecks in which 320 seamen have died along this section of shoreline.

The Great Lakes Shipwreck Historical Society, a group of divers researching the wrecks, opened the museum in 1986 in abandoned buildings of the Coast Guard station, whose light, beaming since 1849, is the oldest active one on Lake Superior. In the main museum, each display is devoted to a different shipwreck. Visitors see a drawing or photograph of the vessel and artifacts that divers have collected, and read the story of its fatal voyage. The ships range from sailing schooners of the early 1800s to the *Edmund Fitzgerald*, the latest and largest shipwreck, which continues

International Bridge Walk

The International Bridge that connects Sault Ste. Marie in Michigan with Ontario's
Sault Ste. Marie is a 2-mile-long toll bridge that was built in 1962 and financed
by both the American and Canadian governments. The bridge rises to 124 feet
above the St. Mary's River, and from the middle of it, you can see the famous St.
Mary's Rapids and the Soo Locks, which ships use to bypass them. In June Sault
Ste. Marie stages an International Bridge Walk that is similar to, but shorter than,
the well-known Mackinac Bridge Walk on Labor Day. Call the Sault St. Marie
Convention and Visitors Bureau (800-647-2858; saultstemarie.com) for dates and
details.

to fascinate residents of the U.P. A darkened interior with theatrical lights,
soft music, and special sound effects of seagulls and foghorns sends tingles
down the spines of most people.

Another building has been turned into a theater where underwater films
of the wrecks are shown, and the lightkeeper's house has been restored.
The newest addition at the museum is lodging for those who want to spend
a night at the lightstation. The 1923 Coast Guard Lifeboat Station Crews
Quarters is now a bed-and-breakfast, offering 5 rooms with private baths
and televisions, yet possessing the historic charm of the lighthouse era.
Lodging is available Apr to late Nov and the double rooms are $150 per
night and include admission to the museum.

The Great Lakes Shipwreck Museum (888-492-3747; shipwreckmuseum
.com) is open from May through Oct daily from 10 a.m. to 6 p.m. Admission
is $13 for adults, $9 for children, or $35 for a family.

Most of the point is a state wildlife sanctuary, renowned for the variety
of birds that pass through. The Michigan Audubon Society has established
the ***Whitefish Point Bird Observatory*** at 16914 Whitefish Point Rd.,
across from the Point Iroquois Lightstation, where a small information room
tells birders the species to be watching for as they hike along the point's
network of trails. The point is best known for hawks, as up to 25,000 have
been sighted in a season, while in April and May, as many as 7,000 loons
will pass by. Other species seen include bald eagles, peregrine falcons, and
a variety of songbirds. The observatory (906-492-3596; wpbo.org) is open
from 10 a.m. to 4 p.m. daily from mid-Apr through mid-Oct.

TOP ANNUAL EVENTS

JUNE

International Bridge Walk
Sault Ste. Marie
(800) 647-2858

Lilac Festival
Mackinac Island
(800) 451-5227
mackinacislandlilacfestival.org

Straits Area Antique Auto Show
St. Ignace
(800) 970-8717

AUGUST

Les Cheneaux Antique Wooden Boat Show
Hessel
(906) 484-2821
lchistorical.org

Upper Peninsula State Fair
Escanaba
(906) 786-4011
upstatefair.org

SEPTEMBER

Labor Day Bridge Walk
St. Ignace, September
(906) 643-7600

Luce County

The county that lies between Chippewa and Alger is probably best known for the Two Hearted River, used by Ernest Hemingway as the title for one of his most famous short stories. Today it remains a favorite for anglers and canoers, who enjoy the solitude of this remote wilderness river that empties into Lake Superior.

The best place to soak in this wilderness setting is *Tahquamenon Falls State Park,* the second largest state park in the Upper Peninsula. Split between Luce and Chippewa Counties, the 38,496-acre park includes *Upper Tahquamenon Falls,* which spans 200 feet across the Tahquamenon River and descends 50 feet into a sea of mist and foam. You can hear the thunder of the falls the minute you step out of the car.

East of the Mississippi River, only Niagara Falls in New York and Cumberland Falls in Kentucky have longer drops than Tahquamenon.

The falls is a day-use area 21 miles from Newberry on M 123. From the parking lot, it's a quarter-mile walk to the bluffs overlooking the Upper Falls.

The best views, however, are obtained by descending the long staircase into the gorge.

Four miles downriver is **Lower Tahquamenon Falls.** While not as impressive as the Upper Falls, this series of cascades is much more fun because it is best viewed by combining a short paddle across the river with a walk around a small island.

The adventure begins by renting a rowboat from the park concession and then shoving off into the brown waters, which are stained by tamarack trees, of the Tahquamenon River. At the island there is a large dock at which to tie up your boat while a wooden stairway leads to the start of the trail. Step-for-step this is one of the most beautiful footpaths in the state, only there are not a lot of steps. It's a loop of less than a mile that skirts the outside of the island, passing one display of tumbling water after another. Along the way parents and kids kick their shoes off, wade out onto the ledge of one of the many drops, and let the river cascade across their legs.

Frozen Falls

The **Upper Tahquamenon Falls,** a stunning sight in the summer, is equally beautiful in the winter when the Upper Peninsula's frigid temperatures turn the tumbling water into sculptured ice. There is no need to pack snowshoes. The falls is such a popular sight with snowmobilers that the park staff plows the parking lot and keeps the short path and stairs to the viewing decks open.

During most winters the river above the falls remains open and flows to the brink of the cascade where the water in the middle tumbles down across large ice formations. Downriver everything is frozen white, and along the rocky bluffs that enclose the falls are gigantic icy stalactites and stalagmites, some of them 10 to 15 feet long.

The walk in is short. Within a quarter mile from the parking lot, you're standing at the first overlook, viewing the falls from a distance. The best view, however, is reached by descending the 94 steps into the gorge to a platform right above the cascade where you can lean against the railing for a close-up of the ice formations that grow larger with every splash of water heading downstream.

The formations are so varied and intriguing that you could study them for hours. But most winter visitors are scurrying back up the stairs after 10 or 15 minutes before their toes and fingers turn into stalagmites and stalactites, too.

Lower Tahquamenon Falls (906-492-3415) is on M 123, 12 miles west of Paradise and 23 miles northeast of Newberry. A vehicle entry permit is required to enter the state park, and there is a small fee to rent the rowboats.

For travelers in Luce County who want to spend their nights in comfort at a historic inn, they should book a room at **Chamberlin's Ole Forest Inn** right on H 33, a mile north of the blinker light to Curtis. Built in the late 1800s, it was originally a railroad hotel near the Curtis depot. The railroad stopped service in 1909, and 15 years later the building was moved to its present location on a high bluff overlooking Manistique Lake.

The classic 19th-century hotel features a wraparound veranda overlooking the lake; a sprawling lobby complete with wicker chairs, deep sofas, and a 6-foot stone fireplace; and 10 rooms with a unique turn-of-the-20th-century decor. Room rates for the Ole Forest Inn (800-292-0440; chamberlinsinn.com) range from $89 to $130 per night and include a full breakfast in the morning.

Another pleasant spot in Luce County to spend a night is **Muskallonge Lake State Park** at the north end of County Road H 37 in the northwest corner of the county. The park is actually a strip of land between Muskallonge Lake, known for its pike, perch, and smallmouth bass fishing, and Lake Superior. You can camp on a site overlooking the small lake and then wander over to Lake Superior to enjoy its seemingly endless sandy shoreline. There is a vehicle fee to enter Muskallonge Lake State Park (906-658-3338) and an overnight fee of $16 to $18 for one of its 179 campsites.

Alger County

Grand Marais, a booming lumber town of 2,500 at the turn of the 20th century, is a sleepy hamlet of about 500 today and the gateway for the eastern half of Pictured Rocks National Lakeshore.

One spot to see within the national lakeshore is the **Grand Sable Banks and Dunes.** To reach the sandy hills, follow County Road H 58 west of town, first passing the parking lot and short side trail to Sable Falls and then the Grand Sable Visitor Center. From both places there are half-mile trails that lead to the Grand Sable Dunes. Or you can continue following the county road a mile past the visitor center. On one side of the road are the picnic area and beach of Grand Sable Lake, and on the other side is a

Michigan's Most Beautiful Hike

The Lakeshore Trail in Pictured Rocks National Lakeshore is one of Michigan's most popular backpacking treks, a 42.8-mile hike from Grand Marais to Munising with most of it strung along Lake Superior. But if you don't have four days to spare or the desire to haul a backpack for that long, the **Chapel Loop** is the perfect alternative.

This hike begins and ends at Chapel parking lot, 14 miles east of Munising via County Road H 58 and then north on Chapel Road. The entire loop is a 10.2-mile walk over generally level terrain, making it a long day hike, but there are many ways to shorten it.

The first leg of the loop is hiking to Lake Superior along Chapel Falls Trail, an old road that heads north into the woods and in 1.4 miles reaches **Chapel Falls,** one of the most impressive in the park. Two observation decks provide a good view of the 60-foot waterfall that hurls itself over the sharp edge of a cliff into a steep-sided canyon.

In another quarter mile you reach Lake Superior and Chapel Rock, a striking pair of sandstone pillars with a large pine growing on the top of them. Just to the west is Chapel Beach, a half mile of wide, sandy shoreline framed in at one end by colorful sandstone cliffs and at the other by a waterfall where Chapel Creek leaps into Lake Superior.

At this point most people return to the parking lot, following the Chapel Lake Trail for a 6.1-mile loop. Big mistake.

By heading east on Lakeshore Trail, you'll see the most impressive scenery of the day. For the next 4.5 miles, the trail skirts Lake Superior and passes numerous overlooks of the promontories and formations that make up the Grand Portal cliffs. There is no shoreline in Michigan more beautiful than this stretch, where the orange-reddish sandstone contrasts vividly with the deep blue of Lake Superior.

The most interesting spot is a sandy beach just past Grand Portal Point, 4.6 miles into the loop. Only this beach is on top of the cliffs, almost 200 feet above the cold waters of Lake Superior.

From Grand Portal Point you continue along Lake Superior, passing more views of the Pictured Rocks and breaking out at another cliff-top beach, before arriving at Mosquito River. Mosquito Falls Trail, one of the newest trails in the park, will return you to the parking lot in 2.7 miles and along the way pass several waterfalls.

huge dune. No more than 50 yards separate the lake and this mountain of sand. Visitors first tackle the heart-pounding scramble up the dune, where the top offers a magnificent view of the windswept sand, Grand Sable Lake, and Lake Superior off in the distance. Then it's a mad dash down the steep bank of sand and usually right into the lake to cool off.

The dunes are a 4-square-mile area of sandy hills about half as high as Sleeping Bear Dunes in the Lower Peninsula, but no less impressive. They end with the Grand Sable Banks, steep sandy bluffs some 300 feet tall that tower right above the Lake Superior shoreline. The best view is obtained by turning off H 58 onto a marked side road for the *Log Slide* located 8 miles west of Grand Marais. A short boardwalk leads to a breathtaking overlook 300 feet above Lake Superior, where Au Sable Point Lighthouse to the west is silhouetted against the water and the banks to the east curve 5 miles back toward Grand Marais. Down below is the 500-foot wooden slide that loggers used in the 1800s to send trees into Lake Superior on their way to town.

To see shipwrecks without swimming in frigid Lake Superior, continue along County Road H 58 to Hurricane River Campground. East of the campground, Lakeshore Trail becomes an old access road to *Au Sable Light Station,* and near its trailhead is a shipwrecks sign pointing down to the beach. These ruins lie in the water and are hard to spot when the lake is choppy. But walk another 1.5 miles up the trail, and you'll see a second shipwreck sign that directs you to 3 sets of ruins half-buried in the sandy beach.

The lighthouse, which was built in 1874, has been renovated by the National Park Service as a museum and historic site and makes a perfect place to lunch before heading back to the campground. The 40-minute tours are led by park rangers and include climbing the 100 steps to the top of the tower for a stunning view of Lake Superior. Tours are given from 11 a.m. to 5 p.m. Wed through Sun from early June to Labor Day. Admission is $3 per person.

You could continue along H 58, although only about half of it is paved, and end up in *Munising.* The scenic town is the gateway to the *Pictured Rocks,* sandstone cliffs that rise 50 to 200 feet above Lake Superior and stretch for 15 miles to the east. They are one of the top attractions in the U.P., and a *Pictured Rock Boat Cruise* is the best way to view them.

The 3-hour cruises depart from Munising City Harbor, swing past Grand Island, and then skirt the most impressive stretch of Pictured Rocks. Along

Michigan's Smallest State Park

The smallest unit of the Michigan State Park system is *Wagner Falls Scenic Site.* The day-use park is only 22 acres and consists of a small parking area along M 94, 2 miles south of Munising, and a 200-yard trail that ends at an observation deck. The park is small but beautiful as the deck overlooks Wagner Falls, a 20-foot cascade that splashes down several rock ledges.

the way you view such noted formations as Miner's Castle, Battleship Rock, Indian Head, Rainbow Cave, and the Colors Caves, along with waterfalls that leap into Lake Superior and kayakers bobbing in and out of sea arches.

Pictured Rock Boat Cruises (800-650-2379; picturedrocks.com) offers daily trips at 10 a.m. and 1 p.m. Memorial Day through June and Sept through mid-Oct, and daily trips at noon, 1, 2, and 3 p.m., and a sunset cruise at 7:30 p.m. from July through Aug. The best time for a trip is in late afternoon or early evening when the sun setting in the west makes the cliffs even more colorful. The cost is $35 for anyone age 12 or older, $10 for children ages 6 to 12, and free for kids age 5 or younger. For a closer and more adventurous way to view the Pictured Rocks, contact *Northern Waters* (906-387-2323; northernwaters.com). The Munising outfitter offers a guided day paddle on Lake Superior that begins with the drive out to Miners Beach in the national lakeshore where they stage a half-hour kayak lesson. You then hop in your kayak and head east for an intimate view of the towering sandstone cliffs not possible on the boat cruises. Overnight guided kayak tours from 3 to 7 days also are offered with primitive camping. Cost is $355 to $635.

No previous kayaking experience is required and the 3-hour paddle is broken up with a shoreline lunch. The cost is $125 per adult and $95 per child and includes all equipment, kayaks, transportation from Munising, and guides.

Waterfalls abound in the Munising area, some right on the edge of town. One of them is *Munising Falls.* From H 58 head up Sand Point Road a short way to the National Park Visitor Center, where a quarter-mile path takes you into the woods and up a shaded sandstone canyon. The first viewing platform provides a fine overview of the 50-foot cascade that tumbles straight down a sandstone cliff; a nearby stairway lets you walk up to the falls for a most unusual view of the falling water.

Munising is also on the edge of another park, the *Alger Underwater Preserve,* a graveyard of shipwrecks that date to the 1800s and early 1900s. The 113-square-mile preserve also includes underwater sea caves hollowed out of the Pictured Rocks cliffs by waves, and between the wrecks and the caves this slice of Lake Superior has become a popular destination with scuba divers.

Not a diver? Not a problem. Non-divers and even non-swimmers can enjoy the treasures of Lake Superior through *Grand Island Shipwreck Tours.* The company uses a 42-foot vessel with a specially designed hull glass viewing area to let passengers see wrecks in Lake Superior. The 2-hour tours depart from Munising daily during the summer and glide over

A Diner in the U.P.

Grand Marais at the end of M 77 is a peaceful oasis of unexpected delights. Officially the town serves as the eastern gateway to Pictured Rocks National Lakeshore but is also home to several museums, the most unusual being the *Pickle Barrel House.* The highly unusual summer home with its peek-a-boo windows belonged to William Donahey, creator of the Teenie Weenies in the 1920s, which was the longest running cartoon series continuously drawn by the same artist. The home was originally located on Sable Lake but has since been moved downtown to Lake and Randolph Streets and is open 1 to 4 p.m. daily in July and Aug by the Grand Marais Historical Society.

Along with a house that looks like a giant pickle barrel, Grand Marais is also the unlikely site of a 1949-vintage diner. The diner was once located in Pennsylvania and hosted such notables as John F. Kennedy and heavyweight champ Floyd Patterson. Eventually it was moved to New Jersey, New York, and finally a vacant field north of Grand Rapids before Rick Guth and Ellen Airgood transported it across the Mackinac Bridge in 1997 and renovated it into *West Bay Diner.* The atmosphere is retro and food is excellent, hamburgers on homemade onion rolls, hand-tossed pizza, classic malts, and Airgood's deep-dish cherry pie. The West Bay Diner (906-494-2607) is at the corner of Woodruff and Veterans Streets and hours are "open to close." That's as committed as anybody gets in Grand Marais.

Tasty Trenary Toast

Finnish culture has heavily influenced the Upper Peninsula, from their winter sports like the luge and ski jumping to what they nibble for breakfast, *Trenary Toast.* A carryover from the Finnish cinnamon treat called korpu, Trenary Toast is slices of bread covered with a layer of cinnamon-and-sugar, then toasted.

The result is a hard, sweet, and very long-lasting slice of bread. Even without any preservatives, Trenary Toast has a shelf life of at least six months and longer if you keep it in a cool, dry place. During a long, cold U.P. winter that's important. When you don't have the energy to battle a raging snowstorm outside, you just reach for the Trenary Toast to sustain you until warmer days arrive.

And Yoopers do. *Trenary Home Bakery,* the sole producer of the famous toast, has 18 employees who make between 3,000 and 4,000 bags a week, most of it consumed in the U.P. If passing through the hamlet of Trenary, you can stop to visit Trenary Home Bakery (906-446-3330; trenarytoast.us) at E. 2914 M 67 and purchase a bag of toast for only $3.19. Don't worry, it will still be good by the time you get home.

3 wrecks as well as sail past the historic lighthouse and the intriguing rock formations of Grand Island.

The most intriguing wreck is the Bermuda. The wooden schooner was loaded with 488 tons of iron ore when it left Marquette in 1870 and sank in Grand Harbor during a fierce storm. In 1884 a Canadian salvage company raised the ship, removed its cargo, and resank it in Grand Island's Murray Bay. The Bermuda lies only 10 feet below the surface, and in the clear, protective waters of the bay, you can glide right over it and view an entire 19th-century ship.

"Everything is still there," says one guide, "everything except the sails and the crew."

Grand Island Shipwreck Tours (906-387-4477; shipwrecktours.com) departs from the Munising Dock 1.5 miles west of downtown off M 28. Tours are offered at 10 a.m. and 1 p.m. daily from June through Sept, weather permitting. In July and Aug there is also a 12:30 and 4 p.m. trip. The cost is $32 for adults and $12 for children ages 6 to 12 (5 and under are free).

Schoolcraft County

Blaney Park is the town that refuses to die. It's been foreclosed on, boarded up, even auctioned off building by building, but today the village is surging back as a quiet resort with an ideal location for touring the Upper Peninsula. No more than 90 minutes from this one-road hamlet are the U.P.'s most popular attractions: Tahquamenon Falls, Pictured Rocks, the historic town site of Fayette, and miles of Lake Michigan's sandy shoreline.

Originally a logging camp, Blaney and the area around it were logged out by 1926, so its owners searched for another endeavor for the town's residents. With all the lakes and sandy beach nearby, recreation was the answer, and soon Blaney became Blaney Park. Tourists began arriving from all over the Midwest to spend their vacations on the Upper Peninsula. The resort featured a 9-hole golf course, tennis courts, riding stables, daily excursions to Lake Michigan beaches, and a lighted swimming pool for those who preferred to stay close to their cottages. A lumber baron's mansion was renamed Celibeth and was described in one brochure as "a beautiful club-type hotel." The boardinghouse where loggers had lived was turned into a 21-room lodge, and in 1934 the Blaney Inn was built, a huge dining facility that featured stone fireplaces, walls paneled in knotty pine, and seating for 400.

Improved roads in the Upper Peninsula were Blaney Park's downfall. The family that owned the town tried twice to sell it, only to end up with it again when the buyers defaulted on their payments. The last tourist season was in 1972, after which many of the buildings were boarded up, and Blaney Park finally was auctioned off in 1985.

Today Blaney Park has come back to life again as a tourist destination. It can be reached from the Mackinac Bridge by following US 2 west for 66 miles and then north on M 77 for 1 mile.

The 22-room **Celibeth** is a beautiful bed-and-breakfast with 7 rooms decorated in antiques and furnishings from the resort era of the 1920s. There is an enclosed porch that overlooks the front lawn and features a row of rocking chairs and a sunroom in the back where breakfast and afternoon tea are served. The bed-and-breakfast (906-283-3409; celibethhousebnb.com) is open from May through Oct, and the rooms range from $80 to $125 per night.

The loggers' boardinghouse just down the street is now *Blaney Lodge* (906-283-3883, 888-252-6395; blaneylodge.com), offering budget accommodations. Rooms in the historic lodge are $59 a night, cabins in the back $79. The price includes a breakfast of homemade muffins and fruit in the sunporch in the morning and fresh pie and ice cream in the evening. Blaney Lodge also has a 2,700-foot paved airstrip behind the lodge. Every year pilots come to Blaney from the Oshkosh Air Show.

The heart of Schoolcraft County, some 96,000 acres, has been preserved as the largest wildlife refuge east of the Mississippi River. The *Seney National Wildlife Refuge* was established in 1935 by the US Fish and Wildlife Service to provide a habitat for wildlife, primarily waterfowl migrating to nesting grounds in Canada. The refuge surrounds the Great Manistique Swamp, which endured rough treatment beginning in the 1870s when loggers were intent on stripping every tree from the area. Fires were then set deliberately to clear away the debris of the lumbering operation, preventing new forests from taking root. Finally a land development company came through, drained acre after acre of the swamp, and sold the land to farmers for agriculture in 1911. The farmers lasted about a year before discovering they had been swindled—the soil would grow little.

Seney was a wasteland that nobody wanted. The state ended up with it, and during the Great Depression, deeded it to the federal government with the recommendation that it be turned into a refuge. Civilian Conservation Corps workers came in and built dikes, dug ditches, and used other water-control devices to impound 7,000 acres of water in 21 major ponds, almost miraculously restoring the marsh. Seney again became a habitat for waterfowl when 332 Canada geese were released in 1936 and established its present nesting flocks. Still more geese and other species of birds depend on the area as an important rest stop on their long migration to and from nesting sites in Canada.

trivia

Manistique boasts a bridge "below the level of the river." Built in 1919, the 300-foot-long Siphon Bridge crosses the Manistique River and is actually below the river because water is atmospherically forced under it. The bridge became famous when it was featured in the *Ripley's Believe It or Not* newspaper series. The bridge is on M 94 at the north end of the downtown area.

Other wildlife—timber wolves, deer, black bears, moose, and coyotes—live in the refuge, but the Canada goose has clearly become the symbol of Seney's return to wilderness. You will see the "honkers" the minute you drive into the parking lot of the visitor center, as a few tame ones are always around looking for a handout from softhearted tourists. The center overlooks one of the many ponds in the refuge, and a telescope at its large viewing window lets you search the marsh area for some of the more than 200 species of birds that can be found here. The center has displays, a children's touch table, and an auditorium that hosts nature movies and slide programs each hour. It is open from mid-May through mid-Oct from 9 a.m. to 5 p.m. daily.

A Hemlock Cathedral

When we entered the cathedral it was quiet, a little dark, and almost spiritual. It was a place to ponder, maybe even meditate, but this was no church. It was a stand of hemlocks that somehow survived the logging era Michigan experienced at the turn of the 20th century.

Today the **Hemlock Cathedral** is part of the **Little Bay de Noc Recreation Area,** and it's where you go to see what a 300-year-old tree looks like. Trees that old are so tall you can't see the tops of them, so big that two people can't link arms around them, so rare that all that's left are pockets scattered across a state that was once blanketed by them.

In Escanaba residents could see the giant hemlocks on the other side of Little Bay de Noc, and by the late 1800s the spot was a popular weekend retreat known as Maywood. When a small resort hotel was built there in 1904, this pocket of old growth was preserved from the loggers advancing down the Stonington Peninsula.

Today the Hemlock Cathedral in the Little Bay de Noc Recreation Area is as quiet and impressive as it was a century ago. The virgin hemlocks are seen by hiking the Maywood History Trail, an easy half-mile loop that includes almost a dozen interpretive plaques.

The recreation area also includes a sandy beach, picnic area, 36 rustic campsites, and 2 other trails. The Hiawatha National Forest facility is on County Road 513, 7 miles south of US 2 on the Stonington Peninsula. There is a vehicle entry fee and a nightly fee for camping. For more information call the Rapid River Ranger Station at (906) 474-6442.

The best way to view the wildlife is to follow the 7-mile *Marshland Wildlife Drive* in your car as it winds its way among the ponds, starting near the center and ending at M 77 just south of the refuge entrance. Pick up a free guide that points out items of interest at a number of marked stops, including an active bald eagle nest that can be seen clearly from the drive. Timing is important for spotting wildlife, and it is best to follow the drive either in early morning or at dusk when the animals are most active. Often during the peak of the tourist season, the refuge will stage guided evening tours that depart around 6 p.m. and last for almost 2 hours. Call the visitor center (906-586-9851) for information about the auto tours.

Another unique way to view more remote areas of the refuge is to paddle the handful of rivers that flow through it. *Northland Outfitters* (800-808-3386; northoutfitters.com), located in nearby Germfask, offers canoe rentals for the area. It will supply canoes, paddles, life jackets, and transportation to the Manistique River, which runs through the southeast corner of Seney. The trips are self-guided, last either 2 or 4 hours, and offer the possibility of spotting beavers, deer, otters, and a variety of birds, or of fishing for walleye or pike in the river.

On the opposite scale of parks is *Palms Brook,* a state park of only 388 acres located 12 miles northwest of Manistique on M 149. The park may be small, but it's equally intriguing because of *Kitch-Iti-Kipi,* Michigan's largest spring. The natural spring pours out more than 10,000 gallons of water per minute from fissures in the underlying limestone, and has created a crystal clear pool 200 feet wide and 40 feet deep. Visitors board a wooden raft with observation holes in the middle and pull themselves across the spring to get a good view of the fantasy world below. Between the swirls of sand and ghostly bubbles rising up, you can view ancient trees with branches encrusted in limestone, huge brown trout slipping silently by, and colors and shapes that challenge the imagination. The spring is especially enchanting in the early morning, when a mist lies over the water and the trout rise to the surface. Palms Brook has a picnic area but no campsites, and there is a vehicle fee to enter. The raft is free.

Delta County

In the mid-1800s iron ore was shipped from the Upper Peninsula mines to foundries in the lower Great Lakes area at a tremendous cost to companies.

The high price of shipping was due to the inefficient method of transportation coupled with the nearly 40 percent waste the ore contained. Fayette Brown, general manager of the Jackson Iron Company, studied the problem and decided the solution was to build a company-owned furnace not far from the mine, where the ore could be smelted into pig iron before it was shipped to the steelmaking centers. The town he planned to build at the smelter had to be a reasonable distance from the Escanaba ore docks, possess a natural harbor, and be near large amounts of limestone and hardwood forests to smelt the iron ore. In 1866 Brown chose a spot on the Garden Peninsula overlooking Big Bay de Noc, and the town of *Fayette* was born.

A year later work began on the furnace and charcoal kiln, and by Christmas the first iron from Fayette was cast. Quickly a town emerged. There were the superintendent's house on a bluff overlooking the harbor, a company office, 9 frame dwellings for the engineers and skilled workers, and 40 log cabins for the laborers. Eventually Fayette featured a machine shop, a small railroad, barns, a blacksmith shop, a hotel, and even an opera house. It was a total community that in 1884 had a population of almost 1,000 and turned out 16,875 tons of iron. Toward the end of that decade, however, Fayette's fate was sealed. The price of pig iron fell, and newly developed coke blast furnaces produced a higher-quality iron at a much cheaper cost. In 1891 the company closed down the furnaces, and within a few years Fayette became a ghost town.

Fayette changed hands several times; at last the state of Michigan obtained the area in 1959 and turned it into *Fayette State Park.* The town booms again now as a scenic ghost town overlooking Snail Shell Harbor, with its towering white cliffs. The 365-acre park is reached from US 2 on County Road 483 and contains an interpretive museum with information, guide maps, and a scale model of Fayette during its heyday. From there you leisurely wander among 22 existing buildings, of which 9 are open. The renovated structures, which are furnished, include the company office, the hotel, the opera house, and a home of one of the skilled employees. More will be opened up in the future.

Fayette State Park (906-644-2603) also has 80 campsites, a beach and picnic area, and boat-launching facilities. The museum is open daily mid-May through June and Sept to mid-Oct from 9 a.m. to 5 p.m. and in July and Aug from 9 a.m. to 8 p.m. There is a vehicle fee to enter the park and a per-night fee to camp.

Another spot worth searching out on the Garden Peninsula is **Portage Bay State Campground,** which is reached from County Road 483 (before the state park) by turning off on County Road 08 and carefully following the signs. Getting to the rustic campground (no electricity, pit toilets) is a bumpy 5-mile ride along dirt roads, but the camping area is worth it: You pitch your tent or park your trailer among the pine trees that border the sandy beach of the bay. You can stroll along the beach, follow the hiking trails in the area, or take a dip in the clear water of Lake Michigan.

A delightful picnic area in Delta County is **Peninsula Point Lighthouse,** the guiding light at the very tip of the Stonington Peninsula that was built in 1865. Congress authorized the funds the year before, because the wooden sailing ships hauling lumber, iron ore, and fish from Escanaba and Fayette were no match for the treacherous shoals and reefs that separated Big Bay de Noc from Little Bay de Noc. The light went out for the last time in 1936, and the house portion of the lighthouse burned to the ground in 1959. But the view from the point was so spectacular that the Forest Service made it into a public picnic area in 1937.

Climb the 40 steps to the top of the square brick tower and you're greeted with a 360-degree panorama that includes the Escanaba waterfront to the west, the limestone bluffs of Fayette State Park to the east, and the length of Lake Michigan in front of you. You can either hike to it or drive in. The 1.5-mile hike is a scenic walk, while the final mile to the 19th-century light is a narrow, winding, and very bumpy one-lane road not recommended for vehicles more than 16 feet long or 8 feet high.

trivia

Gladstone, a small town just north of Escanaba, is home to the world's largest manufacturer of pet caskets. **Hoegh Industries Inc.,** 317 Delta St., produces a line of pet caskets that range in price from $50 to more than $350. You can tour the small plant and "learn the history of the pet burial phenomenon" weekdays from 8 a.m. to 4 p.m. Among the things you learn is that pet caskets are also used by amputees to bury their severed limbs. Contact Hoegh Industries (906-428-2151; hoegh-petcaskets.com) in advance to arrange a tour.

To reach the lighthouse from Rapid River, head east on US 2 to the Stonington exit. Go south 19 miles on County Road 513 to Stonington, and then take Forest Road 2204. The RV parking area and trailhead are reached before the forest road turns into a narrow, one-lane road in the final mile.

Places to Stay in the Eastern Upper Peninsula

AU TRAIN

Pinewood Lodge Bed and Breakfast
M 28
(906) 892-8300
pinewoodlodgebnb.com

BLANEY PARK

Blaney Lodge
M 77
888-252-6395
blaneylodge.com

Celibeth House Bed & Breakfast
M 77
(906) 283-3409
celibethhousebnb.com

ESCANABA

Sandy Shores
E4717 M 35
(906) 786-3625

Terrace Bay Resort
7146 P. Road
(906) 786-7554
terracebay.com

GRAND MARAIS

Sunset Cabins
County Road H 58
(906) 494-2693
sunset.grandmarais
michigan.com

MACKINAC ISLAND

Chippewa Hotel
Main Street
(800) 241-3341
chippewahotel.com

Cottage Inn of Mackinac Island
7267 Market St.
(906) 847-4000
cottageinnofmackinac
.com

Grand Hotel
1 Grand Ave.
(800) 334-7263
grandhotel.com

Lilac Tree Hotel
Main Street
(866) 847-6575
lilactree.com

Mission Point Resort
6633 Main St.
(800) 833-7711
missionpoint.com

MANISTIQUE

The Hotel Peninsula Pointe
905 E. Lakeshore Dr.
(906) 341-3777

Northshore Motel
801 E. Lakeshore Dr.
(906) 341-2420
northshoremotel.com

MUNISING

Cherrywood Lodge of Munising
10160 M-28 East
(877) 424-6423
cherrywoodlodgemunising
.com

Super 8 Motel
County Road H 13 and M 28
(906) 387-2466

NEWBERRY

Comfort Inn
13954 State Hwy M 28
(906) 293-3218
comfortinn.com

PARADISE

Harmon's Birchwood Resort
8442 N. Whitefish Point Rd.
(906) 492-3320

SAULT STE. MARIE

Comfort Inn
4404 I-75 Business Loop
(906) 635-1118

Kewadin Casino Hotel
2186 Shunk Rd.
(800) 539-2346
kewadin.com

Ramada Ojibway Hotel
240 W. Portage
(800) 654-2929
ojibwayhotel.com

ST. IGNACE

Boardwalk Inn
316 N. State St.
(800) 254-5408
boardwalkinn.com

K Royale Lakefront Inn
1037 N. State St.
(906) 643-7737
(800) 882-7122
kroyale.com

Places to Eat in the Eastern Upper Peninsula

AU TRAIN

Brownstone Inn
E 4635 M 28
(906) 892-8332
brownstoneinn.net
American

SELECTED CHAMBERS OF COMMERCE AND TOURISM BUREAUS

Bays de Noc Convention & Visitors Bureau
230 Ludington St.
Escanaba 49829
(800) 533-4386
travelbaysdenoc.com

Mackinac Island Tourism Bureau
P.O. Box 451
Mackinac Island 49757
(800) 454-5227
mackinacisland.org

Newberry Area Tourism Association
P.O. Box 308
Newberry 49868
(800) 831-7292
newberrytourism.com

Sault Ste. Marie Convention and Visitors Bureau
1808 Ashmun St.
Sault Ste. Marie 49783
(800) 647-2858
saultstemarie.com

St. Ignace Visitors Bureau
6 Spring St.
St. Ignace 49781
(800) 338-6660
stignace.com

OTHER ATTRACTIONS

Grand Island Recreation Area
Munising
(906) 387-3503
grandislandmi.com

Mackinac Island Butterfly House
Mackinac Island
(906) 847-3972
originalbutterflyhouse.com

Mackinac Island Carriage Tours
Mackinac Island
(906) 847-3325
mict.com

Sand Point Lighthouse
Escanaba

Seul Choix Point Lighthouse
Gulliver

Tahquamenon Logging Museum
Newberry
(906) 293-5777

BRIMLEY

Wilcox's Fish House
1232 S. Wilcox Lane
(906) 437-5407
Seafood

ESCANABA

Hereford & Hops
624 Ludington Ave.
(906) 789-1945
herefordandhops.com
Brewpub

GRAND MARAIS

Lake Superior Brewing Company
M 77
(906) 494-2337
grandmaraismichigan.com/LSBC
Brewpub

The West Bay Diner
E. 21825 Veterans Street
(906) 494-2607
Breakfast & Sandwiches

MACKINAC ISLAND

Carriage House
Hotel Iroquois
298 Main St.
(906) 847-3321
iroquoishotel.com
Fine Dining

The Gate House
286 Grand Ave.
(906) 847-3331
grandhotel.com
Outdoor Dining

Goodfellow's Italian Chop House
1359 Hoban St.
(906) 847-0260
goodfellowsrestaurant.com
Italian

Mary's Bistro
7463 Main St.
(906) 847-9911
mackinacmarysbistro.com
Outdoor Dining

MUNISING

Camel Riders
5609 N. Camel Rider Dr.
(Wetmore)
(906) 573-2319
Outdoor Dining

Muldoon's
1246 M 28
(906) 387-5880
Pasties

NEWBERRY

Pickelman's Pantry
14045 County Road 460
(906) 293-3777
American

PARADISE

Tahquamenon Falls Brewery
Tahquamenon Falls State Park
M 123 Upper Falls Dr.
(906) 492-3300
tahquamenonfallsbrewery.com
Brewpub

SAULT STE. MARIE

The Antlers Restaurant
804 E. Portage Ave.
(906) 253-1728
saultantlers.com
American

Freighters
Ojibway Hotel
240 W. Portage Ave.
(906) 632-4100
ojibwayhotel.com
Fine Dining

Studebaker's
3583 I-75 Business Spur
(906) 632-4262
American

ST. IGNACE

Galley Restaurant
241 N. State St.
(906) 643-7960
galley-rest.com
American

Village Inn
250 S. State St.
(906) 643-3364
viofmackinac.com
American

WESTERN UPPER PENINSULA

Michigan's most remote and rustic region is the rugged western Upper Peninsula. Two small ranges located here constitute the only true mountains in any of the Great Lakes states; between Baraga and Marquette lie the Huron Mountains, and along the Lake Superior shoreline, from west of Ontonagon to Copper Harbor, is the Copper Range. Within these rugged hills are Mount Arvon, the highest point in Michigan at 1,979 feet above sea level, and the Porcupine Mountains, between whose ridges and peaks lies the stunning Lake of the Clouds.

It was in these hills of the western U.P. that the great iron and copper mines flourished from the 1800s to the 1940s, bringing boatloads of immigrants from Norway, Finland, and Italy to work in the shafts. Today the remnants of the mining era are ghost towns, abandoned mines, and communities with strong ethnic heritage and pride.

For most Michigan residents, this region of the state is a remote, distant place; driving to Copper Harbor from Detroit is the same distance as traveling to Washington, DC. But once it is "discovered," travelers marvel at the western U.P.'s natural wonders. More than for its mines, pasty

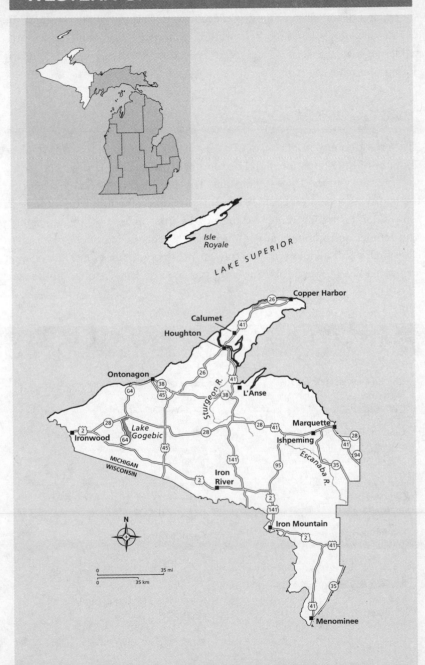

Isle
Royale

LAKE SUPERIOR

Copper Harbor

Calumet

Houghton

Ontonagon

L'Anse

Marquette

Ironwood

Lake
Gogebic

Ishpeming

MICHIGAN
WISCONSIN

Iron
River

Iron Mountain

Menominee

Sturgeon R.

Escanaba R.

N

0   35 mi
0   35 km

shops, and historical museums, you come to this region of Michigan for the beauty of nature's handiwork: cascading waterfalls, panoramas of forested wilderness, a lake set in a sea of reds, yellows, and oranges painted by autumn leaves.

Marquette County

The largest county in Michigan consists of 1,873 square miles, 1,800 lakes, 73 miles of Lake Superior shoreline, and *Marquette,* the largest (and, some say, only) city in the Upper Peninsula. The city of 21,524 became a spot on the map with a post office in 1849, and it bloomed the following decade as the port and shipping center for the nearby iron mines and logging camps. The lumber and mining barons graced the streets of Marquette with mansions, many still standing today. From Front Street turn east onto Ridge Street and you'll head toward Lake Superior, passing one late-Victorian home after

AUTHOR'S TOP TEN PICKS

Black River Harbor Drive
Bessemer
(906) 667-0261

Canyon Falls and Gorge
L'Anse
(906) 524-7444

Fort Wilkins
Copper Harbor
(906) 289-4215

Hanka Homestead
L'Anse
(906) 334-2601

Iron County Historical Museum
Caspian
(906) 265-2617
ironcountyhistoricalmuseum.org

Lake of the Clouds
Silver City
(906) 885-5275

Michigan Iron Industry Museum
Negaunee
(906) 475-7857

Piers Gorge
Norway
(906) 774-2002

Quincy Mine
Hancock
(906) 482-3101
quincymine.com

Sand Hills Lighthouse Inn
Eagle River
(906) 337-1744
sandhillslighthouseinn.com

another until you end up in the parking lot of the *Marquette Maritime Museum* on the waterfront.

The museum is housed in the red sandstone Old Water Works Building at 300 Lake Shore Blvd. and features displays on shipwrecks, antique outboard motors and boats, 3 Fresnel lenses, commercial fishermen who worked the area, and other facets of the city's maritime days, which fed many and made some (from the look of their homes) incredibly wealthy. The museum (906-226-2006; mqtmaritimemuseum.com) is open from mid-May through Oct from 10 a.m. to 5 p.m. daily. Admission to the museum and lighthouse is $9 for adults and $5 for children 12 and under.

The largest and most interesting structures on Marquette's waterfront are the iron ore docks that load the rock into Great Lakes freighters for a journey south. The Lake Superior and Ishpeming Railroad docks are still operating today, and the best vantage point is *Presque Isle Park.* The 328-acre city park is not an island but a peninsula that juts out into Lake Superior on the north side of Marquette. A road circles the park shoreline, beginning on the south side, where you can see the ore docks and, if your timing is right, watch a freighter take on its load (1 to 3 times a week).

The drive continues and passes the steep red cliffs of Lookout Point and then the view at Sunset Point, where residents gather to watch the end of another day. The park also has an outdoor band shell with weekly events, a small zoo, a beach and bathhouse, picnic areas, and bicycle paths. Hiking trails crisscross the forested interior of Presque Isle and become a favorite spot for Nordic skiers during the winter. The park is open daily from 7 a.m. to 11 p.m., and perhaps the best time of year to visit it is the last weekend in July during its Art-on-the-Rocks Festival, when local artists gather to display and sell their work in this picturesque setting. For the days and times to watch iron ore boats being loaded, call the Michigan Department of Transportation Welcome Center (906-249-9066) in Marquette.

trivia

The Superior Dome on the Northern Michigan University campus is the largest wooden dome in the world. Dedicated in 1991, it is 150 feet high and covers 272,330 square feet. It contains more than 100 miles of Douglas fir tongue-and-groove decking.

In Marquette's Lower Harbor are the Old Ore Docks, no longer operating, which have been designated a state historic site. An excellent place to view the docks is from a table in the *Vierling Restaurant* at Front and Main Streets. The saloon was opened in 1883 by Martin Vierling, an art lover and saloonkeeper who headed north with his paintings after running an establishment in Detroit. Later the art lover's bar became just another cafe during Prohibition, but the present proprietors, Terry and Christi Doyle, have turned back the clock by renovating the interior and returning the building to its original function as a saloon, brewpub, and fine restaurant. The brick walls inside once again feature paintings and prints, as the owners exhibit the works of a different artist every month. There are also old photographs and artifacts of early Marquette, and the large windows in the rear of the restaurant overlook the iron ore docks. A pair of binoculars hangs on the back wall for anyone wanting a closer look at the massive structure.

The fare is "fresh and homemade," and the dinner menu features whitefish, shrimp, and chicken entrees, but its most popular requests are for the baked French onion soup and the home-brewed blueberry wheat beer. In December 1995, the Vierling became one of Michigan's first brewpubs with the addition of a 5-barrel micro-brewing system. The brew equipment, direct from Budapest, Hungary, is configured to produce some of the finest ales and lagers in 155-gallon hand-crafted batches. The relatively small-sized batches of beer ensure a fast product turnover, which enables the Vierling to serve the freshest beer possible with a multitude of varieties. The Vierling Restaurant (906-228-3533, thevierling.com) is open daily except Sun from 11 a.m. to 10 p.m. Dinner is served after 4 p.m., and prices range from $19 to $27.

For an excellent view of all of Marquette, head north of town on County Road 550 for a few miles and turn into the dirt parking lot marked by the large SUGAR LOAF sign. This is the start of the *Sugar Loaf Recreation Trail,* a wide and easy path that winds 0.6 mile up the peak of the same name. You actually climb 315 feet through forest and over granite ridges by a series of steps until you reach the rocky knob marked by a stone monument. The view is spectacular on a clear day, a 360-degree panorama that includes the city, Lake Superior, the rough coastline, and the many offshore islands.

By continuing north on County Road 550 for another 26 miles, you reach its end in the small village of Big Bay on the shores of Lake

A Cabin in the Woods

The most unusual lodging accommodations in Marquette County come without a flush toilet, a shower, or any plumbing, for that matter. There are no mattresses, telephones, or televisions with HBO. Heat is a stack of logs and a wood-burning stove. Hopefully you brought some matches.

But what a view!

From the porch of Cabin No. 3 in the *Little Presque Isle State Forest Recreation Area,* you can watch the rays of an early morning sun spread across Harlow Lake. In the background is the rocky crown of Hogsback Mountain, and when the rising sun paints it in a light shade of pink, it's the closest thing we have to alpenglow in Michigan.

Built in 1996, the 6 rustic cabins are scattered in Little Presque Isle, a 3,040-acre tract located 5 miles northwest of Marquette and split in the middle by County Road 550. You can't drive to them, but the walk in is not far. Cabins No. 1, 2, and 3 are a mere 200 yards from where you park the car. Cabin No. 5, the farthest from the trailhead, is only a half mile away.

Yet for the price of a little boot leather and the $65-per-night rental fee, you're ensured of solitude and peace of mind in one of the most picturesque settings in the Upper Peninsula. To reserve the cabins or obtain a brochure on Little Presque Isle State Forest Recreation Area, call the Department of Natural Resources office in Marquette at (906) 228-6561 or (800) 447-2757.

Independence. Big Bay is best known as a place where scenes for the 1959 film *Anatomy of a Murder*, starring Jimmy Stewart and Lee Remick, were shot. The story is true, with the murder taking place at the *Lumberjack Tavern* (906-345-9912), a classic north woods bar on CR 550 that was used for one scene in the movie. You can still see the famed bullet hole in the wall of the tavern and visit other movie location sites with the help of an *Anatomy of a Murder* self-guided tour brochure available free online from the *Marquette County Convention and Visitors Bureau* (800-544-4321; travelmarquettemichigan.com).

An interesting place to stay in Big Bay, in fact one of the most interesting bed-and-breakfasts in the U.P., is the *Big Bay Point Lighthouse,* the secluded retreat 3.5 miles north of town on Lighthouse Road. The light at Big Bay was built and put into service in 1896 and included a 2-story, redbrick dwelling with 18 rooms. The house was divided in half, with the lightkeeper living in one half and his assistant in the other. The Coast Guard automated the light in 1941 and then sold the structure in 1961 after building a new steel tower nearby.

In 1986 the lighthouse became a unique bed-and-breakfast offering guests the rare opportunity to stay overnight in one of its 6 bedrooms. The lights stand high above Lake Superior on a rocky point in the middle of 40 wooded acres that include 2 miles of trails. You can climb the narrow staircase to the top of the tower for a splendid view of the area, catching a sunrise over Lake Superior at daybreak, a sunset over the Huron Mountains at dusk, or possibly the Northern Lights at night. The interior has been

TOP ANNUAL EVENTS

JANUARY

Noquemenon Ski Marathon
Marquette
(866) 370-7223
noquemenon.com

Winter Carnival
Houghton
(800) 338-7982
mtu.edu/carnival

FEBRUARY

Pine Mountain Classic
Iron Mountain
(800) 236-2447

Snowburst
Porcupine Mountains Wilderness
State Park
(906) 885-5209

U.P. 200 Sled Dog Race
Marquette
(800) 544-4321
up200.org

JUNE

PastyFest
Calumet
mainstreetcalumet.com

Pine Mountain Music Festival
Iron Mountain
pmmf.org

JULY

Art on the Rocks
Marquette
(906) 250-6156
artontherocks.org

U.P. Championship Rodeo
Iron River
(906) 265-9938
upprorodeo.com

AUGUST

Ore to Shore Mountain Bike Epic
Ishpeming
(906) 486-4841
oretoshore.com

completely renovated and refinished, showing its natural wood and brick, and the various rooms include a delightful sauna.

The lighthouse is open year-round, with special rates for the off-season, weekdays, and package stays. The basic rate for the summer ranges from $151 to $213 for rooms that sleep from 2 to 4 people. For reservations contact Big Bay Lighthouse (906-345-9957; bigbaylighthouse.com).

One of the most unusual Michigan historical museums is tucked away in the woods near Negaunee and is probably passed up by many visitors. That's a shame. The *Michigan Iron Industry Museum* is an interesting stop that lets you leisurely explore the history of the Upper Peninsula's iron industry. The museum lies in the forested ravines of the Marquette Iron Range and overlooks the Carp River, where the first iron forge in the Lake Superior region was built in 1848. The U.P.'s iron deposits had been discovered 4 years earlier when William Burt, leader of a US Geological Survey party near the area, noticed the magnetic needle of his compass jumping wildly about. He instructed his men to search the ground, and they immediately turned up outcroppings of almost pure iron among the roots of pine trees. The iron era of the U.P. had begun, and in 1846 the Jackson Mine, the first operation in the U.P., was opened near Negaunee.

The museum at 73 Forge Rd. does an excellent job of leading you through the history of iron, from its beginnings to its most robust era to the decline of the industry in the 1960s. Inside are several levels of displays, a reconstructed mine shaft to walk through, and an auditorium that presents a short introductory program. Outside are more artifacts, including a mine locomotive, and trails leading to the old forge site on the Carp River. Expanded by 4,000 square feet in 2006, the Michigan Iron Industry Museum (906-475-7857; michigan.gov/ironindustrymuseum) is now open year-round. Hours from June 1 to Sept 30 are 9:30 a.m. to 4:30 p.m. daily; from Oct 1 to Oct 31 from 9:30 a.m. to 4 p.m.; from Nov 1 to Apr 30 Mon through Fri from 9:30 a.m. to 4 p.m. and the first Sat of each month from 9:30 a.m. to 4 p.m.; from May 1 to May 31 from 9:30 a.m. to 4 p.m. The museum is reached from US 41 by turning onto County Road 492 about 3 miles east of Negaunee, and admission is free. From the state mining museum it's only a short drive to more mining history at *Cliffs Shaft Mine Museum* in Ishpeming. Cliffs Shaft Mine was opened in 1879 by the Iron Cliffs Co. and became the nation's largest producer of hard, spectacular hematite, a type of

Upper Peninsula Cuisine

The Upper Peninsula's finest cuisine has been hooked, picked, or includes, among other things, rutabaga. If traveling the U.P. here are three specialties to try:

Pasties: These pies combine ground beef, potatoes, onions, and rutabaga in a flaky crust, baked until golden brown. Cornish immigrants are credited for introducing them to the U.P. while miners made them a staple because they are incredibly filling and practical to carry.

You can purchase pasties in almost any town in the U.P., but three places that stand out are *Muldoon's Pasties* (906-387-5880, 1246 W. M 28; muldoonspasties.com) in Munising, *Jean Kay's Pasties* (906-228-5310, 1635 Presque Isle Ave.; jeankayspasties.com) in Marquette, and *Joe's Pasty Shop* (906-932-4412, 116 W. Aurora St.; joespastyshop.com), in Ironwood.

Smoked Fish: You'll see small shops and fish houses selling a variety of smoked fish, ranging from lake trout to herring, and most of it caught locally. Start with whitefish, which has the most delicate flavor and is not as greasy as lake trout.

Wilcox's Fish House (906-437-5407, Lakeshore Drive) near Bay Mills sells a delicious smoked fish spread and whitefish sandwiches as well as a variety of smoked fillets.

Thimbleberry Jam: A thimbleberry looks like an overgrown raspberry but is found only in the Keweenaw Peninsula and the western U.P. The jam it makes is divine but hard to find, the reason it usually costs $8 to $10 for a half-pint jar.

The Jampot (societystjohn.com/store, 6500 M 26), located 3 miles east of Eagle River and operated by the Society of St. John monks, is renowned for its wild thimbleberry jam.

iron ore. When it closed in 1967, Cliffs Shaft was the last operating mine in Ishpeming and included 3 shafts that reached depths of 1,358 feet and more than 65 miles of tunnels running under most of the town.

The museum opened its doors in 2002 with former miners guiding visitors through the Dry Building, where workers used to change into their work clothes, the Shop Building, which houses historic equipment, and across the grounds. Among the displays is the Ishpeming Rock and Mineral Club room with its extensive mineral collection and model of the sprawling mine complex from the 1960s.

The Cliffs Shaft Mine Museum (906-485-1882) is at 501 W. Euclid St. and is reached from US 41/M 28 in Ishpeming by heading south on Lakeshore Drive. The museum is open from 10 a.m. to 4 p.m. Tues through Sat June through Sept. There is a small admission.

To view a real working iron mine, join a *Tilden Mine Tour* near Ishpeming. The popular, 2.5-hour tours give visitors a firsthand look at how iron ore is mined from open pits and includes a walk through the plant where the ore is processed and pelletized. You leave with souvenir taconite pellets from the processing plant.

The tours are offered once a day, Tues through Sat, from mid-June through Aug, with a bus leaving the Lake Superior Community Partnership office at 501 S. Front St. in Marquette at noon. Reservations are highly recommended and can be made by calling (906) 226-6591 or (888) 578-6489. The cost is $15 per person.

Though it might surprise a few people, especially avid skiers, Ishpeming is home of the *US National Ski Hall of Fame.* The hall was established here in 1954 because the Ishpeming Ski Club is "the oldest active ski club in the country."

Formed in 1887, the club was founded by Scandinavians who had emigrated to the U.P. to work the Marquette Range iron mines and brought their love of skiing with them. They were soon hosting ski jumping tournaments and in 1926 moved their ramps and competition site to a large bowl owned by Cleveland-Cliffs, Inc. When a skier badly injured himself in practice that first year, a local reporter dubbed the area "Suicide Hill" and the name stuck, much to the alarm of club officials who were trying to promote the new jumps.

In the early 1990s the Hall of Fame was relocated to a new building in Ishpeming that features an impressive roofline in the shape of a ski jump. Inside are exhibits and displays that detail the history of skiing from medieval times to the latest Winter Olympics. All three forms of skiing are included—Nordic, Alpine, and ski jumping—and many visitors are amazed to learn that Alpine skiing is a relatively new version of the sport.

The Ski Hall of Fame (906-485-6323; skihall.com) is on US 41 between Second and Third Streets at 610 Pams Ave. and is open from 10 a.m. to 5 p.m. Mon through Sat. Admission is free.

Chilling Tales at Ski Museum

With a baby strapped to his chest, the brave skier headed out in the coldest, darkest, most dangerous time of the year. By his side was another of the village's skilled skiers. Their mission seemed impossible. They were the original *Birkebeiners*. They were the people who spirited out to safety the crown prince of Norway during the Norwegian Civil War.

Peasants and fierce warriors, the Birkebeiners (Birch Legs) got their name because they were so poor they had to tie bark from birch trees around their legs as footwear. Their enemies, the Baglers, were a rich, powerful dynasty who needed to get rid of the baby—the king's son—and then all of Norway would belong to them.

Of course, the Birkebeiners succeeded or there probably wouldn't be a display honoring them at the US National Ski and Snowboard Hall of Fame and Museum. In 1206, the Birkebeiners saved the child who went on to become King Haakon Hakonsson IV. As king, he ended Norway's civil wars and brought stability to the country.

Another display spotlights the development of the chairlifts to carry skiers up mountains, instead of skiers having to climb the steep slopes. Getting people to the top of the hill is very important. Before the creation of chairlifts, would-be skiers had to climb to the top of the mountain and had to be tough do it. The chairlifts made it easier for more people to enjoy the sport.

Installed in 1936 in Sun Valley, Idaho, the world's first known chairlifts were based on a system for loading bunches of bananas onto boats. Instead of hooks for the bananas, the design called for chairs for skiers to sit on while wearing skis. The chairs were suspended from a single cable running above the chair.

The Modern Ski Warfare exhibit honors the American 10th Mountain Division troops of World War II. The division started as an experiment to train skiers and climbers to fight in the most difficult mountain terrain in Europe. The 10th Division was deployed to the mountains of northern Italy, where for six months the Germans had stymied the US Army atop a dangerously high mountain. On February 18, 1945, when night fell, the steep mountain was covered in snow and ice. The Germans didn't even bother to post a guard, believing that no American unit could climb such a difficult ridge. They were wrong. The soldiers of the 10th climbed silently to the top and secured Riva Ridge. The next day's assault on the mountain proved victorious for the American soldiers. But the victors paid a high cost. They lost 1,000 men in the process. After the war, veterans of the 10th Division created most of the first generation of US ski resorts. Contact the Ski Hall of Fame at (906) 485-6323; skihall.com.

Baraga County

Most roadside rest areas in the Upper Peninsula consist of little more than picnic tables, a pair of pit toilets, and a hand pump for water. Then there is the one on US 41, 8 miles south of L'Anse. It consists of picnic tables, a pair of pit toilets, a hand pump for water, and one of the most beautiful canyons in Michigan. The state's Department of Transportation maintains the tables and the toilets, but it was forestry students from Michigan Technological University who built the wooden boardwalks and observation platforms that make **Canyon Falls and Gorge** such a pleasant stop.

From the large display map in the rest area, the path departs into the woods, crosses a bridge over Bacco Stream, and within a half mile comes to the impressive Canyon Falls formed by the Sturgeon River. The falls mark the beginning of the canyon by thundering over a rock ledge to the river 30 feet below. Handrails have been erected here, and you can lean over the top of the cascade to listen to its roar or to feel the mist the falling water creates.

At this point there is a TRAIL ENDS sign, but the best part of the area, the gorge itself, can be seen only by following the original path, which snakes around a huge rock face. This path hugs the half-mile-long canyon and lets you view the Sturgeon River, a stretch of roiling white water that rushes through sheer rock walls 50 feet high. All visitors, especially families with young children, should be extremely careful if they choose to continue to the end of the old trail, a mile-long one-way hike. The original log handrails are still up, but they're flimsy and weak in places, and after they end there is nothing between you and the sharp edge of the gorge.

To reach the roof of the state, you have to find **Mount Arvon** in the Upper Peninsula, which at 1,979 feet is 21 feet short of being a true "mountain" but still the highest point in Michigan. The outing involves following unmarked logging roads in a remote section of Baraga County and hoping you can find your way back. Once on top there is no majestic view, just a yellow box in a forest with a register book inside.

But enough people undertake this adventure that the **Baraga County Convention and Visitors Bureau** (800-743-4908; baragacountytourism .org) publishes a map and a set of detailed directions to the highpoint. The association visitor center is right off US 41 as you enter L'Anse from the east and is open 9 a.m. to 5 p.m. Mon through Fri.

Strange as it Sounds

Highpointers are a group of adventurers whose mission in life is to stand on the highest point in all 50 states. They used to come to L'Anse from every corner of the country looking for *Mount Curwood,* which for two decades was thought to be Michigan's highest point at 1,996.4 feet. They would fly to Marquette, drive to Baraga County, and then search out some local for detailed directions on how to follow a maze of logging roads to the top of the peak.

Imagine their shock when the Department of the Interior conducted a survey in 1982 and concluded that Mount Curwood is really only 1,978.34 feet in elevation and actually the second highest spot in the state. Michigan's loftiest peak is nearby *Mount Arvon,* which at 1,979.238 feet above sea level is 11 inches higher than Curwood.

Many highpointers, who had climbed Mount Curwood 15 or 20 years earlier, were forced to return to Michigan and climb Mount Arvon. And when they finally reached the peak, what did they see? Most of the time nothing more than the trees at the top. The exception is in late fall after the leaves have dropped and a view through the trees is possible.

What there is on the summit of Arvon is a USGS brass marker verifying the elevation. There is also a small yellow mailbox containing a logbook so you can document your achievement of not getting lost as well as noting how many other highpoints you have reached.

Although serious research on the subject has never been done, many say the largest and best sweet rolls in the state are found at the *Hilltop Restaurant,* on US 41 just south of L'Anse at 18047 US Hwy. 41. One roll is an ample breakfast for most people since it measures more than 5 inches across and 3 inches thick and arrives filled with cinnamon and dripping in glaze. The restaurant has been baking the sweet rolls for more than 60 years and on a good weekend will serve more than 1,000. On a typical busy weekend, the Hilltop will use about 3,000 pounds of flour and 150 pounds of sugar, plus other ingredients, to make the famous sweet rolls. The record so far is 204 dozen sweet rolls baked in the kitchen in the course of one long day. The eatery also has other items on its menu (including good pastries), but who has room for anything else after devouring its sticky specialty with a cup of fresh-brewed coffee? The Hilltop (906-524-7858; sweetroll.com) is open from 7 a.m. to 8 p.m. daily.

One of Baraga County's most interesting attractions is the **Hanka Homestead,** a "living outdoor museum" where visitors learn about and see the lifestyle of the early Finnish farmers who immigrated to what was then a remote and isolated region of the state. The farm dates back to 1896, when the Hanka family applied for a homestead on two 40-acre parcels along the military road to Fort Wilkins at the tip of the Keweenaw Peninsula. The first thing Herman Hanka built was an 18- by 24-foot log house. But he was Finnish, so the second thing he constructed was his *savu,* or smoke sauna. Eventually he added barns, a self-cooling milk house that straddles a small spring, a horse stable, a blacksmith shop, and a granary.

The amazing thing about the farm is that it's never been wired for electricity, even though the youngest son, Jalmer Hanka, lived there until 1966. It was added to the National Register of Historic Places in 1984 and opened to the public the next year. Today there are 10 buildings and a root cellar to explore, each filled with the Hanka possessions. From US 41 in L'Anse, head north toward Houghton, and in 12 miles turn west on Arnheim Road. Follow the small museum signs. If you pass Otter Lake, you've gone too far west. The homestead (906-334-2601; pasty.com/crhm/pages/hanka) is open Tues, Thurs, Sat, and Sun from noon to 4 p.m. from Memorial Day to Labor Day. At other times, visitors are welcome to take a brochure for self-guided tours of the grounds. Admission is $3 for adults and $1.50 for children 5 to 12.

Houghton County

One of the most spectacular areas of the U.P.'s interior is relatively unknown to travelers who are hesitant to leave paved roads. The **Sturgeon River Gorge Area** is located just inside Houghton County along its border with Baraga County south of M 3838. The wilderness area includes the gorge cut by the Sturgeon River, which in some places is more than 400 feet deep, making it the largest and deepest in the Great Lakes states. For the best view of it, follow M 3838 west of Baraga and turn south onto Prickett Dam Road (also called Forest Road 193), marked by a NATIONAL FOREST sign. Within 11 miles the road merges into Sturgeon Gorge Road (Forest Road 191), and a few hundred yards to the right there is a sharp 90-degree curve. At this bend an extremely rough Jeep trail leads west to the edge of the gorge. It is best to walk the quarter mile that ends at one of the most beautiful panoramas in the U.P. You see the deep gorge below and miles of forested ridges and hills to the west.

Before reaching Sturgeon Gorge Road, you will pass a directional sign for *Silver Mountain.* Located on the edge of the Sturgeon River Gorge Wilderness in Houghton County, Silver Mountain is a 1,312-foot peak, once the site of a fire tower. At a small parking lot, you'll find a long stairway— long as in 250 steps—but once on top you'll see the foundation of the old fire tower, two USGS markers, and a view that includes miles of the rugged Sturgeon River Gorge Wilderness.

There are a handful of mine tours in the Upper Peninsula, but the best one is at the *Quincy Mine.* The Quincy Mining Company was organized in 1846 and for almost 100 years it mined the Pewabic copper lode located just north of Hancock. It was such a moneymaker that the mine was nicknamed Old Reliable, and today it is part of the new Keweenaw National Historical Park.

The 2-hour tour begins with the world's largest steam hoist, a giant spool that holds 13,200 feet of cable and lowered workers into Shaft No. 2 of the underground mine to a depth of 9,200 feet. You then board a cog tram for a journey down the steep Quincy Hill to the entrance of Shaft No. 5. Here tractor-drawn wagons take you a half mile into a horizontal tunnel 400 feet below the surface.

trivia

In Laurium, where Tamarack Street joins M 28, is the George Gipp Memorial. Better known as "the Gipper," Laurium's most famous son went on to become a football star at Notre Dame University. Legend has it that from his deathbed, he uttered the famous line to coach Knute Rockne, "Tell the boys to win one for the Gipper." The part of the Gipper and the deathbed scene gave Ronald Reagan his most memorable movie role.

Exhibits and videos in the hoist house round out a visit to the mine. The Quincy Mine (906-482-3101; quincymine.com) is open from the end of April to the first week of June, and full tours are $18 for adults and $9 for children. Winter hours are 9:30 a.m. to 5 p.m. on Fri, Sat, and Sun. In nearby Lake Linden, right downtown on Calumet Avenue, is *Lindell's Chocolate Shoppe.* Joseph Bosch had the building erected in 1893 for his Bosch Brewing Company, but in 1918 it was refurbished with wooden

Toledo for the Upper Peninsula

By 1835 Michigan had grown sufficiently to qualify for statehood, but Congress held it up because of a boundary controversy with Ohio over a sliver of land that included Toledo. The so-called Toledo War resulted in both states' calling out their militias but, fortunately, no bloodshed. When Michigan gave up claims to the city, it was awarded the Upper Peninsula and statehood, becoming the 26th state in 1837.

ceiling fans, 20 high-backed oak booths, a nickelodeon, leaded glass windows, and a 6-foot-long marble food preparation table that took 4 people to lift. It became the Chocolate Shop, and though the entire building was moved down the street in 1928, little of the interior has changed since then.

The menu has, however, but the shop still makes some of the best homemade ice cream in the U.P. The 1943 ice-cream maker is still proudly displayed in the front window. Lindell's Chocolate Shoppe (906-296-8083; lindellchocolateshoppe.net) is also a restaurant and bar with a full menu, but unquestionably it is the ice cream and the malts, milk shakes, sundaes, and banana splits that are its most popular items. The shop at 300 Calumet St. is open Mon through Thurs 6 a.m. to 4 p.m., Fri and Sat 6 a.m. to 8 p.m., and 6 a.m. to 2 p.m. Sun.

Keweenaw County

Under the forceful will of President Andrew Jackson, Michigan became a state in 1837, when it grudgingly accepted the entire U.P. in exchange for surrendering Toledo to Ohio. In only six years, this "worthless wilderness" became a land of incredible wealth after Douglas Houghton, the first state geologist, explored the Keweenaw Peninsula and reported finding chunks of pure copper. Miners began arriving by 1841, and within two years there was a lively copper rush to this small section of the U.P., forcing the US Army to build Fort Wilkins in Copper Harbor (today a state historical park) to maintain law and order. As in all stampedes for a precious metal, many mines quickly died, and thousands of miners went home disillusioned and broke. Nevertheless, substantial lodes of copper were uncovered, and by the 1860s this area was producing 15 million pounds annually, or almost 90 percent of the national total. Two of the most profitable mines were Calumet and Hecla, and near them sprang up the town of Red Jacket. Later renamed *Calumet,* this city of 66,000 in 1898 had wealth, importance (it was considered as a new site for the state capital), and a peculiar problem.

Because of large contributions to the city budget from the mines, the council found itself with a surplus of funds. Already the community had paved streets, electric lights, and telephones, so the town decided to build an opera house, the grandest theater in the Midwest, one that would rival the stages of the East Coast. The *Calumet Opera House* was built in 1899 at Sixth and Elm Streets, and no expense was spared. It was designed in an Italian Renaissance style and inside featured two balconies, private viewing chambers along the walls, and rococo plaster ornamentation of gilt, cream, and crimson. The acoustics were nearly perfect: An actor could whisper on the stage and be heard in the last row of the top balcony.

On March 20, 1900, the first performance was given to a packed house of 1,100 and was described by the Copper Country Evening News as "the greatest social event ever known in the copperdome's metropolis." A string of legendary performers arrived at the famed opera house, including John Philip Sousa, Sarah Bernhardt, Douglas Fairbanks, and Lillian Russell. Eventually the theater, like the town, fell upon hard times. The local mines, the last to operate in the Keweenaw Peninsula, were closed for good because of a labor strike in 1968; by then Calumet's population had dwindled to 1,000.

The mines are still closed, but the opera house has reopened. Declared a National Historic Site in 1974, it was fully restored, and its opulence can be viewed on a guided tour from mid-June through mid-Oct. Guided tours are offered from noon to 3 p.m. Mon through Fri; it's $6 for a peek into Calumet's past. The building has also returned to live theater after a stint showing motion pictures of the 1920s and 1930s; major performances are scheduled from Mar through Oct. Contact the Opera House at 340 Sixth St. (906-337-2610; calumettheatre.com) for information.

At one time or another in the late 1800s, there were 14 active copper mines in the Keweenaw Peninsula, and today a number of them have been preserved, offering a glimpse of the underground world of the miners. The least promoted but perhaps the most intriguing is the *Delaware Mine* on

US 41 between Calumet and Copper Harbor. To reach it you pass through Delaware, a ghost town of a few abandoned buildings and a sobering reminder that when the copper ran out, so did the lifeblood for boomtowns throughout the peninsula.

Interest in the copper at Delaware began in 1845 and involved one early investor by the name of Horace Greeley. The famous newspaper editor actually made a trip to the Keeweenaw Peninsula but never traveled much farther than Eagle River. A mining company was organized in 1848, and actual mining began the following year. From 1849 to 1851 the mine produced 522,541 pounds of copper, but the Northwest Copper Mining Company lost almost $100,000 on the operation. The mine was sold again and again to new investors, with one company building a huge hoist house in 1870 to pull the cars out of the deep shafts that were being dug. Despite all efforts, the Delaware never really turned a profit, and the shafts were sealed for good in 1887. The town of Delaware, which in 1879 had 300 residents, also disappeared.

trivia

Lake Superior is the largest and deepest of the Great Lakes, and its 31,700 square miles make up the largest surface area of any body of freshwater in the world. Measuring 383 miles long and 160 miles wide, Superior holds half of all the water in the Great Lakes.

Now a tourist attraction, the Delaware offers 2 different tours during the summer. A 40-minute tour takes you down a 100-foot staircase into Shaft No. 1 to the first level. The top level is 900 feet of tunnel from which other passages, shafts, and a huge cavern can be viewed. The Rustic Lantern Tour goes deeper into Shaft No. 3—without the aid of a staircase—and usually lasts 90 minutes. There is still plenty of copper lying around in this level, and in the information center visitors are told how to recognize and search for it in the mine. They are also given tips afterward on cleaning any metal they find.

The Delaware Mine (906-289-4688; copperharbor.org) is open from 10 a.m. to 6 p.m. daily June through Aug and 10 a.m. to 5 p.m. Sept and Oct. Admission is $10 per adult, $6 per child.

The men who actually worked the mines were often immigrants from the Cornwall area of England or from Finland or Norway, and they brought

Copper Country Cruising

Locals love to refer to the Keweenaw Peninsula as Copper Island because it is surrounded by water; Portage Canal on one side and Lake Superior on the rest. And departing from this "island" are numerous scenic cruises.

Docked at Copper Harbor is the 100-foot-long **Isle Royale Queen IV,** best known for its trips to Lake Superior's largest island, Isle Royale National Park. But from July 4 through Labor Day the *Isle Royale Queen* (906-289-4437; isleroyale .com) also departs between 7:30 and 8:30 p.m. (depending on when the sun sets) Tues, Wed, Thurs, and Sat, weather permitting, for a sunset cruise in which the passengers are treated to the sun melting into the Great Lake on one side of the boat and the rugged Keweenaw shoreline on the other. The fare for the 1.5-hour cruise is $25 for adults, $20 for seniors, and $15 for children.

Lighthouse Ferry Service offers cruises on a considerably smaller vessel, a historic double-ender hull launch that was designed especially for lighthouse keepers traveling through the Keweenaw's treacherous, shoal-lined waters. The cruise is a 15-minute ride across Copper Harbor followed by a tour of the museum at the Copper Harbor Lighthouse. Lighthouse Ferry Service (906-289-4966; copper-harborlighthouse.com) offers the tour at 10 a.m., noon, 2 p.m., and 4 p.m. May, June, Sept, and Oct, and on the hour from 10 a.m. to 5 p.m. July and Aug. The fare is $16 for adults and $11 for children. Lighthouse sunset tours are $20.

In Houghton, the 110-foot-long **Keweenaw Star** (906-482-0884; keweenaw-excursions.com) offers a variety of 2-hour tours, including a sunset cruise that departs daily at 7 p.m. during the summer and includes traveling the Portage Canal and Lake Superior. The cost is $25 for adults and $12 for children.

to Copper Country their strong ethnic heritages. Traces of that heritage can be seen in the Cornish pasties that are sold throughout the U.P. and in the popularity of Finnish saunas. For years the sauna took the place of bathtubs and showers in homes, as early settlers would build their sauna huts first and worry about their cabins later. A good sauna begins with a shower to open up the pores, followed by a stay in a cedar-paneled room where a small pile of rocks is heated. As water is tossed on the rocks, a dry heat emerges that makes the body perspire profusely, flushing out dirt and grime from the skin. The temperature ranges from 160 to 180 degrees, and the old miners used wicker sticks to beat their backs to get the blood moving. The entire ordeal ends with a cold shower to close the pores.

In Copper Harbor you can experience this Finnish ritual at *Finnish Sauna House,* operated by the Harbor Lights Inn in the heart of town on US 41. The public sauna is across the street from the resort and consists of 2 private suites. Each is completely paneled in cedar and features a dressing area, shower, and sauna that will seat 4 to 6 people. The building is not that far from Lake Superior, and occasionally a local resident will finish the sauna with a mad dash into the chilly lake, a tradition most visitors pass up. The Finnish Sauna House (906-289-4741; harborlightsinn.biz) is open daily from May 15 through Oct 15 from 1 to 10 p.m. The price is $25 per person and includes use of a room, towel, soap, and a wicker stick if you request it.

The copper rush of the Keweenaw Peninsula began in 1843, and Copper Harbor quickly became the center of exploration parties, newly formed mining companies, and a "rough population of enterprising prospectors, miners, and speculators." Because of the seedy nature of the miners and the constant threat of Chippewa Indians wanting to reclaim their lost land, Secretary of War William Wilkins dispatched two companies of infantry to the remote region of Michigan. They arrived in late May of 1844, and by November *Fort Wilkins* was built.

Sand Hills Lighthouse Inn

Built in 1919, Sand Hills Lighthouse is one of the largest along the Great Lakes and had enough rooms to house three lightkeepers and their families. The lighthouse was so big that the US Coast Guard used it as a training base during World War II and housed 200 guardsmen on the grounds.

In 1954 Sand Hills' beacon was made obsolete by new navigational technology, and the building was abandoned. In 1961 Bill Frabotta purchased the 3-story brick building and its 7-story beacon tower, and after 30 years of careful renovation, opened it up as the Sand Hills Lighthouse Inn. The bed-and-breakfast offers 8 guests rooms, a hearty breakfast in the morning, and more than 3,000 feet of Lake Superior shoreline from which to watch both sunrises and sunsets. Or you can climb the tower and enjoy the panoramic view from its walk-out roof.

Sand Hills Lighthouse Inn (906-337-1744; sandhillslighthouseinn.com) is 4 miles west of Eagle River at Five Mile Point. Rooms range from $165 to $225 per night. Make reservations well in advance if planning a trip from May through Oct.

The threat of Indian hostilities never materialized, and the troops discovered the Upper Peninsula winters were long and cold. Isolated from the rest of the world with little more than duty and drill to occupy their time, the garrison of 105 men ran into problems of boredom, low morale, and illegal whiskey. The following year half the troops were transferred to Texas in preparation for the Mexican War, and in 1846, less than two years after it was built, Fort Wilkins was abandoned. In 1921 Fort Wilkins was recognized as a historic landmark by the state, and in 1923 it was designated a state park. Today the structure is noted for being one of the few surviving wooden forts east of the Mississippi River.

Although the fort was insignificant militarily, it's an outstanding example of a mid-19th-century frontier outpost, with 12 of its 16 buildings from the original structure. You can wander through the fort year-round, even ski through it in the winter, but the buildings are open mid-May through mid-Oct. Ranging from kitchen and mess room to the bakery, company barracks, and hospital, many contain restored furnishings and artifacts depicting the rough life troops endured here. From mid-June through Labor Day, interpreters in period dress give tours daily from 9 a.m. to 5 p.m., adding a touch of realism to the fort.

The main entrance to the park and the fort is a mile east of Copper Harbor on US 41. A vehicle pass is required to enter the park and the fort. For more information on Fort Wilkins or on camping in the state park, call (906) 289-4215.

Keweenaw is the smallest county in the U.P., but it has more than its share of scenic drives, where every curve reveals another striking view. The most famous is the ***Brockway Mountain Drive,*** a 10-mile stretch to Copper Harbor that is the highest above-sea-level drive between the Rockies and the Alleghenies. Less traveled but almost as scenic in its own way is the ***Sand Dune Drive*** between Eagle River and Eagle Harbor. From Eagle River this portion of M 26 heads west along the Lake Superior shoreline, climbing high above the water along sandy bluffs. The road provides sweeping views of the Great Lake on the horizon and the sandy shoreline below, and the best turnoff looms above Great Sand Bay. The road returns to the lake level at Cat Harbor, a delightful beach for sunning and swimming if you can handle Superior's chilly waters, and then swings through Eagle Harbor, passing the picturesque ***Eagle Harbor Lightstation,*** which is now a museum open to the public.

Built in 1871, the lighthouse and the lightkeeper's residence have been renovated and furnished to reflect an early-20th-century lightstation. Next door is a small museum that contains, among other things, a display on Keweenaw's prehistoric copper culture. Signs from M 26 lead you to the

lighthouse (906-289-4990; keweenawhistory.org), which is open daily from noon to 5 p.m. June and Sept and 10 a.m. to 5 p.m. July and Aug. Admission is $5 for adults and free for children.

From Eagle Harbor M 26 continues east, first passing the junction to Brockway Mountain Drive and then returning to the edge of Lake Superior, whose shoreline becomes a rugged mass of red sandstone gracefully carved by the pounding waves. Along this segment you will pass ***Devil's Wash Tub,*** a huge depression in the shoreline that echoes the waves crashing in and out of it.

Ontonagon County

Three miles west of Silver City is ***Porcupine Mountains Wilderness State Park,*** a preserve of 58,000 acres of primitive forests, secluded lakes, and the rugged "Porkies." For most visitors, this state park is a quick drive to the end of M 107, where they follow a short wooded path to the escarpment overlooking ***Lake of the Clouds,*** a watery gem between the peaks and ridges of the mountains. Those willing to don a pair of hiking boots can enjoy some of the most unusual accommodations found in the U.P. with a night in one of the park's rustic cabins.

Within the Porkies is a trail network of more than 85 miles, and scattered along the footpaths are 16 wilderness cabins, each located in a scenic setting along a stream or lake or on the shore of Lake Superior. You can reach them only on foot, and some take an all-day hike while others lie only 30 or 40 minutes from the nearest parking lot. The cabins have no electricity, running water, or toilets that flush. Modern conveniences are replaced by candles, woodstoves, and an outhouse up the hill—ideal for anybody who wants to spend a night in the woods without having to "rough it" in a tent, sleeping on the ground.

Copper Peak Adventure Rides

North of Bessemer along Black River Harbor Drive is **Copper Peak,** a mountain that's impossible to miss because it's crowned by a ski ramp.

Built in 1969, the 469-foot slide rises 241 feet above the summit and is so immense they needed 300 tons of steel grids to support the ramp, the reason it's dubbed "the Eiffel Tower of the U.P." Despite being the world's largest ski jump, Copper Peak has always been used more in the fall by leaf peepers, who have no intention of leaving the ramp, than in the winter by daredevil skiers, who do.

You begin with a chairlift ride to the summit and then step into an 18-story elevator to continue the upwards journey. When the cage door swings open, you walk still higher, to the top of the ramp, to almost 1,800 feet in elevation, where the wind blows in sudden gusts and the faint-of-heart, who had to be coaxed out of the elevator, are clutching the railing in a death grip.

But from Sept through mid-Oct the ski ramp is a $14 ticket to a million-dollar view. From the top there is a 360-degree panorama that includes Minnesota, Wisconsin, Canada, even Isle Royale National Park. What isn't the deep blue of Lake Superior is foliage painted in a palette of fall colors, from crimson reds to dazzling golds. This is autumn at its best; dramatic and colorful.

Copper Peak Adventure Rides (906-932-3500; copperpeak.org) are offered from 10 a.m. to 4:30 p.m. Tues through Sun from mid-June to Labor Day and on Sat and Sun from Sept to mid-Oct. Admission is $14 for adults and $7 for children.

The cabins provide bunks, mattresses, cooking utensils, and for those on an inland lake, a small rowboat. You must provide a sleeping bag, clothing, and food. The park rents the cabins, which hold from 4 to 8 people, from Apr through Nov at $35 to $60 per night. Stop at the park visitor center (906-885-5275) just off S. Boundary Road (open daily from 10 a.m. to 6 p.m. from mid-May through mid-Oct) for maps and a list of open cabins. You can reserve the cabins up to a year in advance through the **Michigan Campground Central Reservation System** (800-447-2757; midnrreservations.com).

Thanks to a rich history of loggers and miners, Michigan is blessed (cursed?) with a scattering of ghost towns throughout the state. Fayette is the most famous and most visited, but **Old Victoria** can be an equally interesting stop. The Ontonagon County town was originally named Cushin and established in 1849 after the discovery of an ancient miner's pit that still contained a mass of copper. In 1858, a new group of investors came in and renamed the mine town Victoria, and the company town grew to more than 2,000 residents.

Victoria became a ghost town when the copper ran out. Most of the buildings date to the late 19th century. There are classic hand-hewn log cabins, ruins of a rock house, and mining equipment lying all over the place. Old Victoria (906-886-2617; oldvictoria.net) is located 4 miles west of Rockland in Ontonagon County, with an entrance road that is clearly posted on US 45. Historical tours are given from Memorial Day through fall colors in October daily from 10 a.m. to 5 p.m. Guided tours range from $5 to $10 for adults and $2 to $5 for children.

Upper Tahquamenon Falls in Luce County is the largest waterfall in the state, but many cascade connoisseurs think **Bond Falls** in southern Ontonagon County near Paulding is much more beautiful. The cascade is a drop

Camping in Michigan

With more than 14,000 campsites, the Michigan state park system ranks third in the country for total number of sites. Add almost 5,000 more sites in its national and state forests, and it's easy to understand why camping holidays are a time-honored tradition in Michigan, especially in the Upper Peninsula.

I prefer rustic campgrounds because they are smaller and more remote. For a list of and directions to all public campgrounds in the U.P., pick up a copy of the U.P. Travel and Recreation Association's Four Season Travel Planner. It's free and can be obtained by calling the association at (800) 562-7134; uptravel.com. Here are my favorite rustic campgrounds in the U.P.

- *Norway Lake National Forest Campground,* Iron County
- *Gene's Pond State Forest Campground,* Dickinson County
- *Big Knob State Forest Campground,* Mackinac County
- *Big Eric's Bridge State Forest Campground,* Baraga County
- *Mouth of Two-Hearted River State Forest Campground,* Luce County
- *Kingston Lake State Forest Campground,* Alger County

Black River Drive—The Waterfall Road

Departing from Bessemer, Black River Drive (also labeled CR 513) heads north for 15 miles to end at Black River Harbor, one of the few access points to Lake Superior and the site of a National Forest campground. It's a scenic drive past 5 waterfalls all located a short walk from the road.

The cascades are linked together by a portion of the North Country Trail, which hikers can walk from Copper Peak Ski Flying Hill to the campground, a 5.5-mile trip. But it's more convenient if you drive the road, stopping at the trailhead of each individual falls. The hikes are short, the longest being a 1.5-mile round-trip, but do include a number of long staircases.

The first cascade, Great Conglomerate Falls, is reached 12 miles north of Bessemer and is followed by Potawatomi Falls, Gorge Falls, Sandstone Falls, and Rainbow Falls. The drive to view the falls makes an excellent side trip any time of the year, even in the winter, but autumn, especially from late September through early October, is by far the most spectacular time to go.

of more than 50 feet where the Middle Branch of the Ontonagon River fans out and leaps down a series of steplike rocks and around a small island of large boulders in the middle. It's the constantly tumbling water that makes Bond Falls so alluring.

Lake Superior

Black River
Harbor
Campground

To Porcupine
Mountains

North Country Trail

Ottawa
National Forest

Rainbow Falls

Sandstone Falls

Black River Drive

Gorge Falls

Black River

Potawatomi Falls

N

To US 2 and
Bessemer

Great
Conglomerate
Falls

0   0.5 mi

North Country Trail

To Copper
Peak Trailhead

Trailhead and
parking area

From US 45 in Paulding turn east onto Bond Falls Road and in 3.2 miles you'll come to the trailhead to the cascade and a small parking area. The falls are a half-mile hike that includes numerous stairways, some steep, and boardwalks. Nearby are a picnic area, beach, and campground.

Gogebic County

Waterfalls of every type and description are the gems of the Upper Peninsula, and there are more than 150 of them scattered across this region of
Michigan. ***Black River Harbor Drive*** (also known as Black River Road
and County Road 513) in Gogebic County is virtually a parkway of whitewater splendor. The 15-mile road departs from Bessemer on US 2 and enters
Ottawa National Forest, ending at scenic Black River Recreation Area on
Lake Superior. Heading north you first pass ***Copper Peak Ski Flying Hill,***
the largest artificial ski slide in the world and the site of 500-foot jumps during the winter.

Pine Mountain Ski Jump

Known as the King of Hills, Pine Mountain Ski Jump is an awesome sight. Built
in 1938 as a Works Progress Administration project and upgraded several times
since, the 90-meter ski ramp features a 186-foot-high scaffold and a 381-foot
slide. It sits majestically on top of a landing hill with a vertical drop of another 349
feet. Add it all up and you have a 1,440-foot run that sends skiers through the air
at speeds of 55 to 65 miles an hour. In Iron Mountain they tell you it's like jumping
off a 29-story building, of which there are none in the U.P.

Jumpers use skis that are wide, heavy, and often 265 centimeters or longer. Both
their boots and bindings are much more closely related to Nordic skiing than
Alpine, especially with the ability to lift the heels off the skis.

The jumpers are able to defy gravity by basically turning themselves into airplane
wings when they lift out of the back of their bindings on takeoff and lean forward
until their bodies are almost parallel to the skis. In 1994, an Austrian set a US
record at Pine Mountain when he leaped 400 feet.

If you're around Iron Mountain in mid-February, you can see the jumpers in action
during the annual Pine Mountain Classic, which draws almost 20,000 spectators. In the summer you can climb the 280 steps to the top of the jump and be
rewarded with a panoramic view that includes seven lakes.

To reach the ski jump from US 2, turn west on Kent Street and follow it past the
Cornish Pump Engine and Mining Museum. Turn north on Upper Pine Mountain
Road, which will wind to the ski ramp at the top of the hill.

From Copper Peak, Black River Road enters the heart of the national forest and winds near 5 waterfalls, each lying at the end of a trail from a marked turnoff. Gorge and Potawatomi Falls are among the most spectacular and easiest to reach. The 2 falls are within 800 feet of each other and only a 5-minute walk from the parking lot. Potawatomi is the larger, with a 130-foot-wide cascade that drops 30 feet into the Black River. Gorge, smaller with a 24-foot drop, is encased in a steep and narrow red rock canyon—a spectacular setting. A well-marked path with stairs and observation decks leads you past both falls.

At the end of the road, you can camp at Black River Harbor Recreation Area, or those who want a little more luxury can rent a log cabin at **Bear Track Inn** nearby. The small resort has been around since the 1930s, when it catered to lumbermen and commercial fishermen. Its name came from a hungry bear who wandered in one night while the main cabin was being built and walked in the wet cement of the front steps. The name stuck, and the tracks can still be seen today. The inn has only 3 cabins for rent, but 2 are authentic log structures, and all 3 feature natural wood interiors, woodstoves and stone fireplaces, and kitchen facilities. The large cabin can sleep 10, the others hold 4 people each, and during the summer the rates range from $85 to $170 per night for double occupancy. For reservations call the inn at (906) 932-2144 or write Bear Track Inn, 15325 Black River Rd., Ironwood 49938.

The most famous statue in Ironwood is **Hiawatha,** the world's tallest and largest Indian that overlooks the downtown area at the end of Burma Road. At 50 feet high and 16,000 pounds, this Indian can withstand winds of up to 140 mph. But this city's newest statue is equally out of proportion; a red **Stormy Kromer** cap along US 2 that is 6 feet tall and 8 feet wide. A hat so big it would fit Paul Bunyan.

Why a Stormy Kromer?

This distinctive cap with its quirky, Elmer Fudd–like six-panel design is as much a part of the Upper Peninsula as pasties and deer hunting. It has been an indispensable part of the Yooper wardrobe since 1903 when George "Stormy" Kromer, a semi-pro baseball player turned railroad engineer, asked his wife to fix his baseball cap so it would stay on his head better and keep his ears warm. That's when the famous cap with ear flaps and slightly downward visor was born.

Going Underground in the Upper Peninsula

Mining has had a long and colorful history in the Upper Peninsula, and there are many places where you can experience from a miner's point of view what it was like to go underground. Some of the following mines are covered in greater detail in this chapter:

Iron Mountain Iron Mine: Guided tours that begin on a rail tram (miner's train) take you through 2,600 feet of underground drifts and tunnels in this iron mine on US 2 in Vulcan, east of Iron Mountain; (906) 563-8077; ironmountainironmine.com.

Adventure Mine: This mine near Greenland, just off M 38, operated from 1850 to 1920 by the same board that oversaw the highly profitable Quincy Mining Company. Although at one point the copper mine consisted of five shafts, including Shaft No. 3 that contained 13 levels and extended down 1,300 feet into the ore body, it was never profitable. Today Adventure Mine offers a variety of tours, ranging from a 45-minute walk through Shaft No. 2 (adults $12.50, children $7) to the 3-hour Miners Underground Tour that includes rappelling down a mine shaft in darkness ($55 per person); (906) 883-3371; adventureminetours.com.

Delaware Mine: Located in Keweenaw County east of Mohawk on US 41, this is the only mine offering a self-guided tour into its shafts. You descend 110 feet into the mine and then follow a horizontal shaft where you can look for nuggets of pure copper. Find any and they're yours; (906) 289-4688; copperharbor.org.

Quincy Mine: This is the best mine tour in the Upper Peninsula. The Houghton County copper mine is just a mile north of Hancock on US 41 and includes an underground tour 400 feet into the No. Two Shafthouse and a scenic ride on a rail tram; (906) 482-3101; quincymine.com.

Tilden Mine Tour: This is the only tour in the Upper Peninsula of a working mine. Tilden Mine is an open-pit iron mine near Ishpeming in Marquette and includes walking more than a mile on steel grating around the gigantic pit and viewing the taconite processing plant; (906) 486-4841 or (888) 578-6489.

Since then the ***Stormy Kromer Mercantile*** has grown from a northern Wisconsin mom-and-pop operation producing a North Country favorite to a national company with a 30,000-square-foot facility in Ironwood, manufacturing more than 50,000 Stormy Kromer caps per year in 6 styles and 12 colors, including blaze orange for hunters, a green and gold cap for Green Bay Packers fans, and a Lil' Kromer for infants and toddlers.

At Stormy Kromer Mercantile (888-455-2253; stormykromer.com) at 1238 Wall St. east of Ironwood along US 2 you can hear the history of the hat during a free factory tour that is offered at 1:30 p.m. Mon through Fri. The store is open Mon through Fri 8 a.m. to 5 p.m. and Sat 9 a.m. to noon. Or skip the tour and just shop for a new Stormy Kromer. You'll fit in with the locals and your ears will never be cold again.

Iron County

Perhaps the U.P.'s largest and least-known historical complex is the ***Iron County Museum,*** located in the village of Caspian on County Road 424, 2 miles south of US 2 at Iron River. The grounds include almost 20 buildings, many a century old, in a Greenfield Village–like setting that lacks some of the polish of the famous Dearborn attraction but is no less interesting. The park occupies the site of the Caspian Iron Mine, and the head frame that hoisted cars out of the mine in the 1920s still towers over the complex. The main museum is the former engine house, which has been considerably enlarged and today is a maze of displays and three-dimensional exhibits. The favorite is the iron ore mining model that, for a nickel, will automatically run through the process of the rocks being rinsed from the mine and loaded into railroad cars above ground. Other interesting exhibits are the renovated saloon, blacksmith shop, schoolroom, and a hand-carved model of a logging camp that fills an 80-foot display case with hundreds of figures and pieces.

Outside you can wander through one historic building after another: a logging camp bunkhouse with a table set for supper and mackinaw shirts (made of a heavy plaid wool) still hanging up near the door, a barn filled with plows and threshers of the 1800s, a completely furnished homesteaders' cabin, and many other exhibits. You could easily spend an entire day exploring this fascinating folklife complex. The Iron County Museum (906-265-2617; ironcountyhistoricalmuseum.org) is open from mid-May to Sept from 10 a.m. to 4 p.m. Mon through Sat, and in Sept Mon through Sat, noon to 4 p.m. Admission is $8 for adults and $3 for children.

Dickinson County

As in the copper fields, many workers in the iron mines were immigrants from Europe. At Iron Mountain, many Italians came to work the Chapin Mine, which opened in 1879 and went on to become the second-leading ore producer in the U.P. You can learn about the miners' life and work at the ***Menominee Range Historical Museum*** and see the huge water pump that was built for the exceptionally wet mine at the ***Cornish Pump Engine and Mining Museum.***

The pump engine was built for the Chapin Mine, and while Chapin led iron ore production in the Menominee Range, it was also one of the wettest mines ever worked. To dry things out, the E.P. Allis Company of Milwaukee was commissioned in 1889 to build a pumping system for the excess water. The centerpiece of the museum is the 725-ton steeple compound condensing engine that rises 54 feet from the floor and features a 40-foot flywheel. It has been documented as the largest steam-driven pumping engine in the United States.

There are also photos and exhibits on the underground mining days of Iron Mountain and an intriguing exhibit on Henry Ford's World War II gliders, which were manufactured in the area and used to secretly deploy troops behind enemy lines. The museum (906-774-1086) is in downtown Iron Mountain, 1 block west of US 2 on Kent Street. Hours are 9 a.m. to 5 p.m. Mon through Sat and noon to 4 p.m. Sun from mid-May to mid-Oct. Admission is $5 for adults and $3 for children or $8 for adults and $4 for children for a ticket that includes the Menominee Range Historical Museum (906-774-4276; menomineemuseum.com), which is open when volunteers are available.

The Menominee River forms almost half of the border between Wisconsin and Michigan's Upper Peninsula, beginning west of Iron Mountain and extending to its mouth on Green Bay. Two miles south of Norway, the river flows through Piers Gorge, a whitewater area of large falls, holes, and swirls as the river tumbles through a scenic forested canyon. The gorge picked up its name in the 1840s when loggers built piers along this section of the river to slow the current and prevent logs from jamming and splitting on the jagged rocks. You can view this spectacular stretch of wild water by heading south of Norway on US 8; just before its bridge across the Menominee, turn left onto Piers Gorge Road. The paved road quickly turns into a dirt one, and then after 0.6 mile it ends at *Piers Gorge Nature Trail.* The trail is a round-trip of 3 miles but swings past a series of viewing points above the falls.

During the summer you can also experience the gorge and what many rafters call the "Midwest's premier whitewater river" through *Kosir's Rapid Raft.* The company offers a 3-hour raft trip that takes you through Piers Gorge and over its falls. On Sat and Sun, the rafters meet nearby and then proceed to the river with their large inflated rafts. It's a wild ride, one that will leave you soaking wet but exhilarated. The company provides the rafts, guides, helmets, life jackets, and a paddle for each passenger.

Kosir's Rapid Raft (715-757-3431; kosirs.com) is based in Wisconsin. The raft trips, which also can be set up during the week by advance reservation, cost $45 per person.

Menominee County

One of the products of Michigan's white pine era was hardwood floors by the IXL Company of Hermansville. Established by C. J. Meyer in the 1870s as part of his Wisconsin Land and Lumber Company, IXL became world-renowned for its floors after machines were invented in Hermansville that could precision-manufacture tongue-and-groove hardwood flooring in one operation. By the early 1900s IXL had the largest such plant in the country, and its flooring could be seen (and walked on) in the main lodge at Yellowstone National Park and the Mormon Temple in Salt Lake City.

In 1881 Meyer erected a huge office building to manage his sprawling lumber operation, and today it's one of the most intriguing museums in the Upper Peninsula. The *IXL Office Museum* is literally a step into a 19th-century business office. On the first floor visitors wander through the payroll and accounting departments as well as the private offices of the company executives. All are fully furnished and appear as if the workers had just stepped out for lunch. In one room are dictaphones, mimeographs, typewriters, and other machines complete with instruction booklets, while across the hall beautiful rolltop desks and an ornate walk-in vault can be seen. On the second floor several rooms are devoted to the machinery and equipment used in the flooring industry, and on the third floor visitors can still flip through original payroll records and see what a worker earned each week (along with deductions) in the 1890s.

The museum is located in the heart of Hermansville, a small town on US 2, 26 miles west of Escanaba and 30 miles east of Iron Mountain. The museum (906-498-2181; hermansville.com/IXLMuseum) is open from Memorial Day through Labor Day from 12:30 to 4 p.m. daily. Admission is $3 for adults.

Places to Stay in the Western Upper Peninsula

BIG BAY

Big Bay Depot Motel
301 Depot Rd.
(906) 345-9350

Big Bay Point Lighthouse
3 Lighthouse Rd.
(906) 345-9957
bigbaylighthouse.com

BLACK HARBOR

Bear Track Inn
15325 Black River Rd.
(906) 932-2144

CALUMET/LAURIUM

Americinn
56925 S. Sixth St.
(906) 337-6463

Laurium Manor Inn Bed and Breakfast
320 Tamarack St.
(906) 337-2549
lauriummanorinn.com

Victorian Hall Bed & Breakfast
305 Tamarack St.
(906) 337-2549
laurium.info/victorianhall

COPPER HARBOR

Keweenaw Mountain Lodge
US 41
(906) 289-4403
atthelodge.com

Mariner North Resort
255 Gratiot St.
(906) 289-4637
manorth.com

EAGLE RIVER

Eagle River Inn
5033 Front St.
(906) 337-0666
eagleriverinn.com

Sand Hills Lighthouse Inn
Five Mile Point Road
(906) 337-1744
sandhillslighthouseinn.com

HOUGHTON

Franklin Square Inn
820 Shelden Ave.
(888) 487-1700
houghtonlodging.com

Travelodge Houghton
215 Shelden Ave.
(906) 482-1400
travelodgeofhoughton
.com

IRON MOUNTAIN

Comfort Inn
1555 N. Stephenson Ave.
(906) 774-5505
comfortinn.com

Edgewater Resort Cabins
N4128 US 2
(800) 236-6244
edgewaterresort.com

Woodlands Motel
N3957 US 2
(800) 394-5505

SELECTED CHAMBERS OF COMMERCE AND TOURISM BUREAUS

**Baraga County Convention &
Visitors Bureau**
755 E. Broad St.
L'Anse 49946
(800) 743-4908
baragacountycc.org

Dickinson Area Partnership
600 S. Stephenson Ave.
Iron Mountain 49801
(906) 774-2002
dickinsonchamber.com

**Keweenaw Convention and Visitors
Bureau**
56638 Calumet Ave.
Calumet 49913
(800) 338-7982
keweenaw.info

**Marquette County Convention and
Visitors Bureau**
337 W. Washington St.
Marquette 49855
(800) 544-4321
travelmarquettemichigan.com

**Upper Peninsula Travel and
Recreation Association**
P.O. Box 400
Iron Mountain 49801
(800) 562-7134
uptravel.com

**Western U.P. Convention and
Visitor's Bureau**
648 W. Cloverland Dr.
Ironwood 49938
(800) 522-5657
explorewesternup.com

IRONWOOD

Classic Motor Inn
1200 E. US 2
(906) 932-2000
westernup.com

Comfort Inn
210 E. Cloverland Dr.
(906) 932-2224
comfortinn.com

ISHPEMING

Jasper Ridge Inn
1000 River Parkway
(906) 485-2378
bwjasperridgeinn.com

MARQUETTE

Cedar Motor Inn
2523 US 41
(906) 228-2280
cedarmi.com

Landmark Inn
230 N. Front St.
(888) 752-6362
thelandmarkinn.com

SILVER CITY

Americinn
120 Lincoln Ave.
(906) 885-5311
americinn.com

Mountain View Lodges
34042 M 107
(906) 885-5256
mountainviewlodges.com

Watersmeet
Vacationland Resort
E 19636 Herbert Rd.
(906) 358-4380
vacationlandresort.com

Places to Eat in the Western Upper Peninsula

CALUMET/LAURIUM

Toni's Country Kitchen
79 Third St.
(906) 337-0611
American

COPPER HARBOR

Keweenaw Mountain Lodge
14252 US 41
(906) 289-4403
atthelodge.com
Fine Dining

Pines Restaurant
174 Gratiot Ave.
(906) 289-4222
pinesresort.net
American

EAGLE RIVER

Fitzgerald's Restaurant
Eagle River Inn
5033 Front St.
(906) 337-0666
eagleriverinn.com
Lakeview Dining

HOUGHTON

Keweenaw Brewing Company
408 Shelden Ave.
(906) 482-5596
keweenawbrewing.com
Microbrewery

Library Restaurant
62 N. Isle Royale St.
(906) 487-5882
librarybrewpub.com
Brewpub

Suomi Home Bakery
54 Huron St.
(906) 482-3220
Finnish

OTHER ATTRACTIONS

Coppertown USA
Calumet
(800) 338-7982

Houghton County Historical Museum
Lake Linden
(906) 296-4121
houghtonhistory.org

Marquette County Historical Museum
Marquette
(906) 226-3571
marquettecohistory.org

Menominee County Historical Museum
Menominee
(906) 863-9000
menomineehistoricalsociety.org

Old Depot Park Museum
Ironwood
(906) 932-0287

Shrine of the Snowshoe Priest
L'Anse
(906) 524-7021

Upper Peninsula Children's Museum
Marquette
(906) 226-3911
upcmkids.org

IRON MOUNTAIN

Fontana's Supper Club
115 S. Stephenson Ave.
(906) 774-0044
Italian

IRON RIVER

Alice's
402 W. Adams St.
(906) 265-4764
Italian

Depot Restaurant & Bakery
50 Fourth Ave.
(906) 265-6341
American

IRONWOOD

Joe's Pasty Shop
116 W. Aurora St.
(906) 932-4412
Pasties

Manny's
316 E. Houk St.
(906) 932-0999
Italian

Mike's
106 E. Cloverland Dr.
(906) 932-0555
mikesironwood.com
American

ISHPEMING

Jasper Ridge Brewery
1075 Country Lane
(906) 485-6017
countryvillageresort.com
Brewpub

L'ANSE

Hilltop Restaurant
18047 US 41
(906) 524-7858
sweetroll.com
American

MARQUETTE

Donckers
137 W. Washington St.
(906) 226-6110
donckersonline.com
Soda Fountain & Sandwiches

Jean Kay's
1639 Presque Isle
(906) 228-5310
jeankayspasties.com
Pasties

Landmark Inn Capers
230 N. Front St.
(888) 752-6362
thelandmarkinn.com
Fine Dining

Sweet Water Cafe
517 N. Third St.
(906) 226-7009
Bakery & Cafe

Union Grill
1651 S. Front St.
(906) 225-5564
Barbecue

The Vierling Restaurant
119 S. Front St.
(906) 228-3533
thevierling.com
Brewpub

Index